# BUILDING CHINA INTO A CYBER SUPERPOWER

This book provides a comprehensive look into China's emerging cyberspace strategy. It highlights the prime drivers of China's desire to be a cyber superpower and discusses the ways in which China is turning resources into cyber power.

The book analyses China's domestic cyber policy initiatives, strategy documents, censorship measures, and the rationale behind its strong advocacy for sovereignty in cyberspace. It examines China's position on the prominent issues of cyberspace governance, norms and security in cyberspace, and key diplomatic initiatives. The book also discusses next-generation networks, artificial intelligence, quantum information sciences, and cyber warfare.

An important contribution to the study of China's cyber policy, the book will be of interest to students and researchers of international relations, Chinese digitalisation, security studies, Chinese politics, international security, Chinese foreign policy, and Chinese economy. It will also be useful to the policymakers and corporate professionals engaged with China's digital sphere.

**Munish Sharma** currently works as an advisor on cyber and emerging technology areas at a foreign diplomatic mission in New Delhi. He has worked in the private sector, held a research position at the Institute for Defence Studies and Analyses, India, and consulted with India's Ministry of External Affairs. He has a PhD from Jawaharlal Nehru University, New Delhi.

# BUILDING CHINA INTO A CYBER SUPERPOWER

## Desires, Drivers, and Devices

*Munish Sharma*

Routledge
Taylor & Francis Group

LONDON AND NEW YORK

First published 2024
by Routledge
4 Park Square, Milton Park, Abingdon, Oxon OX14 4RN

and by Routledge
605 Third Avenue, New York, NY 10158

*Routledge is an imprint of the Taylor & Francis Group, an informa business*

© 2024 Munish Sharma

*British Library Cataloguing-in-Publication Data*
A catalogue record for this book is available from the British Library

ISBN: 978-1-032-75334-8 (hbk)
ISBN: 978-1-032-75333-1 (pbk)
ISBN: 978-1-003-47351-0 (ebk)

DOI: 10.4324/9781003473510

Typeset in Sabon
by Deanta Global Publishing Services, Chennai, India

*In loving memory of my grandfather, Dev Dutt Sharma, who taught me two values I hold dearly – reading and working hard in silence.*

# CONTENTS

# ACKNOWLEDGEMENTS

I extend my deepest gratitude to Prof. Srikanth Kondapalli for his steadfast guidance and supervision during my doctoral research, which laid the foundation for this book.

I am thankful to Dr. Ajey Lele, who initially encouraged me to undertake doctoral research and later motivated me to transform my thesis into the form of this book. My gratitude also goes to Dr. Cherian Samuel for lending an academic ear to scrutinising the key ideas and graciously reviewing the first draft. The contributions of these two individuals, along with Rama Vedashree's flexibility during the manuscript preparation phase, were instrumental in bringing this book to publication.

My profound appreciation goes to the two anonymous reviewers whose insightful suggestions greatly improved the transition from the initial version to the book now in your hands.

I am also thankful for the assistance provided by the library staff at the Manohar Parrikar Institute for Defence Studies and Analyses in accessing research materials.

Lastly, I wish to express my heartfelt thanks for the unwavering love and support of my parents and particularly my wife Savita who has shown incredible patience and understanding throughout the writing of this book.

## Author's note

The views and opinions expressed in this book are the author's own and do not reflect the views or positions of his current or previous employers. This book is developed from a doctoral thesis submitted at the Jawaharlal Nehru University, New Delhi.

# ABBREVIATIONS

| | |
|---|---|
| **AI** | Artificial Intelligence |
| **BRI** | Belt and Road Initiative |
| **CAC** | Cyberspace Administration of China |
| **CAICT** | China Academy of Information and Communications Technology |
| **CAS** | Chinese Academy of Sciences |
| **CMC** | Central Military Commission |
| **CNGI** | China Next-Generation Internet |
| **CNNIC** | China Internet Network Information Center |
| **CPC** | Communist Party of China |
| **GDP** | Gross Domestic Product |
| **IANA** | Internet Assigned Numbers Authority |
| **ICANN** | Internet Corporation for Assigned Names and Numbers |
| **ICT** | Information and Communication Technology |
| **IETF** | Internet Engineering Task Force |
| **IEU** | Information Engineering University |
| **IGF** | Internet Governance Forum |
| **IP** | Internet Protocol |
| **ITU** | International Telecommunications Union |
| **MIIT** | Ministry of Industry and Information Technology |
| **NDRC** | National Development and Reform Commission |
| **NUDT** | National University of Defense Technology |
| **OEWG** | Open-Ended Working Group |
| **PLA** | People's Liberation Army |
| **PLASSF** | PLA Strategic Support Force |
| **RMB** | Renminbi |

| | |
|---|---|
| **SCIO** | State Council Information Office |
| **SCO** | Shanghai Cooperation Organisation |
| **SEP** | Standards Essential Patent |
| **TD-SCDMA** | Time Division-Synchronous Code Division Multiple Access |
| **TSAG** | Telecommunication Standardization Advisory Group |
| **UN GGE** | United Nations Group of Governmental Experts |
| **VPN** | Virtual Private Network |
| **WCIT** | World Conference on International Telecommunications |
| **WIPO** | World Intellectual Property Organization |
| **WSIS** | World Summit on the Information Society |

# 1

# INTRODUCTION

With the rising strategic relevance of cyberspace, particularly in the economic, technology, and military spheres, states are developing strategies to gain and demonstrate their superiority in this domain. The advent of cyber as a priority compels states to create new institutions and structures to effectively govern cyber affairs and defend their interests in cyberspace. Cyber power – the ability to exert power and influence decisions and outcomes in and through the cyber domain – stems from the growing sense of contestation and competition among states in cyberspace. None of the states is oblivious to this unfolding reality in the conduct of its statecraft and international relations. States understand the growing importance of cyberspace to their prosperity and security, and are conscientious of the vast possibilities of cooperation, competition, and confrontation in cyberspace.

In recent times, China is known to have made significant strides in the fields of information and communication technologies, computer networking, telecommunications, supercomputing, artificial intelligence, and other emerging technology areas having strategic importance. China has the world's largest internet user base, and it also operates the largest communications infrastructure in the world. Telecommunication equipment and personal computer and networking device manufacturers of Chinese origin not just compete head-on with established global players now, but their leadership in some of the market segments and technology domains is widely acknowledged. China is also the largest consumer of semiconductors in the world, driven by the burgeoning domestic mobile handsets and computing devices manufacturing industry.

Cyber features heavily in China's economic planning now. The 13th Five-Year Plan, for the first time in the history of Five-Year Plans, carried a

DOI: 10.4324/9781003473510-1

dedicated section on Cyber Economy. The 14th Five-Year Plan dedicated an entire section to the initiative of building a digital China. The political leadership perceives digital economy as a key driver of China's economic growth, mainly as the share of digital economy in China's gross domestic product increased from 14.2 per cent in 2005 to 39.8 per cent by 2021 (CAICT, 2020, 2021, 2022).

While taking over the reins of informatisation and cyber policy at the first meeting of the then newly created Central Leading Group for Cybersecurity and Informatization in February 2014, Xi Jinping had called for collective efforts to build China into a cyber superpower. The phrase *wǎngluò qiángguó* thereafter gained salience as it continued to find repeated reference in many speeches of Xi Jinping thereafter and eventually made inroads into several statements and policy analyses on cybersecurity and digitalisation. The Fifth Plenary Session of the 18th Central Committee of the Communist Party of China (CPC), held in 2015, proposed implementation of the strategy to build China into a cyber superpower (Xi, 2022). The phrase featured in Xi Jinping's speech at the 2016 and 2018 editions of the National Cybersecurity and Informatization Work Conference. It was the central theme of the book *Excerpts of Xi Jinping's Discussion on the Power of the Internet* published in 2021. DigiChina translates the phrase *wǎngluò qiángguó* as "cyber superpower" and observes that *qiángguó* could either be understood as a slogan, a desired state of strength, or a process of strengthening (Creemers, Webster, et al., 2018).

According to a 2017 article published by Theoretical Studies Center Group of the Cyberspace Administration of China in *Qiushi* (theoretical journal published by the CPC Central Committee), the strategic thought behind the objective of building China into a cyber superpower is an outcome of the union of the basic principles of Marxism and the practice of internet development in China under the new circumstances (CAC, 2017b). The article regarded the objective as an ideological guide and a plan of action to steer the development of cybersecurity and informatisation industry, as well as global internet governance. China's priorities and policies related to its activities in cyberspace are anchored in the strategic concept of cyber power, guided by the vision and principles espoused by the highest echelons of political leadership. It steers China's plans for informatisation, strategies for cyberspace governance in both domestic and international realms, efforts to build an independent information technology base or leapfrog in the technology competition, and the quest to mould online public opinion. The prime motive is to transform China from a major cyber power into a cyber superpower.

With Xi at the helm of cyber affairs in China, a series of initiatives and measures have been rolled out to help realise this ambition, to be advanced in tandem with the "two centenary goals." China provisioned a

*Cybersecurity Law*, published its *National Cyberspace Security Strategy* and an *International Strategy of Cooperation on Cyberspace*, initiated the flagship annual event – the World Internet Conference, and at the same time reinforced state control and censorship on online content and information. The Central Leading Group brought cyber policy in China under the direct authority of the General Secretary of the CPC. Since then, cyberspace governance and cybersecurity have remained to be the priorities in the informatisation agenda of the political leadership and China has also started playing a proactive role in international cyber affairs. As part of the wide-ranging military reforms initiated in 2015 end, the Strategic Support Force was raised with the objective of augmenting space and cyber operations capabilities of the People's Liberation Army.

Cyberspace has gradually acquired a central role in China's economic growth, foreign policy, and the modernisation of its armed forces. These imperatives have been underscored time and gain by the political leadership at different forums and various occasions. After the landmark speech of 2014 where Xi Jinping prescribed the prime areas of work to build China into a cyber superpower, in 2015 at the opening ceremony of the second edition of the World Internet Conference he called on the international community to work together to foster a peaceful, secure, open, and cooperative cyberspace. Also, at this occasion, he promulgated a few principles to transform the global internet governance system and urged states to respect sovereignty in cyberspace. In a 2016 collective study session of the Political Bureau, Xi Jinping proposed "six accelerations" to catapult China as a cyber superpower. At the National Cybersecurity and Informatization Work Conference in 2018, he further outlined six areas for future work on cybersecurity and informatisation.

China has witnessed rapid growth in digital economy over the last two decades owing to the aggressive policy measures devised to expand the information and communication technologies (ICTs) infrastructure and integrate information technology with the traditional sectors of the economy. The idea is to modernise China's traditional industries by leveraging developments in emerging technologies such as mobile broadband, big data, the internet of things, and cloud computing. Informatisation has long been pursued as a national priority in China given its vast potential for driving economic growth and elevating the living standards of the society; primarily under the rubrics of digital economy and information society. Security also has had a deep influence on the thought process, whether internet and computer security previously or cybersecurity in the recent past.

China's demonstrated ability to drive advanced large-scale scientific endeavours and its growing prowess in the advanced technology space underpins its desire to shape international discourse on the future and governance of technology, including the internet and cyberspace. Cyber has emerged as a key element in the conduct of China's foreign policy, especially related to negotiations and technology for the future and governance of cyberspace at the United Nations and the International Telecommunication Union. Cyber and digital technologies are also a prime aspect of China's Belt and Road Initiative. Moreover, in the wake of the increase in intensity and sophistication of cyber intrusions or espionage attempts attributed to China globally, its intent to leverage cyberspace to advance political and military objectives has become quite apparent. China's rapid growth in the fast-paced technology domain, whether driven by intrinsic factors, security imperatives, or its geopolitical environment, has placed China on a pedestal where it aspires to occupy the so-called "commanding heights" of competition in cyberspace. The quest to build China into a cyber superpower – a cyber power to be reckoned with – is the focal point of this book.

China's desire to exploit the cyber domain has stirred strategic and scholarly discussions alike. The existing scholarly efforts to interpret China's behaviour in cyberspace examine one or a few of these broad aspects amongst the vast scope of the concept of cyber power. The concept of cyber power itself spans multiple dimensions as it encapsulates elements from the varied fields of technology, public policy, economics, diplomacy, military, and international relations. Moreover, analyses on this subject tend to focus on China's malicious behaviour in cyberspace, and the threat to American leadership in the technology realm and the military and security implications thereof, basically against the backdrop of the strategic competition between China and the US. When the subject is analysed from a technology perspective, the international relations or geopolitical contexts seem to lose focus. Similarly, while deliberating on security and international relations aspects of cyber power in the context of China, economic and social aspects are generally not touched upon. Likewise, military aspects have not received due attention in the analyses focused on China's cyber diplomacy.

The book begins by examining the concept of cyber power and identifying the constituents in the form of capabilities and resources that tend to shape the cyber power of a state. The book then attempts to gather a better understanding of how does the Chinese political leadership perceive the concept of cyber power and derive a few benchmarks which could be used to make a qualitative assessment of the progress made thus far towards the goal of building China into a cyber superpower. It takes a historical account of China's digital revolution before analysing China's domestic cyber policy initiatives, strategy documents, censorship measures, and the rationale behind its strong advocacy for sovereignty in cyberspace. The book delves both into China's perspective on cyber power and the international views on China's cyber power. Since international engagement is slated to play an important role in garnering support for China's views and vision for the future of cyberspace, the book analyses China's positions on the prominent issues of governance, norms, and security in cyberspace and the key diplomatic initiatives. On the emerging technology aspect, the book limits discussion to the disciplines of next-generation networks, artificial intelligence, and quantum information sciences. The military dimension examines the thought within People's Liberation Army (PLA) on information and cyber warfare, and the efforts dedicated to building cyber military capabilities.

The book takes an objective and multidimensional approach and does not analyse China's cyber power merely from the security lens. It refrains from drawing inferences about China's cyber power from the widely reported malicious cyber activities attributed to China. Most importantly, the book does not seek to provide an assessment of China's cyber power, but rather to illuminate the prime drivers of China's desire to be a cyber superpower, how is China translating resources and capabilities into cyber power, and from where China is likely to derive cyber power.

The book has examined publicly available data for qualitative analysis of the subject under consideration. It has relied on white papers, reports, and strategy documents published by the State Council of the People's Republic of China and key state agencies such as the Ministry of Science and Technology, the Ministry of Industry and Information Technology, the Ministry of Foreign Affairs, and the Cyberspace Administration of China. The Five-Year Plans, the reports at the National Congress of the CPC, and the speeches of political leaders on various occasions have also been another important source of information for the book.

The reports on the technology and innovation aspects of China published by the Organisation for Economic Cooperation and Development and the World Intellectual Property Organization have been used extensively to source data on these specific aspects. The reports from premier academic institutions and think-tanks in China such as the Chinese Academy of Sciences, Tsinghua University, and the China Academy of Information and Communications Technology have also been consulted. The research publications from leading international think-tanks on cybersecurity and China's cyber policy have been extremely helpful. The websites providing translations of important government documents which do not have official English translation have been of immense help.

## Chapters walkthrough

To prepare the ground, the second chapter first explains the concept of cyber power reviewing the existing conceptual frameworks, global perspectives, scholarly literature on cyber power, and looks at the prevalent views on the classification of cyber power and its assessment. The chapter introduces a model for cyber power based on various attributes, resources, or constituents of cyber power to elucidate how cyber power builds up from a wide range of measures and strategies and policy decisions across different state functions. The chapter then builds a framework based on key speeches and statements of political leaders to interpret China's conceptualisation of cyber power.

The third chapter presents a historical account of the evolution and consolidation of China's informatisation effort, discusses the priorities, and sheds light on the institutional changes brought in by the leadership since taking over the reins of the government a decade ago against the backdrop of the unprecedented leadership supervision of cyber affairs. Subsequently, the chapter illuminates China's conceptualisation of cyber power and investigates the developments pertaining to national cyberspace strategy, legal frameworks, controls and censorship, and China's advocacy for sovereignty in cyberspace. Towards the end, the chapter brings in international perspectives of China's cyber power.

In the context of China's international engagement on internet or cyber governance issues, the fourth chapter examines how China's diplomatic efforts have sought to promote its position at various platforms, beginning with the case of the *International Code of Conduct for Information Security* and then looking at the World Internet Conference. It also highlights how China's *International Strategy of Cooperation on Cyberspace* tethers the ideas and principles China has for the future of cyberspace with a clear plan of action. The chapter thereafter dissects the technology dimension of China's Belt and Road Initiative (better known as Digital Silk Road), the plan for a Digital Renminbi, and the Global Initiative on Data Security.

Regarding emerging digital technologies, the fifth chapter delves into select technology areas to discuss China's advancements. Under next-generation networks, the chapter covers China's Next-Generation Internet initiative, 5G mobile communications, and Network 2030. The chapter then touches upon China's breakthroughs in the research and technology aspects of quantum information sciences and artificial intelligence.

The sixth chapter expands on the military dimension of China's cyber power, and to begin with, the chapter traces the origins and the subsequent evolution of information and cyber warfare in the Chinese military thinking, doctrine, and strategy. As a key element of China's force structuring in cyberspace, the chapter discusses the raising of Strategic Support Force in the PLA and the corresponding cyber and asymmetric warfare capabilities. The chapter thereafter looks at how China is synergising the capacities of the civilian and military sectors in the case of cyber and emerging digital technologies as part of the military–civil fusion strategy. The efforts to fulfil the training and educational requirements of PLA for cyber and related disciplines are discussed towards the end of the chapter. The concluding chapter draws insights from the discussion in preceding chapters.

# 2
# CYBER POWER
## Concept and framework

The rising influence of cyber domain on virtually every function of statecraft and the conduct of interstate relations has triggered scholarly efforts in the discipline of international relations, broadly trying to make strategic sense of this phenomenon. Theoretical examination of the confluence of "cyber" with the concepts such as power (Gray, 2013; Kuehl, 2009; Nye, 2010), deterrence (Libicki, 2009; Lupovici, 2011; Morgan, 2010), warfare, and securitisation (Buzan et al., 1998) has expanded scholarly understanding on the outcomes of interaction of cyberspace with the functions of the state. Scholars have leveraged, and even improvised, the established theoretical frameworks applying the abovementioned concepts, as well as concepts such as anarchy, balance of power, complex interdependence, and institutionalism to gain a better perspective on the evolving dynamics in global cyber affairs.

Moreover, cyberspace has unequivocally been termed as the fifth domain of warfare, alongside the physical domains of land, air, sea, and space – rendering it susceptible to contestation arising from exercise of power to gain control or defend interests in and through the domain. Development of strategies for cyberspace is therefore conditioned by the traditional power structures. To prepare the ground for the forthcoming chapters in the book, it is important to first introduce the concept of cyber power.

### The concept of cyber power

Power, in dictionary terms, is the ability to act, or to control people and events (*Cambridge English Dictionary*, n.d.). Power is synonymous with the possession of control or influence over others. Power also denotes strength

DOI: 10.4324/9781003473510-2

and authority, and it is considered to be the ability to influence the behaviour of others or the course of events. Power in the political context is an old-age concept, but the meaning and intuitive understanding of power have remained fluid. In modern times, theories explaining how operating environments or domains affect national power came to prominence at the turn of the 20th century. Beginning with the 1890 publication *The Influence of Sea Power upon History: 1660–1783*, the American naval strategist Admiral Alfred Thayer Mahan advanced the concept of sea power – attributing the emergence of Britain as a dominant military and economic power to its naval supremacy (Office of the Historian, n.d.). The principles establishing the relationship between a nation's sea power and its overall power shaped the American perspectives and strategies in the maritime domain. Considering world history in the context of conflict between land and sea powers, the British geographer Halford John Mackinder (1904) posited that the control of Heartland – the landlocked region of central Eurasia – is key to world domination. Asserting the prominence of continental power, the Heartland Theory contradicted Mahan's assertion.

The First World War influenced air power theorists, most notably the Italian General Giulio Douhet and the American General William Mitchell who argued for the primacy of air power in future wars through strategic bombing, surprise, and pre-emptive airstrikes. With the advent of satellites for intelligence and communications in the 1960s, the control of space and its impact on military activities, national power, and global issues gave rise to the concept of space power. For national defence and national power, states develop military capabilities for each of the environments, and these are navy, armed forces, air force, and spacecrafts and satellites. Such capabilities are instrumental in establishing control and wield influence across the domains to meet political objectives and secure legitimate interests (Spade, 2012: 6).

Power, according to Waltz, meets four overarching objectives – it provides the means of maintaining autonomy when others wield force, permits wider ranges of action, provides wider margins of safety to the powerful ones in dealing with the less powerful, and renders its possessors a big stake in system (Waltz, 1979: 194–195). Adapting this observation to the cyber domain, cyber power may extend the range of options before a state, allow a state to maintain autonomy in its approach to security in cyberspace, and render it a greater say in the decisions related to the governance of cyberspace or establishing norms of responsible state behaviour in cyberspace. Given the growing imperatives of cyberspace in foreign and security policy and strategic matters, the interpretation, assessment, and mobilisation of cyber power have gained attention of scholars, theorists, and strategists.

The common denominator in the theories related to land, sea, air, and space power, according to Kuehl, is the ability to use and exploit the physical environments to one's advantage or to meet specific purposes and to extend the sphere of influence. His definition of cyber power stems from this inference as, "the ability to use cyberspace to create advantages and influence events in all the operational environments and across the instruments of power" (Kuehl, 2009: 12). In contrast to Mahan's or Douhet's approach to sea power or air power, Kuehl's definition is broader as it encompasses other forms of power and draws emphasis on the synergising effect of cyber power on, and its integration with, other forms and instruments of power across all other domains and in all aspects of the P/DIME (political/diplomatic, informational, military, and economic) paradigm.

Adapting General William Mitchell's succinct definition of air power, Gray describes cyber power as, "the ability to do something strategically useful in cyberspace" (Gray, 2013: 9). Sheldon defines cyber power as, "the sum of strategic effects generated by cyber operations in and from cyberspace," which could be "felt within cyberspace, as well as in the other domains of land, sea, air, and space" (Sheldon, 2011: 96). According to Nye, cyber power rests on "a set of resources that relate to the creating, control, and communication of electronic and computer based information – infrastructure, networks, software, human skills," and in behavioural terms refers to "the ability to obtain preferred outcomes through the use of electronically interconnected information resources of the cyber domain" (Nye, 2010: 3–4). Nye further observes that cyber power could be used to produce preferred outcomes within cyberspace, as well as in other domains outside cyberspace (Nye, 2011: 123). Li defines cyber power as "a country's capability to both take action and exert influence in cyberspace," and deemed it critical to a "country's ability to conduct cyber warfare" (Li, 2012: 802). The concept of power in international relations has influenced the prevalent body of literature on the nature of power in cyberspace, drawing thought on both perspectives: domination ("power over") and empowerment ("power to").

Starr (2009) delves into the commonalities of environmental theories of power (land, sea, air, and space) to propound that "a theory of cyber power should focus on four key attributes – technological advances, speed and scope of operations, control of key features, and national mobilisation." Rattray (2009) also takes the environmental theories of power approach, describing cyber power analogous to the control of land masses, prominent sea lanes, vital airspace, or satellite orbits, and how the environmental theories of power were developed to predict the political–military impact of technological advances elucidating the abovementioned four attributes. Amongst others, emphasis is drawn on national mobilisation as a key measure of cyber power, indicating the need for close coordination with the private sector which houses much of the technical expertise.

Analysing the use of cyber power to impact and influence the elements of power under the P/DIME paradigm, Kuehl (2009) characterises cyber power as an influential military instrument central to the new concepts and doctrines, and pivotal to the development and execution of national policy, be it economic planning, external affairs, or other key governmental operations. Starr (2009) lays down the groundwork for developing a theory of cyber power, drawing from Kuehl's widely referenced definition – appropriating the elements of the P/DIME paradigm as the instruments of power with primary emphasis on the military and informational levers. Starr articulates that as part of their strategy, states employ a mix of P/DIME activities to generate effects in the areas of PMESII (political, military, economic, social, informational, and infrastructure). Rattray (2009) also considers cyber power to be a fundamental enabler for the full range of instruments of power. According to Xie (2018), the control and competence of a country in cyberspace have become the very basis for determining its comprehensive national strength.

The concept of cyber power locates cyberspace amongst the physical domains where states strive to gain control and demonstrate superiority. But unlike other domains, cyber power is generally perceived to have an impact on all the operational environments cutting across the entire spectrum of traditional levers, instruments, or forms of power. Its strategic utility hinges upon the distinctive ability to generate effects or influence events in other domains besides cyberspace. Owing to the cross-domain effect of cyber power, cyber capabilities for governments have emerged as a potent tool. In addition to the traditional military, diplomacy, and economic means, cyber capabilities are another option available to states to be deployed in support of a specific or even multiple national objectives.

Although there is no established theory of cyber power, the scholarly understanding of cyber power is expanding as the efforts to theorise the nature and attributes of cyber power; to explore its facets, dimensions, and constituents; and to attune the prevalent conceptions and classifications of power to the cyber domain have gained momentum. Betz and Stevens (2011) apply Barnett and Duvall's (2005) taxonomy of four types of power (compulsory, institutional, structural, and productive) in the context of cyberspace to derive four distinct forms of cyber power. According to their taxonomy for cyber power, "the use of direct coercion by a cyberspace actor in an attempt to shape or modify the actions and circumstances of another" is a form of *compulsory cyber power*. The use of cyber-attacks, deployment of non-material resources such as economic sanctions or military threats, and direct control could be the means to affect the actions of others. *Institutional cyber power* involves the control of a cyberspace actor by another in indirect ways, mediated by formal or informal institutions. For example, states promote norms and standards of state behaviour in cyberspace through various global institutions to influence the behaviour of other states. *Structural cyber power* works to maintain the structural positions of actors, and these positions essentially "facilitate or constrain the actions of an actor with respect to others to whom they are directly connected."

Cyberspace not just preserves the existing structural forms but also facilitates the forming of new ones, and *structural cyber power* therefore simultaneously conserves and disrupts the status quo. Since cyberspace aids the reproduction and reinforcement of existing discourse, as well as the construction and dissemination of new ones, Betz and Stevens deem *productive cyber power* to be the foundation for other forms of cyber power, or, the most important form of cyber power (Betz and Stevens, 2011: 45–51). One of the examples of it is the discursive construction of threat actors in cyberspace as national security threats. This interpretation of Betz and Stevens captures the nuances of cyber power, direct or diffused, emerging through the social interaction between actors in the structure and rapidly advancing technology, different from the monolithic view of deliberately putting resources into use to meet the objectives in cyberspace.

Nye's interpretation of cyber power encompasses *soft power* in the form of agenda framing, attraction, persuasion, and standards development, and *hard power* which is exercised through the use of malwares, distributed denial of service attacks, intellectual property theft, and disruptions in the critical infrastructure or the industrial control systems (Nye, 2011: 126). Nye expounds on three faces or aspects of relational power, where each has hard and soft power facets in the cyber context. The first face of power is "the ability of an actor to make others do something contrary to their initial preferences or strategies," where denial-of-service attacks, malware, and disruptions are the *hard power* aspects, while persuading hackers or the members of terrorist outfits have a *soft power* outlook.

The second face of power is "agenda setting or framing in which an actor precludes the choices of another by exclusion of their strategies" where the use of firewalls and filters for online content moderation has *hard power* connotation, and self-regulation on part of the search engines or internet service providers and the adoption of software standards and protocols or the rules set forth by multistakeholder institutions have a *soft power* overtone. The third face of power involves "one actor shaping another's initial preferences so that some strategies are not even considered," and *hard power* aspects in this case could be the threats of punishment for online dissemination of censored content, while *soft power* aspects could be the development of norms against the social menaces in cyberspace (Nye, 2010: 7–9). Nye's postulation of the three faces of cyber power provides a broad basis for the classification of a wide range of activities that state and non-state actors pursue in cyberspace. Though this approach does not propose a new nomenclature, it concisely develops a template whose second dimension rests on Nye's own distinction between the soft and hard facets of power.

Recognising cyber as a new form of power, Hu (2016) argues that it has broken the notion of state as the largest independent political unit in the international system and has had a strong impact on the traditional understanding of sovereignty and power structures. Notwithstanding the fact that states continue to be the most influential actors in cyberspace, the domain is much more contested with the presence of a wide spectrum of entities which include civil society organisations, private enterprises, individual citizens, terrorist outfits, insurgent groups, criminal syndicates, multilateral global institutions, and media. Power emanates from their mutual interactions, and since the relations through which it is enacted and constructed are not confined to cyberspace, power extends into, out of, and through cyberspace (Betz and Stevens, 2011: 38–41). For states, cyberspace seems to strengthen existing power structures and present unique advantages, especially as a force multiplier enabling smaller ones to tackle a larger opponent. This makes cyber power both a deterrent and an unconventional weapon (Manjikian, 2010). Military, economic, and technological capabilities have long been seen as the pillars of state power. This view has strongly influenced the early analyses on the concept of cyber power, with frequent reference to the P/DIME activities and instruments of state power.

Cyber power has also drawn from wider perspectives, encompassing the aspects of cybersecurity, cyber defence, civil-government relations, and even soft power as in the ability to shape global cybersecurity discourse by persuasive diplomacy, and setting agenda, standards, and norms. On the relation of cyber power to the broader concept of power, Cavelty notes two different notions – one finds cyber power to be a measure of readiness or preparedness such as the level of cybersecurity, resilience to cyber-attacks, and the ability to shape the environment as per own interests, while the other deems cyber power as a supplement to the political power (Cavelty, 2018: 13). Cyber power is often deemed to be an enabler for the instruments of power or having a formidable impact on the other operational domains, though argued widely to be devoid of having independent war-winning capacity.

Sheldon views cyber power to be subservient to the needs of policy, and strategy as the bridge between policy and exploitation of the cyber instrument. He argues that it is best used in support of, and in conjunction with, other military and national instruments of power (Sheldon, 2011: 103–104). Gray also deems cyber power to be useful as an enabler of joint military operations, and asserts that it should be understood as just another category of weapon, but it is devoid of applying force itself and has limited stand-alone usability in generating coercive strategic effect (Gray, 2013: 54). Borghard and Lonergan do not recognise cyber power as an ideal independent tool of coercion, or in other words, not so effective a tool when used in isolation from the conventional instruments of power to undermine adversary's ability or willingness to resist (Borghard and

Lonergan, 2017: 472, 479). Betz and Stevens (2011) also note that cyber power is fundamentally a manifestation of power in cyberspace, and not a new, or, different form of power. These views essentially call for greater integration of cyber with the conventional conceptions and instruments of power and enhanced synergy between the government, military, civilian, and industry, and among the organs of the state to achieve the desired effects.

Models and classifications help build a nuanced understanding of the concept of cyber power from both theoretical and policy perspectives. Adapting the existing taxonomies or proposing new ones, they collate different facets and perspectives so that the decision-makers or analysts can figure out what kind of power a state demonstrates or experiences in its interactions or relations with other actors in the system. Classifications are also an effective tool to identify the areas or actions that are likely to build a specific characteristic of cyber power. Another mechanism which could be considered critical to decision-making and calibrate own actions commensurate with those of others is assessment of cyber power – basically an evaluation of capability and intent based on a set of indicators.

### Cyber power assessment

The idea of cyber power assessment stems from the effectiveness of established measures of military power, which are based on the assessment of both tangible and intangible attributes. An evaluation of the capabilities of another state to exercise the cyber option in support of its national interests is pivotal to the very decision to exercise its own cyber power. Cyber power is essentially seen as a composite of capabilities spread across the government, industry, military, and civilian spheres, whose effectiveness hinges upon the ability to integrate the resources and draw synergies between these pillars.

Cyber power indices take an evidence-based approach to evaluate the relative cyber power of states. Some of the leading security think-tanks have come up with cyber power indices based on methodologies derived from their respective conceptualisation of cyber power. The earliest effort in this direction was the *Cyber Power Index* published in 2011 – a benchmarking study of digital adoption, cyber security, and the economic and regulatory environment in G20 countries developed by the Economist Intelligence Unit and Booz Allen Hamilton (Booz Allen Hamilton, 2012). The Potomac Institute published *Cyber Readiness Index 1.0* in 2013, followed by an expanded version in 2015 (Hathaway et al., 2015). The index evaluated a country's maturity and commitment to securing its national cyber infrastructure and services against the backdrop of the rising economic cost of cyber insecurity. The *Global Cyber Security Index* of the International Telecommunications Union is a trusted reference that assesses each country's level of development or engagement in cybersecurity, but it mainly focuses on domestic cyber resilience and is based on member states' self-assessment (ITU, 2020).

Belfer Center's *National Cyber Power Index 2020* measures cyber capabilities in the context of seven national objectives that countries pursue through cyber means, using intent and capability indicators for 30 countries (Voo et al., 2020). A measure of proven power and potential, the final score of a country in the index assumes that the respective government can wield these capabilities effectively. The International Institute for Strategic Studies published *Cyber Capabilities and National Power: A Net Assessment* in 2021, which provides an assessment of the cyber capabilities of states and how it contributes to the national power. The report provides a qualitative analysis of cyber ecosystem and capabilities of 15 countries based on seven categories (IISS, 2021).

Some of the scholarly writings on cyber power assessment are also noteworthy. Borghard and Lonergan observe that cyber power indices could help ascertain another state's ability to carry out threats or be used as a measure of relative strength, and their absence leaves states with no option of signalling or communicating their capability. According to them, indices of cyber power may encompass budgetary allocation, numbers of personnel in cyber forces and the scope and extent of their training, cyber commands under the armed forces, scope of national-level cyber exercises, and the participation in cyber exercises of international repute (Borghard and Lonergan, 2017: 464–465).

Along the lines of military power assessment, Willett argues for objective quantification and measurement of cyber power and assessment of a nation's ability to develop and use cyber capabilities to understand, influence, disrupt and even destroy adversaries' systems (Willett, 2019: 86). Willett identifies three possible indicators of cyber power – the capacity to join cyber capabilities across government, industry, military, and civilian space; raise a skilled workforce; and the intelligence capability in cyberspace for situational awareness (Willett, 2019: 89–90). In his view, other factors which could be considered for such an analysis include technical capacity, investments in research and development, integration of strategy and doctrine, scope and scale of cyber exercises, experience in defensive and offensive cyber operations, cyber-related legislative provisions, and the political will to use it as an instrument of power.

Bebber breaks down the assessment of cyber power into two parts: one is potential cyber power and the other is cyber effectiveness. The resources of potential cyber power, according to Bebber, include information culture, technology industry, information networks, political institutions, civil–government relations, foreign partnerships, and the capacity for technology diffusion, innovation, and adaptation (Bebber, 2017: 427–430). For cyber effectiveness, Bebber adapts the four central attributes that Brooks has identified in relation to military effectiveness – *integration* (synergies between strategic, operational, and tactical aspects and consistency across policy, strategy, and tactics), *responsiveness* (accommodate internal and external constraints and opportunities), *skill* (motivation and competencies to assimilate new technology, adopt new strategies and tactics, training, etc.), and *quality* (of equipment) (Brooks, 2007: 10–13). Bebber adds reputation as the fifth attribute, which is the perception shared by adversaries and actors of a state's cyber capabilities and willingness to exercise cyber power to achieve its national goals (Bebber, 2017: 426–434).

Li (2012) elucidates seven essential elements of cyber power, which include the ability to innovate and apply research outcomes in IT, leadership in the global IT industry, size of the internet infrastructure, internet penetration and its use in diverse industries, technology and thought leadership in internet governance, and the ability to deter threat actors and conduct offensive operations in cyberspace. Li further argues that merely possessing these capabilities is not sufficient to be a cyber power, and it depends considerably upon the intent or willingness of the country to possess and use that power as part of a well-defined cyberspace strategy (Li, 2012: 802–803). Fang and Hu (2014) identify a globally competitive internet or IT industry, the ability to defend critical infrastructure, and deterrence in cybersecurity and military terms as the key constituents of cyber power. Comprehensive evaluation to measure a country's cyber capability, in Lyu's view, should include technological research and development and innovation capabilities, IT industry companies, cyber diplomacy, cyber military strength, and comprehensiveness of the cyber strategy (Lyu, 2019).

Assessment of cyber power is a complex exercise given the number of factors at play, the intangible nature of many indicators or constituents, and the shrouded character of cyber capabilities due to strategic considerations. Some of the indicators that are comparatively easy to assess as information about these is publicly available include budgetary allocations, the existence of cyber commands or specialised agencies for cyber operations, the numbers of personnel reported to be part of these agencies, the capacity for and investment into technology research and innovation, and the strategies, laws, and policies related to cyber affairs to name a few. Some of the indicators that could be difficult to assess as their basis of assessment is more qualitative in nature include the quality of research and innovation ecosystems, influence at the multilateral or multistakeholder platforms, international partnerships, the ability to integrate capabilities spread across government, industry, military, and civilian space, and the integration of principles of doctrines, strategies, and tactics in the military domain.

Moreover, offensive cyber capabilities and the capabilities residing in the intelligence agencies and armed forces are particularly difficult to gauge. It is equally challenging to capture the full spectrum of elements or components of cyber power of a state, be it capabilities or intentions. Considering these constraints, a universal measure or index of cyber power is not viable and cyber power therefore should be analysed in the specific context of a state. Notwithstanding these challenges, an assessment of one's own cyber power as well as that of the adversaries' is critical to informed decision-making, especially when cyberspace has permeated all the traditional functions of a state and impacted all the instruments of power.

### A model for cyber power

The interaction between various attributes, resources, constituents, or indicators of cyber power discussed above could better be understood with the help of a graphical representation. For this purpose, Figure 2.1 depicts the *Capacities* and *Capabilities* required for a cyber power across the four dimensions over which state efforts of building cyber capabilities are generally spread across. These dimensions are *National Cyber Policy, Cyber Diplomacy, Emerging Digital Technologies*, and *Military Cyber Policy*. *National Cyber Policy* encompasses the efforts in the domestic realm, while *Cyber Diplomacy* surrounds international engagements related to the governance of the internet and cyberspace. Likewise, *Emerging Digital Technologies* relates to the technology development aspects of cyber power and *Military Cyber Policy* pertains to cyber capabilities in the military domain. Cyber power comprises multiple constituents which could either be categorised as *Capacities* or *Capabilities*. Under each of these four dimensions, states may require building and harnessing these *Capacities* and *Capabilities* to achieve certain *Outcomes* or *Objectives*, which in aggregate tend to shape their *Cyber Power*.

The rationale for considering *Capacities* and *Capabilities* together for analysis is that the capacities themselves do not automatically or necessarily translate into power outcomes, and capabilities largely remain intangible and subject to variations in assessment. An entirely either capacity-based or capability-based interpretation of cyber power could therefore be inadequate.

*Capacities* include the attributes which are resource-based or the information about them is either available in the public domain or could be derived from publicly available information. Under *National Cyber Policy*, the *Capacities* may include attributes such as advanced information infrastructure, high expenditure on R&D in technology, and the existence of strategies, policies, or laws related to cybersecurity as well as institutions or agencies dedicated to cyber affairs. A strong intellectual property protection regime and any historical evidence of the use of cyber as an instrument of power by the state could be the other attributes.

Under *Cyber Diplomacy*, the *Capacities* may include historical evidence of the state exerting influence in global governance processes, a stated intent

**National Cyber Policy**

**Capacities Required**
- Advanced Information Infrastructure
- High R&D Expenditure
- Cybersecurity Strategies/Policies/Laws
- Institutions/Agencies for Cyber Affairs
- Strong IP Protection Regime
- Historical Evidence of Using Cyber as an Instrument of Power

**Capabilities Required**
- Support/Disposition of Leadership
- Effective Implementation of Policies
- Prominent Positioning of Cyber Affairs Agencies within the Government
- Existence of Information Society

**Cyber Diplomacy**

**Capacities Required**
- Historical Evidence of Influence in Global Governance Processes
- Clear/Stated Intent to set Agenda for Internet/Cyber Governance
- Ability to Forge/Leverage Global Partnerships/Alliances
- International Cyber Strategy in Place

**Capabilities Required**
- Ability to Establish New Institutions
- Influence in Cyber Governance Processes
- Influence in Multilateral Organisations
- Ability to Synergize International Cyber Strategy with National Strategies/Policies

**Emerging Digital Technologies (ETs)**

**Capacities Required**
- High Investment in the R&D of ETs and Corresponding Infrastructure
- Availability of Highly-Skilled Workforce in Technology Research and Development
- Advanced Technology Industrial Base
- Focus on Technical Education & Training
- Easy Access to Capital/Investment

**Capabilities Required**
- Ability to Conduct High-Quality R&D
- Effective Academia-Industry Collaboration/Interface
- Globally Competitive Innovation Ecosystem and Industry

**Military Cyber Policy**

**Capacities Required**
- Existence of Cyber Forces/Cyber Command
- Access to Quality Training
- Participation in International Cyber Exercises
- Prominence of Cyber in Military Thought/Doctrine/Strategy/Education

**Capabilities Required**
- Deeper Civil-Military Integration
- Experience in Conducting Cyber Ops
- Jointness in Military Operations
- Integration of Cyber with Military Doctrines, Strategies, and Tactics

**Expected Outcomes/Objectives**

- Accelerate Digital Economy & Social Development/Prosperity
- Ensure Security & Resilience of National Infrastructures and Services
- Protect & Promote Interests/Values and Tackle Risks to National Security
- Strengthen Cybersecurity Ecosystem

- Shape Interests, Opinions and Preferences of Other Actors
- Shape Cyber Governance and Norms According to Own Interests and Values
- Leverage Multilateral Organisations/Partnerships/Alliances to Promote Interests
- Enhance Capacity of Partners/Allies

- Build Intellectual Property Assets
- Develop National Standards
- Gain Leadership Role in International Standards-Setting Bodies
- Accelerate Technology Diffusion and Commercialization
- Achieve Technology Supremacy

- Execute Cyber Ops/Cyber-Enabled Information & Psychological Ops in support of Geopolitical/Security Goals
- Develop a Credible Cyber Deterrence Posture
- Defend Military Information Systems
- Support Joint Military Operations

## Cyber Power

**Purposes of Exercising Cyber Power**

| Cybersecurity | Influence | Persuasion | Coercion | Inflict Punishment | Meet Political Ends |
|---|---|---|---|---|---|
| Deter State/Non-State Actors | Prevent Foreign Interference | Preserve Political System | Improve International Standing | Defend Sovereignty | Shape the Outcome of Geopolitical Events |

**FIGURE 2.1** Graphical depiction of cyber power constituents.

Prepared by the author.

to play an influential role in the internet or cyber governance, a known ability to forge partnerships or alliances and leverage them, and the existence of a strategy for international engagement on cyber issues.

Likewise, under *Emerging Digital Technologies*, the *Capacities* may include high investment in R&D activities pertaining to emerging technologies and building the corresponding research infrastructure, availability of highly skilled workforce for R&D in the priority areas of technology, the existence of an advanced technology industrial base, focus of the state on technical education and training, and easy access to capital or investment for the commercialisation of technology.

As part of *Military Cyber Policy*, the *Capacities* may include the existence of cyber forces or a cyber command, access to quality training for cyber forces, participation in international cyber exercises, and the prominence of cyber in military thought, doctrine, and strategy as well as in professional military education.

*Capabilities*, on the other hand, include those characteristics which are largely intangible in nature, and could broadly be understood as qualities of the state. It is difficult to make an accurate assessment of them. Under *National Cyber Policy*, the *Capabilities* may include support of the political leadership for cyber affairs or its disposition towards cyber affairs, effective implementation of cyber strategies and policies, prominent positioning of agencies charged with cyber affairs within the government hierarchy, and the existence of information society in the state.

As part of *Cyber Diplomacy*, the *Capabilities* may include the ability to establish new institutions for issues of global importance, the influence of the state in existing cyber governance processes as well as in multilateral organisations, and its ability to synergise the international cyber strategy with the national strategies and policies devised for cybersecurity.

Under *Emerging Digital Technologies*, the *Capabilities* may include the ability of the state to carry out cutting-edge R&D of international standards, effective collaboration or interface between the academia and the industry, and the presence of a globally competitive innovation ecosystem and industry in the state.

As part of *Military Cyber Policy*, the *Capabilities* may include deeper Civil–Military integration in the technology sphere, the experience of the armed forces in conducting cyber operations, a higher degree of jointness in military operations, and the integration of cyber with military doctrines, strategies, and tactics.

By harnessing this ensemble of *Capacities* and *Capabilities* spread over *National Cyber Policy*, *Cyber Diplomacy*, *Emerging Digital Technologies*, and *Military Cyber Policy*, states would expect certain *Outcomes/ Objectives* in the respective dimensions. Under *National Cyber Policy*, for instance, these could be accelerating the growth of digital economy and social development or achieving national prosperity, ensuring the security and resilience of information infrastructure and services, protecting and promoting own interests and values in cyberspace, tackling risks to national security, and strengthening the nationwide cybersecurity ecosystem. The expected *Outcomes* from *Cyber Diplomacy* could be shaping the interests, opinions, and preferences of other actors; shaping cyber governance and norms in accordance with own interests and values; leveraging multilateral organisations, partnerships, or alliances to advance interests in cyberspace; and enhancing the capacity of partners or allies in cybersecurity or building digital infrastructure.

As part of *Emerging Digital Technologies*, the expected *Outcomes* could be building intellectual property assets and developing national standards for emerging digital technologies, gaining a leadership position in international standards–setting bodies, accelerating technology diffusion and commercialisation, and achieving technology supremacy. The expected *Outcomes* from *Military Cyber Policy* could be executing cyber operations or cyber-enabled information and psychological operations in support of geopolitical and security goals, developing a credible cyber deterrence posture, defending military information systems from adversaries, and supporting the execution of joint military operations.

The *Outcomes/Objectives* that states seek to achieve from harnessing *Capacities* and *Capabilities* basically shape their *Cyber Power*. In other words, *Cyber Power* could be seen as an ensemble of these *Outcomes/Objectives* which states seek to achieve from their activities and engagements in cyberspace. States can exercise their *Cyber Power* to meet quite a broad spectrum of purposes, and these could be – ensuring cybersecurity, exerting influence, persuading or coercing other actors, inflicting punishment in response to a hostile act, meeting political ends, deterring adversarial state or non-state actors from hostile acts, preventing foreign interference, preserving own political system, improving international standing, defending sovereignty, or shaping the outcome of geopolitical events.

Figure 2.1 tries to depict how cyber power actually builds up from a wide range of activities that states engage in as they execute their functions in the domestic realm, their foreign and security policy, the technology sphere, and in the military domain. It must however be clarified that making an assessment of cyber power is not the objective here, but rather to look in a broad manner at the aggregation of cyber power constituents. Building up on this understanding of cyber power, the forthcoming chapters of the book analyse cyber power in the context of China one-by-one across these four dimensions. The next section explains the framework used for this analysis.

**Framework**

Since the 18th National Congress of the CPC, Xi Jinping in his speeches has consistently outlined the significance of informatisation, the internet, and cyberspace for China. The ideas, advice, and guiding principles for cyber power that Xi has shared in these speeches have in aggregate shaped the strategy and policy decisions of the Chinese Government. The speeches made at different occasions also throw light on the priorities of the Government and help make sense of the contours of cyber power for China. In a way, they help interpret what cyber power means for China and how does the political leadership evaluate the progress of the ambitious task of building China into a cyber superpower. In order to gain a better understanding of the approach to this task, the book looked at the speeches of Xi Jinping at significant occasions along with the speeches and writings of senior leaders and the key strategy documents. Based on a review of these, the key tenets underpinning the overarching objective of building China into a cyber superpower are identified as follows:

1. *Augmenting indigenous innovation in core technology areas*: The strategic importance of core technologies that underpin the internet architecture, infrastructure, and applications has been highlighted time and again, especially in view of the advantage the United States (US) has over China in this segment. Indigenous innovation in core technology areas was mentioned in the first meeting of the Central Leading Group. Xi Jinping in his speech at the 2016 *National Cyber Security and Informatization Work Conference* underscored that core technology controlled by others is a risk and the prominent Chinese enterprises lack the clout of their American counterparts such as Microsoft, Intel, Google, or Apple (China Copyright and Media, 2016b). Indigenous innovation in information technology is amongst the "six accelerations" that Xi Jinping stressed on to move towards the goal of building China into a cyber superpower while presiding over the 36th collective study session[1] of the Central Political Bureau in October 2016. He even went on to say that "core technology is the most important weapon of the country" at the 2018 *National Cyber Security and Informatization Work Conference* (Xinhua, 2018a). Speaking at a Politburo study session on the digital economy in October 2021, Xi reiterated the imperatives of self-reliance and indigenous innovation in critical and core technologies (Creemers, Costigan, et al., 2022; Xi, 2022).

   The *National Medium- and Long-Term Program for Science and Technology Development (2006–2020)* identified the core technology areas in the information industry as integrated circuits and key components, major software, high-performance computers, broadband mobile telecommunication, and the next-generation internet. The 14th Five-Year Plan, as part of innovation in key digital technologies, lays down cutting-edge computer chips, operating systems, cloud computing systems, quantum computing and communications, etc., as the priority areas of technology development (NDRC, 2021). The recent 2022 *Report on the Work of the Government* speaks of building digital industries such as integrated circuits and artificial intelligence, and enhancing China's technological innovation and capacities for key software and hardware (K. Li, 2022). Narrowing the technology gap with the West has been a long-standing goal of the party-state, engendered by the strong conviction that leadership in technology paves the way for dominance in global governance systems and elevates a country's status in the international system. The fifth chapter examines this tenet with the case studies of select emerging digital technologies.

2. *Strengthening cybersecurity*: Ensuring network security/cybersecurity remains to be one of the key objectives and the leadership perceived it as a precondition to development. This echoes the famous quote of Xi Jinping which goes as, "security and development are like the two wings of a bird or the two wheels of a cart. Security ensures development, and development is what security is aimed at" (Xi, 2015). The focus on cybersecurity was apparent in the first meeting of the Central Leading Group. Cyber defence capabilities also feature amongst the "six accelerations." Protection of critical information infrastructure, cybersecurity monitoring, defensive and deterrence capability, and a slew of other cybersecurity measures featured in the speech made by Xi Jinping at the 2016 *National Cyber Security and Informatization Work Conference*.

A 2017 article published by the Theoretical Studies Center Group of the Cyberspace Administration of China in *Qiushi* had also identified ensuring cybersecurity and critical information infrastructure protection as one of the four major dimensions of China's strategy for cyber power (CAC, 2017b). On cybersecurity, the former Minister of Industry and Information Technology Miao Wei in his speech at a Theoretical Study Center Group meeting in 2016 had brought up the significance of core technologies for network security, situational awareness, and defence and deterrence capabilities (Miao, 2016).

Zhuang Rongwen, the director of the Cyberspace Administration of China, in a 2021 article elucidated measures such as cybersecurity assurance system, supply chain security, and the protection of personal information and data to strengthen national cyber defence (Zhuang, 2021). Zheng Bijian, the former executive vice president of the Central Party School, in a 2021 article mentioned enhancing cyber defence and deterrence capabilities amongst other measures to build China into a cyber superpower (B. Zheng, 2021).

Strengthening cybersecurity, data security, and personal information protection featured as one of the action items in the *Report on the Work of the Government* for both 2021 and 2022 (K. Li, 2021, 2022). The 14th Five-Year Plan indicated continuity in the efforts to improve national cybersecurity laws, regulations and standards, and develop cybersecurity infrastructure and the capacity to implement cybersecurity measures (NDRC, 2021). Cybersecurity is deemed to be a precondition to development, and hence it weighs heavily in China's conceptualisation of cyber power and is prioritised in the informatisation agenda warranting direct supervision of the highest echelons of political leadership. The third chapter discusses some of the aspects of this tenet in detail.

3. *Influencing internet/cyber governance*: Since 2014, Xi Jinping has categorically emphasised the importance of international cooperation and influence in global cyberspace governance decision-making. At the opening ceremony of the second edition of the World Internet Conference in December 2015, Xi promulgated "four principles" and "five proposals" to transform the global internet governance system (Xi, 2015). Respect for cyber sovereignty is one of the four principles and it forms the premise of China's international engagement. Reform of the global internet governance system was also discussed at the 2018 *National Cyber Security and Informatization Work Conference,* while international discourse power or the influence in global cyberspace governance decision-making was one of the "six accelerations." The 2017 article of Theoretical Studies Center Group had also discussed increasing China's role in building, governing, and operating the internet globally as one of the four dimensions of China's strategy for cyber power.

At the 2018 *National Cybersecurity and Informatization Work Conference,* Xi Jinping categorically said that China should take the "Belt and Road Initiative as an opportunity to strengthen cooperation with countries along the route, in building network infrastructure, digital economy, and cybersecurity, and build the 21st Century Digital Silk Road" (Xinhua, 2018e). At the Politburo study session on digital economy held in 2021, Xi pressed on active participation in negotiations at international organisations on digital economy and asserting China's voice at these platforms (Creemers, Costigan, et al., 2022; Xi, 2022). On China's international engagement, the 14th Five-Year Plan prioritises reforming the global cyberspace infrastructure and resource governance mechanism, developing international rules and digital technology standards, and providing assistance in technology, equipment, and services to less developed countries. China's cyber diplomatic engagement envisions providing Chinese solutions to the reform of the global cyber governance system, with the end goal of increasing China's normative influence and garnering international acceptability of its multilateral approach to cyberspace governance. China's concept of sovereignty in cyberspace is discussed in the third chapter and its cyber diplomatic efforts are the focal point of the fourth chapter.

4. *Strengthening CPC's control over information and leadership over cybersecurity and informatisation work*: One of the talking points in Xi Jinping's speech at the 2016 *National Cyber Security and Informatization Work Conference* was related to online content, propaganda, and public opinion. He further remarked that "the internet is not a land outside the law", and the use of the internet for subversion, stirring religious extremism, propagating ethnic separatism, or instigating terrorist activities must be firmly curbed (China Copyright and Media, 2016b). Later, at the 2018 *National Cyber Security and Informatization Work Conference,* he stressed on strengthening online positive propaganda and public opinion orientation. The 2017 article by Theoretical Studies Center Group listed managing internet content as one of the four major dimensions of China's strategy for cyber power. The article reiterated the action items such as innovation in positive propaganda online, guidance of online public opinion, and management of the online ecosystem.

Zhuang Rongwen has also laid strong emphasis on guiding public opinion over the internet in his articles and supported taking online public opinion work as the top priority of propaganda and ideological work (Zhuang, 2021). He further stressed that the internet has increasingly become the main battlefield and the forefront of ideological struggles, and spoke about maintaining the ideological and political security of the internet. The end goal of this task of managing online content and public opinion is information control, and this has engendered the rigorous censorship regime to curb freedom of expression and freedom of access to information online. It also plays an important role in maintaining the supremacy of the CPC. China's designs for controls and censorship over the internet are discussed in the third chapter.

Strengthening CPC's leadership over cybersecurity and informatisation work in China found a mention in Xi Jinping's speech at the 2018 *National Cyber Security and Informatization Work Conference* as the means to advance in the correct direction. Highlighting the challenges emanating from the internet, the 2017 article of Theoretical Studies Center Group noted that if the CPC "cannot traverse the hurdle represented by the internet, it cannot traverse the hurdle of remaining in power for the long term" (CAC, 2017b). Denoting strong leadership of

CPC as the fundamental requirement for building a world-class cyber power, Zheng Bijian in an article advocated preparing the CPC for this opportunity with a sense of urgency. The decision to upgrade the Central Leading Group for Cybersecurity and Informatization to the Central Cyberspace Affairs Commission in March 2018 could also be seen as a step towards strengthening the leadership and role of the CPC on overall cybersecurity and informatisation work within China (Xinhua, 2019b).

5. *Accelerating the digital economy*: At the first meeting of the Central Leading Group, Xi Jinping had mentioned comprehensive development of the digital economy, which now contributes significantly to China's economic growth. The digital economy is one of the "six accelerations" as well. At the 2018 *National Cyber Security and Informatization Work Conference*, Xi had mentioned of developing the digital economy and accelerating the promotion of digital industrialisation. In his speech at a Theoretical Study Center Group meeting in 2016, Miao Wei spoke about implementing the *Internet Plus Action Plan* and the State Council's guiding opinions on deepening the integrated development of manufacturing and the internet. In the 2017 article of Theoretical Studies Center Group, development of the digital economy featured as the means to improve productivity and economic development. Speaking at a Politburo study session on digital economy in October 2021, Xi Jinping further emphasised on the task of integrating digital economy and the real economy, recognising the role of digital technologies in the expansion and growth of China's economic development.

   On similar lines, the 2021 *Report on the Work of the Government* also mentioned that digitalisation will be sped up to accelerate the digital economy and transform traditional industries with digital technologies. The 14th Five-Year Plan speaks of building a strong position in digital economy with a focus on the development of key technologies and digital industries and the digital transformation of traditional industries. The recent 2022 *Report on the Work of the Government* speaks of augmenting the digital China initiative and advancing digitalisation of industries. China has witnessed a rapid growth in digital economy over the last two decades owing to aggressive policy measures for the expansion of ICT infrastructure and integration of IT with the traditional sectors of the economy. Digital economy has become one of the prime drivers of China's economic growth and China attaches great importance to further enhancing its digital economy. The third chapter devotes some discussion to digital economy.

6. *Building cyber military capabilities*: At a Political Bureau meeting held in 2014, Xi Jinping called on the PLA to develop a new strategy for "information warfare" and said that China must promote innovation

in the armed forces. He also urged for a "change in the mindset dominated by mechanized warfare and pressed on the need to establish a new military doctrine, institutions, and strategies and tactics for information warfare" (*China Daily*, 2014b). A year ago, the 2013 edition of *Science of Military Strategy* – a joint publication by military scholars at the PLA Academy of Military Science – had taken notice of the emergence of space and cyberspace as the domains of warfare and the shift in the control of battlefield from land and sea to space and cyberspace (Academy of Military Science, 2013).[2] China's Military Strategy – released in 2015 – articulated the intent to raise a cyber force and adjusted the basic point for preparations for military struggle of the armed forces to 'winning informationized local wars' (State Council, 2015b). The 2020 edition of *Science of Military Strategy* published by the National Defense University notes that "the victory of the war begins with the victory of cyberspace." The edition features cyberspace as part of the discussion on "military conflict in new domains", and includes an entire section on how to develop a cyber force (National Defense University, 2020).[3]

One of the key aspects of building cyber capabilities in the military domain is the integration of efforts with the civilian domain – dubbed as military–civil integration and prioritised heavily by the Chinese leadership in its cybersecurity and informatisation work. At the 2018 *National Cyber Security and Informatization Work Conference*, Xi Jinping had pointed out that cybersecurity and informatisation are the frontiers of military–civil integration (Qiushi, 2018). The 2017 article of Theoretical Studies Center Group had also mentioned of augmenting military–civil integration for cybersecurity and informatisation and working towards relevant policies. The 14th Five-Year Plan seeks to boost collaborative military–civil efforts in cyberspace, artificial intelligence, and quantum science and technology amongst other areas. The sixth chapter focuses on PLA's efforts to build cyber military capabilities in China.

Speeches and authoritative writings from the Chinese leadership commend the progress made so far, especially in terms of the number of internet users in China, but simultaneously present its diagnosis on the lacunae in some of the critical aspects. Though largely qualitative in nature, these concern capabilities gaps such as those in core technologies of the internet, dependence on technologies of foreign origin, and relatively limited influence of China over global internet governance institutions. The abovementioned tenets of the objective of building China into a cyber superpower form the premise of the next four chapters of the book. They inform the scope of the discussion on China as each of the chapters delves into one specific dimension of the cyber power model introduced earlier.

## Notes

1 Initiated by Hu Jintao in 2002, collective study sessions are delivered by leading experts to the members of the Political Bureau of the CPC Central Committee. Covering a wide range of disciplines, collective study sessions can provide some cues to the key strategic and policy issues that China's top leadership is pondering over.
2 Translated into English by the China Aerospace Studies Institute.
3 Translated into English by the China Aerospace Studies Institute.

# 3

# CHINA'S TRYST WITH CYBERSPACE

## Priorities and perspectives

China's pursuit of "informatization" has unfurled a digital revolution. China has made great strides in the field of information and communication technologies, and the political leadership has now set the vision of taking China to new heights of economic and social development leveraging cyberspace and digital technologies. China has its own perspectives of cyberspace, which define its expectations from this domain and its vision for the governance of cyberspace. The chapter takes a historical account of the evolution and consolidation of China's informatisation plans, efforts for the nationwide implementation of these vast plans, and the specialised agencies, ministries, and administrative bodies established in the due course of time to spearhead policy-making and execute the key technical functions.

The chapter elucidates China's earlier cybersecurity (or internet security) efforts and the high priority attached to cybersecurity since the current leadership took over the reins of the Chinese Government in 2012–2013. It looks at the economic imperatives of cyberspace for China, before making an attempt to interpret cyber power connotations from the slew of measures taken by the Government such as cybersecurity strategy, laws, and controls and censorship for online content. The principle of cyber sovereignty, China's conception of cyber power, and the international perspectives on China's cyber power are discussed towards the end of the chapter.

## A historical account of China's digital revolution

Recognition of the importance of communications in the affairs of the state runs deep in the history of China. The efforts to build a communication infrastructure in China date back to 1877, in the form of a

DOI: 10.4324/9781003473510-3

telegraph line in Taiwan during the rule of the Qing dynasty (Harwit, 1998). The Qing Government, as early as 1906, had raised a ministry – the Ministry of Posts and Communications – to supervise the functioning of telegraphs, posts, and railways (Bowman, 2000). A robust information infrastructure is the cornerstone of a modern society, economy, and the state as they depend heavily on information and communication technologies (ICTs) for a wide range of functions and activities. The systems built to collect, process, and disseminate information have themselves advanced in leaps and bounds ever since they have become digitalised. The growth of technology in the cyber and digital spheres continues to outpace policy measures. The realisation of the economic, security, and strategic imperatives of advancing ICTs; internet and the associated technologies; and the dynamics of cyberspace reflects in the prominence the Chinese government has placed in the development and nurturing of globally competitive electronics and information technology industries. Ever since the foundation of science and technology in modern China was laid, a strong emphasis has been placed on the fields of communications, electronics, computing, and information technology, ushering China into a digital revolution.

Informatisation, or digitalisation, is generally viewed as the means to enhance economic and social advancement, widely recognised by states as integral to national development. Jiang Zemin in 1991 categorically pointed out that none of the four modernisations can be achieved without informatisation. Jiang Zemin – an electrical engineer by education – brought with him the exceptional experience as a Minister of Electronics Industry which he headed from 1982 to 1985. The layout of key projects of informatisation for the Tenth Five-Year Plan elaborated informatisation as an integrated system, with the extensive application of information technologies as its aim, information resources as its nucleus, information network as its basis, information industry as its pillar, information talents as its reliance, and regulations, policies and legal standards as its safeguard (Xu, 2004).

The six pillars of informatisation identified were – information resources, national information network, information technology applications, information technology industry, talent, and policies, regulations, and standards. All these pillars of informatisation have received ardent support from the leadership in China, be it at the level of national, provincial, or municipal governments. In one of the first and key policy decisions towards informatisation, the State Council established the National Economic Informatization Council under the chairmanship of Vice-Premier Zou Jiahua in December 1993.

The Chinese Government initiated the famous Golden Projects in the 1990s in order to accelerate the adoption of information technology in key governmental functions. The first three of the Golden Projects were the Golden Bridge, Golden Customs, and Golden Card. Announced in March 1993, the Golden Bridge aimed to construct an information network to connect various ministries and commissions of the State Council with the geographically spread provinces, autonomous regions, and cities. It also intended to connect 12,000 large and medium-sized enterprises and 100 leading business conglomerates. Along with connectivity, applications such as e-mail, electronic data exchange, electronic databases, and information sources were also part of the Golden Bridge project (CNET, 1997).

Started in 1995, the Golden Card project formed the foundation of a cashless economy as it established a nationwide banking network to execute financial transactions electronically, replacing cash transactions in payments and withdrawals with credit and debit cards. The Golden Customs project linked government departments of foreign trade administration, foreign exchange control, and customs services to foreign trade enterprises and state corporations. The project facilitated paperless transactions as it automated the process of customs checks, thereby eliminating transactions in cash (CNET, 1997). The Golden Tax project computerised China's tax collection system, and it built a network for the accounts-clearing system of the People's Bank of China connecting centres in 50 major cities.

China reportedly began working on the idea of connecting the computer networks at its research institutions towards the late 1980s. The China Academic Net project was however launched in 1988 to connect the computers at the Chinese universities and research institutions with those from outside, and in 1991 the Institute of High Energy Physics of the Chinese Academy of Sciences (CAS) was connected with the Stanford Linear Accelerator Center (CNNIC, 2012a). On 20 April 1994, with the international line of the National Computing and Networking Facility of China[1] (an information infrastructure project financially supported by the World Bank) becoming operational and accessing the internet, China became the 77th country in the world to have access to the functioning global internet (Xinhua, 2014a). The following year, the Ministry of Posts and Telecommunications started providing internet services to the public (*China Daily*, 2016), opening the floodgates for the commercial expansion of the internet and associated services in China. As the internet picked exponential growth in China and commercial interests grew, the next few years witnessed a rise in high-level policy and regulatory decisions.

The State Council Leading Group for Informatization Work – a cross-ministerial group to lead and coordinate the nationwide informatisation efforts – was set up in January 1996 chaired by Vice-Premier Zou Jiahua and consisting of over 20 ministers and commissions. The Leading Group was responsible for – laying down work principles and informatisation development strategies; planning for the development of information infrastructure, information industry, and major informatisation projects; supervising their implementation; and coordinating the work related to the drafting of relevant laws and regulations, and formulation of technology standards (China Copyright and Media, 1996). It had replaced the Office of the National Joint Conference for Economic Informatization.

At the National Informatization Working Conference in 1997, the Leading Group defined "national informatization" as "under the uniform planning and organizing of the state, the wide application of modern information technology in agriculture, industry, science and technology, national defense, social life and so on, deeply developing and utilizing information resources to accelerate the process of national modernization" (Bin & Taylor, 2005). This view too closely associated informatisation with the four modernisations and looked at informatisation as the means to accelerate the development process. As informatisation gained traction, informatisation leading groups chaired by local leaders were founded in a majority of the provinces and municipalities across China (Lu, 2002).

The swelling number of users and the proliferation of internet across the length and breadth of China, especially beyond the government and academia to the wider public, propelled the idea of China as an "information society." Providing services through the internet infrastructure for public interests was a key policy objective, and to meet that, the China Internet Network Information Center (CNNIC) was established in June 1997 (CNNIC, 2012b). The CNNIC was tasked with the management of technical functions of the internet in China, and the construction, operation, and administration of infrastructure in the Chinese information society. The CNNIC is China's national internet registry which coordinates Internet Protocol (IP) address and autonomous system number allocations, and it performs other internet resource management functions at the national level. It is also responsible for national-level root server setting and maintenance. The CNNIC operates and manages the .CN country code top-level domain and the Chinese domain name system, and provides services for domain name registration and resolution. The wide gamut of CNNIC's functions and responsibilities includes operation, administration and security of fundamental internet resources, and research on the latest developments in policies and technologies pertaining to the internet (CNNIC, 2012b).

The *Outline of the National Informatization Development Plan*, released in 1997, established the broader framework for the Government to proceed in the different aspects of informatisation promotion, formulation of relevant policies and regulations, and the development of information resources, network infrastructure, the information technology industry, and skilled human resources (Qiang, 2007). As part of the restructuring plan of the State Council adopted at the first session of the Ninth National People's Congress, the Ministry of Electronics Industry, the Ministry of Posts and Telecommunications, and the information and network management functions of the Ministry of Radio, Film, and Television were consolidated to form the Ministry of Information Industry (MII) in March 1998.

The MII began supervising the development of China's information industry, which mainly encompassed manufacturing of electronics and information technology products, telecommunications, and software. It was responsible for charting out development strategies and plans, technical policies, and regulations; laying down products' quality criteria; managing domain and website resources; supervising the enforcement of laws and administrative rules; and ensuring information security (FAS, 2000). The Ministry was also responsible for all the functions of the State Council Leading Group for Informatization, which was upgraded to a National Informatization Leading Group in December 1999 chaired by Vice-Premier Wu Bangguo as the strategic importance and relevance of information, information infrastructure, and the internet grew for the governments globally (China Copyright and Media, 1999; CNNIC, 2012b).

The electronics industry was designated as the topmost pillar industry of the national economy as the scale of the industry touched one trillion Yuan in the year 2000 (*People's Daily*, 2001). By 2000, China's most prominent technology firms of the present times were already founded – Tencent in November 1998, Alibaba in April 1999, and Baidu in January 2001. Then President Jiang Zemin reiterated the idea "informatization driving industrialization" at the World Computer Congress held at Beijing in August 2000. It was one of the first major conferences related to computers and the internet held in China.

Informatisation was further integrated with economic planning as the Tenth Five-Year Plan (2001–2005) underscored the need to leverage information technology to stimulate industrialisation and committed government support over the next five years to high-tech projects such as high-speed, wide-band information networks and integrated circuits. The Plan envisaged industrialisation and information revolution to go hand in hand as informatisation permeated through the production sector, public services, and government administration (Zhu, 2001). Setting forth the long-term agenda of integrating informatisation with the national economy, the Plan triggered China's transition from a user of ICTs for administrative purposes only to that of an information society, drawing emphasis on service-oriented uses of ICTs for the wider sections of society.

A specialised plan for the information technology industry was promulgated as part of the Tenth Five-Year Plan in 2002 (CNNIC, 2012b; State Council, 2010). The national informatisation effort received further thrust with the creation of the State Informatization Leading Group in August 2001. With the Premier (Zhu Rongji) replacing a Vice-Premier as chair of the Leading Group, the topmost leadership began driving the informatisation work. The Leading Group was empowered to make policy proposals, coordinate implementation of the strategy, develop informatisation plans, and draft new laws and regulations. The year 2001 also saw China's accession to the World Trade Organization, paving the way for China's deeper integration with the global political and economic systems and opening vast opportunities for investment, trade, and commerce.

In 2001, China unveiled its own "National Informatization Index" – a statistical system to scientifically evaluate and quantify the degree of informatisation across national, provincial, and municipal areas. Work on the idea of such a unified index – which could provide scientific and quantitative basis for the evaluation of the levels of national and regional informatisation, forecasting trends and further direction of the policy measures for informatisation programmes – began in 1993 in the form of a series of research projects conducted by the experts at the China Information Economy Academy, CAS, Development Research Center of the State Council, and the former Ministry of Posts and Telecommunications, and later spearheaded by the National Bureau of Statistics. An outcome of eight years of extensive research and consultations and multiple iterations, the final version consisted of 25 indices divided across the following five aspects (Yang et al., 2003):

1. Information resources
2. Information infrastructure
3. Information human resources
4. Dissemination and application of information technology
5. Development of information industry

With an eye on the future of the internet, China Next-Generation Internet (CNGI) – a research and development programme – was launched in 2003 to contribute to the advancement of next-generation internet. By 2005, the value addition of the information industry to China's gross domestic product (GDP) was to the tune of 7.2 per cent, and the electronics and information products manufacturing sector had a 30 per cent share in the total value of exports. The *State Informatization Development Strategy (2006–2020)* gave major thrust to China's informatisation endeavour, setting forth the priorities and goals of informatisation development in China for the next 15 years and the long-term vision of a prosperous and harmonious socialist society. The strategy took special note of the shortcomings in indigenous innovation capacity and the application of information technology, and the increasing information security risks. The strategy laid down Deng Xiaoping Theory – leveraging informatisation to drive industrialisation and stimulate development in economics, politics, culture, society, and military affairs, and the development of informatisation with Chinese characteristics as the guiding ideology.

The objectives of the strategy were the nationwide expansion of the information infrastructure, strengthening the indigenous innovation capacity in the field of information technology, development of information industry, safeguarding information, building an information-based economy and society, enhancing the application of information technology in governance and among the public, and strengthening defence and war-fighting capacities under the conditions of informatisation. The nine key areas of strategic focus included informatisation of the national economy (transformation of traditional industries and intelligent production processes), e-governance and social informatisation (such as education, healthcare, and telemedicine), information infrastructure (also next-generation networks), competitiveness of the information industry (technology innovation systems), information security (vigilance, surveillance, monitoring, legal protection, and tracking global trends capacities), and human resources (China Copyright and Media, 2006).

Based on these focus areas, the six-point strategic plan encompassed education and training, action plans for e-commerce and e-government, narrowing the digital divide, and indigenous innovation with a focus on integrated circuits, application software, mobile telecommunications, and next-generation networks. In order to achieve them, the strategy proposed nine concise measures which include – research and policy (information technology in industrial policies, funding, new methods of economic growth, industrial policies for integrated circuits, software and information security, financial policies, preferential treatment to domestic products and services); structural reforms, technology standards, and intellectual property rights protection (for e-commerce, e-governance, information security, personal data protection); internet governance (governance mechanisms, participation in international dialogues, coordination between government, enterprises, sector associations, and citizens); human resources (fostering, attracting foreign expertise, and scholarship); and international cooperation (multilateral and bilateral) (China Copyright and Media, 2006).

As part of the institutional reforms of the State Council, the functions of the MII; the Commission of Science, Technology, and Industry for National Defense; the State Council Informatization Office; the State Tobacco Monopoly Bureau; and industry and trade management functions of the National Development and Reform Commission (NDRC) were consolidated to create the Ministry of Industry and Information Technology (MIIT) in 2008 (State Council, 2014; Xinhua, 2008). In addition to industrial planning, policies and standards, and innovation in the communications sector as the administrative authority of the information industry in China, the Ministry is also responsible for information security in general (State Council, 2014).

The Chinese Government released a white paper titled *The Internet in China* in 2010 presenting the status of internet-related developments in China and elaborating on the basic policies and China's views. The white paper listed security, scientific development, and rule-based order as the basic guiding principles and recognised the importance of a healthy and harmonious internet which is safe, reliable, and conducive to economic and social development. For internet administration, the white paper supported the use of laws, regulations, self-regulation, public supervision, and education to aid China's goals of promoting internet accessibility, protecting freedom of speech, building a market, and ensuring information and national security. At the time of its publication, as the white paper noted, the value addition of the information industry to China's GDP had reached 10 per cent (State Council, 2010).

A study published by the CAS in 2010 presented a 40-year roadmap for China to prepare for the advances in information science and technology by the year 2050. With the overarching objective of realising an information society, the focal areas identified in the roadmap included network science, microelectronics, quantum information sciences, supercomputing, future information service, low-cost information systems, information security, and interdisciplinary sciences of intelligence and cognitive science, bioinformatics, and social informatics. The study listed down the following six major objectives that need attention till 2050 (Lu, 2010: 1–2):

1. A ubiquitous information network
2. Upgradation of information systems
3. A data and knowledge base service industry
4. Upgradation of traditional industries using IT
5. Development of information science and interdisciplinary sciences
6. An information security system

Since the beginning of commercial internet services in China around 1994–1995, the government has proactively pursued a long-term agenda for better integration of the internet, information technology, and ICTs, or in other words informatisation, with the national economy and society to drive China's transition into an information society. To that end, high-level informatisation plans devised and coordinated at the highest levels of political leadership have propelled informatisation of the economy, and development of a national information network and infrastructure and a vibrant information technology industry over the span of more than two-and-half decades. China's contemporary informatisation endeavour aspires to meet the objectives set for the 2050 horizon, and the present leadership of China has left no stone unturned to achieve those objectives. The forthcoming section looks at how did the issue of security in cyberspace (or internet) shape China's institutional responses and leadership priorities. It also locates the positioning of some of the prime institutions within the Chinese Government and the perceived economic imperatives from cyberspace.

## Identifying priorities and building institutions

The Central Leading Group for Cybersecurity and Informatization was established in November 2013 with Xi Jinping as its Chair, tasked with the formulation and implementation of national cybersecurity and informatisation development strategies, macro-level plans, and policies (*China Daily*, 2014a). Xi Jinping had earlier indicated towards the problems such as "multiple authorities, overlapping functions, mismatch of power and responsibility, as well as inefficiency in the management system for cybersecurity" (*People's Daily Online*, 2013). The fact that this was the second leading group chaired by Xi Jinping – in addition to the Central Leading Group for Deepening Overall Reform – speaks volumes about the priority the new leadership assigned to this endeavour.

Since then, China has also taken an active interest in the governance and future of cyberspace with proactive measures on multiple fronts. China provisioned *Cybersecurity Law*, published its *National Cyberspace Security Strategy* and an *International Strategy of Cooperation on Cyberspace*, initiated the annual World Internet Conference, and at the same time reinforced state control and censorship on online information. China also laid emphasis on space and cyber domains for information and joint operations as part of the military modernisation plans (Gill & Ni, 2017; Song, 2017; Zhen, 2016). The Central Leading Group for Cybersecurity and Informatization was later upgraded to the Central Cyberspace Affairs Commission in March 2018, providing it with the much-needed bureaucratic grounding.

After ten years into enforcement, the *State Informatization Development Strategy (2006–2020)* received an overhaul in 2016. The new *Outline of the National Informatization Development Strategy* calibrated the existing strategy in accordance with the changing circumstances in the domestic and global realms, also reflecting the vision of the new central leadership and extending its lifespan to 2025. Although the guiding ideology and the identified shortcomings in the new outline by and large remained the same as the previous edition. Noting that "without informatization, there is no modernization," the strategy deemed informatisation to be important to meet the "two Centenaries" objective, to realise the Chinese Dream of great rejuvenation of the Chinese nation, and to break away from the so-called middle-income trap. Split into six sections, the strategy elaborates on the ways and means to strengthen informatisation development capacities (core technologies, infrastructure, skills, collaboration etc.), enhance economic and social informatisation levels (e-governance, people's livelihood, modern military, etc.), and optimise the informatisation development environment (cyberse-curity, cybersecurity law, personal data protection law, etc.) in addition to the principles, objectives, and present circumstances (China Copyright and Media, 2016a).

Two important aspects featured prominently in this version of the strategy – one is emerging technologies, and the other is international engagement and expansion of China's informatisation plans. The strategy document recursively discussed technology research, development, and industrialisation of the fifth-generation mobile telecommunications (5G), big data, next-generation internet, the internet of things, smart manufacturing, and cybersecurity. As far as international engagement is concerned, the strategy outlined support to the Belt and Road Initiative for the development of a Digital Silk Road, and high-speed network interconnection (optical fibre cable connectivity) with neighbouring countries and regions in the Pacific, Central and Eastern Europe, Southeast Asia, Central Asia, and South Asia.

The strategy espoused vigorous participation in the formulation of international cyber norms and technology standards, and ardent support for the principle of cyber sovereignty, multilateral approach for internet governance (led by governments with participation from enterprises, NGOs, technology community, and citizens), and reform of the Internet Corporation for Assigned Names and Numbers (ICANN). The strategy attached great importance to cyber governance, cybersecurity, and security of the critical information infrastructure professing stringent measures of the sorts of administrative supervision, monitoring, self-discipline, censorship, public opinion management, identity management, and behavioural evaluation.

Speaking at the opening ceremony of the Central Leading Group for Cybersecurity and Informatization, Xi Jinping emphasised that "cybersecurity and informatization are mutually constitutive. Security is the precondition of development, development is the guarantee for security, security and development must progress simultaneously." He also pointed out that "without cybersecurity, there is no national security," underscoring the threat from cyberspace to China's national security and attaching a sense of urgency to the effort of cybersecurity.

However, it must be emphasised that China's cybersecurity efforts, though under the paradigm of internet or information security, actually date back to 1994 when the State Council promulgated the *Regulations for Security Protection of Computer Information Systems* (State Council, 1994). The responsibility of this task of security and supervision of the internet was vested with the Ministry of Public Security (MPS). The MPS issued *Measures for Security Protection of the International Networking of Computer Information Networks* in 1997 which brought a whole gamut of activities under the purview of security. These included information that instigates the resistance and disruption of the implementation of the Constitution, laws and administrative regulations; instigates the subversion of the state political power; sabotages national unity; instigates hatred and disrupts social order; disseminates obscenity, pornography, gambling, violence and terror (State Council, 1997).

The MPS also established the Public Information Network Security Monitoring Bureau in 1998 to manage and supervise the security of computer networks and information systems, and monitor the use of internet in China (CNNIC, 2012a). Around the same time, the MPS initiated the Golden Shield Project – a sophisticated nationwide internet censorship and surveillance system (IBM, n.d.). The project laid the foundations of China's present-day practices of content monitoring and censorship over the internet, which will be discussed later in the chapter. Along with monitoring and censorship, combating cybercrime, critical information infrastructure protection, and regulation of virtual private networks (VPNs) also fall under the purview of the MPS.

More regulations were rolled out later in tandem with the growth of internet usage in China, covering a wide canvas of aspects such as encryption, telecommunications, critical infrastructure protection, internet services, domain names, intellectual property rights, electronic signatures, publications, crime, privacy, and personal data protection. The regulations, *inter alia*, are *Measures on Management of Internet Information Services* and *State Secrets Protection Regulations for Computer Information Systems on the Internet* (2000), *Measures for the Administration of Internet Domain Names of China* (2002, 2004), *Measures for the Administrative Protection of Internet Copyright* (2005), *Provisions on the Technical Measures for the Protection of the Security of the Internet* (2006), *Measures for the Administration of Internet E-mail Services* (2006), *Measures for the Multi-level Protection Scheme of Information Security* (2007), *Measures on the Protection of Personal Data of Telecommunication and Internet Users* (2013), *Cybersecurity Law* (2017), *Data Security Law* (2021), and *Personal Information Protection Law* (2021).

China has also raised specialised agencies to effectively manage the technical and administrative functions of cyber and information security. The numbers and powers of the state agencies involved in the management of cyber affairs have increased with the expansion of China's interests in cyberspace. In September 2002, for instance, the National Computer Network Emergency Response Technical Team/Coordination Center of China (known as CNCERT or CNCERT/CC) was founded as a non-governmental technical and coordination centre for cybersecurity. With branches and offices in 31 provinces, autonomous regions, and municipalities across China, CNCERT/CC is tasked with China's emergency response to handle major cybersecurity incidents (CNCERT, n.d.). It functions under the administrative control of the MIIT, and so does the CNNIC. MIIT supervises the technology management aspects of the internet and regulates the internet service providers in China.

State Network and Information Security Coordination Small Group was formed under the State Informatization Leading Group in 2003 to facilitate the management and operations of network and information security protection systems, corresponding policies, and national strategies (Chang, 2014: 16). The Group was later merged with the Central Leading Group for Cybersecurity and Informatization. The Leading Group was established in 2013 to draft and implement national strategies, development plans, and major policies for informatisation, placing informatisation agenda at the heart of the economic and security policy-making. The Office of the Central Leading Group for Cybersecurity and Informatization – commonly known as Cyberspace Administration of China (CAC) – was formed to implement these tasks.

The CAC replaced the State Internet Information Office, which was formed by the State Council in 2011 as a subordinate office under the State Council Information Office (SCIO), separating internet regulatory functions from the State Council and emerged as an authority with significant powers (Samson, 2015). The CAC began coordinating information infrastructure development, informatisation, and spearheading cybersecurity strategies, initiatives, and regulations (Miao & Lei, 2016). Some of the administrative functions of the SCIO related to the internet, such as licensing for internet-based news were transferred to the CAC. It also has regulatory and enforcement functions for internet content management. The Leading Group was later upgraded to the Central Cyberspace Affairs Commission as part of the 2018 institutional reforms to further consolidate its powers to supervise and regulate cyberspace. This change placed CAC under the Office of the Central Cyberspace Affairs Commission.

Since the management and regulation of cyberspace cuts across the scope and interests of several ministries and state functions, the CAC is placed at a position to ensure coordination not just among the ministries but also among the power epicentres of government, military, and the CPC to overcome bureaucratic hurdles. The fact that CAC has representation from all the key ministries of the State Council and commissions of the CPC underscores the priority the Government assigns to this subject, and that also makes CAC one of the most authoritative bodies for cyber policy-making in China. The CAC has representation from the National Development and Reform Commission, People's Bank of China, the Ministry of Finance, Central Military Commission, Central Political and Legislative Affairs Commission, the Ministry of Foreign Affairs, the Ministry of Public Security, and the Ministry of Science and Technology.

Beyond that, the wide range of activities under its fold includes supervision of the National Computer Network and Information Security Management Center (earlier supervised by MIIT), extending funding support (through China Internet Development Foundation), making of laws, formulation of standards, advancement of informatisation and internet economy, international (bilateral or multilateral) collaboration, management of online content, and also hosting the annual World Internet Conference.

The CAC is also a manifestation of the fundamental changes in China's approach to the overall evolution of the matter of cyber policy. It represents a greater centralisation of authority over cyberspace and digital affairs, a process which practically began in 2014 (Creemers et al., 2018). The focus on the development of technology and infrastructure in the earlier phases gradually evolved into wider integration of information technology with the existing processes and functions – what is commonly denoted as informatisation. The term "cyber" found a sparing mention earlier, but in recent times, terminologies like "cyberspace," "cybersecurity," "cyberspace governance," "cyber policy," and "cyber (super)power" have made inroads into work reports, Five-Year Plans, and policy and strategy documents.

The first mention of "cyber" in the National Congress of the CPC was found in Hu Jintao's report at the 17th National Congress (held in 2007). It is worth mentioning that in April 2007, a series of Denial-of-Service attacks on Estonia – one of the most networked or digitised countries in the world – targeting the parliament, major banks, governmental ministries, newspapers, and broadcasters created havoc (O'Neill, 2020). The incident is one of the most cited examples in the brief history of cyber conflicts. Hu Jintao's report endorsed "strengthening of efforts to develop and manage Internet culture and foster a good cyber environment" (Hu, 2007). The report also deemed indigenous innovation to be a crucial link in enhancing China's overall national strength – which was also a lynchpin of the *National Medium to Long-term Plan for the Development of Science and Technology (2006–20)*. Hu Jintao's subsequent report to the 18th National Congress of the CPC recognised cybersecurity among emerging global issues, and in the military context pointed out the importance of cyberspace security alongside maritime and space security. This was the first time "cybersecurity" found a mention in the report to the National Congress of the CPC (Hu, 2012).

Xi Jinping, akin to his predecessors, envisions an agenda for his government to achieve the larger goals of development, economic growth, social prosperity, and modernisation of the armed forces. Enshrined in the "great revival of the Chinese people" and the "Chinese dream of national rejuvenation," the vision encompasses making China a country of innovators, amassing economic and technological strength, and strengthening the armed forces while maintaining political integrity, stability, and unity.

Xi Jinping's report to the 19th National Congress of the CPC made a total of three mentions of "cyber." The first was in the context of innovation – which the report reiterated as a primary driving force. The support to research and development and innovation was assured to "build strength in science and technology, aerospace, cyberspace, and transportation" (Xi, 2017a). The second mention was with reference to public communication in ideological work – indicating better control on online content and "pledging a system for integrated Internet management to ensure a clean cyberspace." The third mention of cyber was regarding the growing uncertainties and destabilising factors in the global environment. Here, "cyber-insecurity" was placed among the common challenges such as the widening gap in economic conditions, terrorism, infectious disease, and climate change (Xi, 2017a). Cyber also features heavily in China's economic planning now. For the first time in the history of Five-Year Plans, the 13th Five-Year Plan carried a dedicated section (part VI) on cyber economy.

Four chapters (Chapters 25–28) in the section aimed at building efficient information networks, implementing the national big data strategy, and developing internet-based industries (State Council, 2016). In line with the tenets of the *State Informatization Development Strategy*, the 13th Five-Year Plan charted out a roadmap for the development of high-speed, mobile, and ubiquitous next-generation information infrastructure. This included optical fibre networks, international communications facilities, land and submarine cable infrastructure, Digital Silk Road, technologies for 5G mobile networks and their commercial applications, next-generation internet, operating systems, industrial software, big data, cloud computing, and artificial intelligence. The plan also intended to implement the *Internet Plus Action Plan* and the *National Big Data Strategy*, instigate internet-based open innovation alliances for sharing of resources, and strengthen China's say in the formulation of international standards.

On the security front, the 13th Five-Year Plan proposed a series of initiatives pertaining to cybersecurity (information security), personal data protection, security laws and regulations, safeguarding sovereignty in cyberspace, and preventing hostile and terrorist activities in cyberspace. It affirmed support to the establishment of multilateral cyberspace (internet) governance systems and formulation of international rules on cybersecurity, cybercrime, and security technology and standards. The plan also mentioned enriching cyber culture, which essentially translates into enhanced control on online content, online public opinion, and online behaviour of the citizens.

Digital transformation is the keystone of 14th Five-Year Plan, as part V of the plan charts out the path to integrate digital technologies with economy, society, and government functions. The 14th Five-Year Plan elaborates the Government's plan to build a strong position in digital economy through innovation and large-scale application of key digital technologies;

breakthroughs in emerging digital industries such as artificial intelligence, big data, blockchain, etc.; and data-driven transformation of traditional industries (NDRC, 2021). The plan envisions ease of access for a wide spectrum of public services, open access to public data, and extensive use of digital technologies in government services and decision-making.

One of the sections of the 14th Five-Year Plan is dedicated to the task of developing a safe and rules-based digital ecosystem. This includes devising data protection regulation and enabling policy environment to find the right balance between the needs of data-enabled development and privacy, public security, data rights, and cross-border flow of data. On the cybersecurity front, the 14th Five-Year Plan reaffirmed the commitment of the Government to strengthen cybersecurity laws, regulations, and standards and protect critical information infrastructure. "Cyber Economy" in the 13th Five-Year Plan was replaced with "Digital China" in the 14th Five-Year Plan – the latter accommodates the changes brought by data-driven technologies globally over the last five years. The economic aspects of digitalisation continue to inform and shape China's social and economic development planning, and they certainly are one of the key considerations for the Chinese Government.

### The economic imperatives

The vast economic activity resulting from the billions of digital connections and transactions among the people, businesses, and organisations, and knowledge and information exchange over the information networks gives rise to the concept of digital economy. It has become one of the important constituents of the national economy and a key driver of economic growth for developed and developing economies alike. China also attaches great importance to the digital economy and it has witnessed a rapid growth in this segment of the economy over the last two decades owing to aggressive policy measures devised to expand the internet and ICT infrastructure and integrate information technology with the traditional sectors of the economy.

The reports from the China Academy of Information and Communications Technology on the development of digital economy in China highlight the increasing role of digital economy in China's national economy. The reports note that the scale of China's digital economy grew from RMB 2.6 trillion in 2005 to RMB 45.5 trillion in 2021, and the share of digital economy in China's gross domestic product rose from 14.2 per cent to 39.8 per cent in that period (CAICT, 2020, 2021, 2022). The growth rate of China's digital economy (16.2 per cent) in 2021 was 4.7 times the nominal growth rate of gross domestic product (3.4 per cent). In 2022, the scale of China's digital economy was reported RMB 50.2 trillion, and its share in the gross domestic product rose to 41.5 per cent (State Council, 2023).

A working paper titled *China's Digital Economy* published by the International Monetary Fund noted that China is leading in some of the new and emerging industries such as e-commerce where China executes close to 40 per cent of the total global transactions, and financial technology where Chinese enterprises account for more than 70 per cent of the total global valuations (Zhang & Chen, 2019). According to the NDRC, digital economy has played an important role in attracting investment and increasing foreign trade, and it has emerged as a driver of China's economic growth (NDRC, 2022). Making a similar observation based on the indicators of digital economy, a report from the United Nations Conference on Trade and Development notes that in terms of the size of digital economy, China is placed second only to the US (UNCTAD, 2022).

Enabled to a greater extent by the internet, digital economy holds endless opportunities and vast potential for elevating China's economic growth as it increases productivity of the enterprises, inculcates innovation, and boosts consumption. Innovative business models adapted to the local needs and market conditions have turned China into a burgeoning market for novel applications and services. It has been supported in no small measure by the central economic planning and a favourable policy environment. In 2015, China charted out another ambitious roadmap to integrate the internet with the real economy – dubbed the *Internet Plus Action Plan*.

The *Internet Plus Action Plan* – seen as a watershed in China's economic transformation – was officially unveiled by Premier Li Keqiang in the 2015 *Government Work Report*. The broader idea behind the action plan is to modernise the traditional industries using technologies such as cloud computing, big data, mobile internet, and the internet of things to catapult economic growth (Li, 2015). Building on the internet as the basic infrastructure, the action plan seeks to integrate it with all the areas of the economy and society in order to promote technological progress, improve efficiency, and enhance productivity. The focus areas of the action plan are manufacturing, agriculture, e-commerce, transportation, energy, public services, logistics, biology, and artificial intelligence (State Council, 2015c).

The salient features of the action plan are – the intent to overcome China's technological weakness in chips, high-end servers, high-end storage equipment etc.; the focus on technological standards for industrial internet, smart networks, smart cities, industrial control systems, etc., and strengthen China's position at international standards-setting organisations; support for open-source software and communities; and the willingness to leverage the Belt and Road Initiative and other national strategies to expand the reach of Chinese enterprises to the international markets in industrial clouds, supply chain management, big data analysis, and other associated services (State Council, 2015d).

Recognising the importance of the manufacturing sector to China's national economy and prosperity, the *Made in China 2025* plan devised China's strategy for the next decade to revolutionise the manufacturing sector. Released in 2015, the plan seeks to build an industrial internet infrastructure using optical fibre networks, mobile networks, wireless local area networks in manufacturing clusters, intelligent control systems, industrial application software, and sensing and communication systems to ensure the provisioning of internet applications for intelligent monitoring, remote diagnosis and management, industrial cloud, and industrial big data. Targeting deep integration of next-generation information technology with the manufacturing sector, the plan is an audacious attempt to build an internationally competitive manufacturing sector and the Chinese Government perceives it important to enhance China's strength and become a world power (State Council, 2015a).

A quantitative analysis of China's informatisation level and its national "well-being" established a positive correlation between the "Informatization Index" and the "well-being index" of 31 provinces, municipalities, and autonomous regions in China (Zhang et al., 2015: 8). The study derived well-being index from the Human Development Index of the United Nations and deduced that improvement in the levels of informatisation further advances national well-being and improves the living standards of people. Since Deng Xiaoping, both national well-being and improving the living standards of people have been part of the overarching vision of the subsequent top leadership in China.

Informatisation has been pursued as a national priority in China given its vast potential for economic development and elevation of living standards of the society. However, security has also had a deep influence on the thought process – whether the internet and computer security previously, or cybersecurity in the present times. The Chinese Government has created agencies specifically mandated to execute functions which include security of computer networks and information systems, and established bodies for effective coordination and implementation of cyber policy. The bodies placed at the apex within the Government are driven by the top political leadership clearly indicating the deep interest of the leadership in China's cyber affairs. Moreover, authoritative powers vested in these bodies go a long way in effective coordination cutting across various ministries and power epicentres, and overcoming bureaucratic hurdles among the stakeholders in China's domestic cyber affairs.

The integration of information technology with the Chinese economy, industry, and society has been pursed aggressively under the umbrella term "informatization" ever since Jiang Zemin mentioned it in his report at the 15th National Congress of the CPC in 1997. However, over the course of the last one decade, the term "cyber" has made significant inroads into

China's strategic thinking, economic planning, and international relations. Within a span of three to four years, China rolled out a *Cyberspace Security Strategy*, an *International Strategy of Cooperation on Cyberspace*, and a *Cybersecurity Law*, amongst a host of other activities focused on cyberspace. The rolling out of these initiatives picked pace following Xi Jinping's taking over the lead of the national cybersecurity initiatives almost a decade ago when he had also explicitly called for collective efforts to "build China into a cyber superpower." The next section looks at the concept of cyber power in China's context. It draws in perspectives on cyber power from China and examines the prime initiatives and the key principles rooted in China's perspectives of cyberspace.

## China's views on cyber power

The term "cyber" is relatively new in Chinese political parlance, but the ability of information technology, in general, to produce an effect or be a determinant of national power was realised quite early on. Jiang Zemin in his book *On the Development of China's Information Technology Industry* enunciates that the information technology industry "epitomizes a country's international competitiveness, national defense capability, and overall national strength", and it "is the strategic high ground for international competition" (Jiang, 2009: xv–xvii). He asserts that competition among states for strength centres mainly on the control of information technology and information resources, and therefore a country's capabilities in information technology have a prominent role to play. The revised outline of the *National Informatization Development Strategy (2006–2020)* underscored the advantages of occupying the so-called "commanding heights" of informatisation so as to gain superiority, enhance security, and play a decisive role in the future. The strategy – wary of the strategic thinking and actions of other countries pertaining to the distribution of internet resources and international norms in cyberspace – pressed on the urgent need for China to consolidate its position as a strong cyber power.

A majority of the articles and points of view on cyber power from Chinese academics focus on the principles and requirements for building cyber power – areas that need attention of the government and the ways and means to speed up building China into a cyber superpower. One of the earliest and notable publications on cyber power from a Chinese academic is a 2012 paper by Li, the then director of the Institute of Information and Social Development Studies. He had analysed the 2011 *International Strategy for Cyberspace* of the US, also referring to the works of American scholars such as Tim Jordan, Joseph S. Nye, Franklin Kramer, Stuart Starr, and Larry K. Wentz on cyber war in particular, and the role of American defence companies such as Northrop Grumman, Lockheed Martin, Boeing, and Raytheon in developing cyber-weapons (Li, 2012). Noting that "the UN Charter and the law of the armed conflict apply to the cyberspace, in particular the principles of non-use of force and peaceful settlement of international disputes," Li professed that the international community should take every measure possible to avoid the use of force or the threat of force in order to prevent the outbreak of war in cyberspace. The paper elucidated seven essential elements of cyber power, and they include (Li, 2012: 802–803):

1. *Internet and information technology capabilities*, which consist of research and development capabilities in the field of information technology, the ability to innovate and apply research outcomes in the industry to transform various industrial and business processes.
2. *Information technology industry capabilities*, to the extent that the country is home to the global industry leaders across products, applications, or services, such as the lead position of IBM, Microsoft, Intel, Google, Cisco, or Apple from the US in the market segments of hardware, software, networking equipment, computers, telecommunication equipment, semiconductors, and mobile phones.
3. *Internet market capabilities*, largely defined by the size or volume of the internet infrastructure, such as internet users and the number of computers or devices they own, the number of mobile phone subscribers, and the integration of the internet infrastructure with key services and governance to name a few.
4. *The influence of internet culture*, in terms of internet penetration; the diversity of its uses, be it communication, networking, education, entertainment, and so on; and the quality of the content available on the internet which has influence domestically as well as internationally.
5. *Internet diplomacy and foreign policy capabilities*, as they are closely associated with the bargaining power and the influence of a country in international platforms for internet governance, be it ICANN, IGF, or the ITU; considering how a country can play a leading role in internet governance, technology, security, and other key aspects by providing technology and thought leadership.
6. *Cyber military strength*, which essentially means the ability to defend critical and military information infrastructure from attacks, and the ability to deter threat actors and conduct offensive operations in cyberspace.
7. *National interest in taking part in a cyberspace strategy*, as merely possessing the abovementioned capabilities, in part or all, is not sufficient to be a cyber power. It depends considerably upon the intent or willingness of the country to possess and use that power as part of a well-defined cyberspace strategy which could provide theoretical guidance, a strategic goal, or a long-term action plan.

Along the similar lines, Fang and Hu (2014) recognise the globally competitive internet or information technology industry, the ability to defend the critical infrastructure, and deterrence in cybersecurity and military terms to be the key constituents of cyber power. They underscore the two aims of the goal of building China into a cyber superpower, "to be a great power in cyberspace, and to acquire national power by realising the full potential of the cyber domain in all the aspects of statecraft." Hu Yuning, faculty at Shanghai Normal University, perceives cyber as a new form of power and argues that cyber power strategy is the only way to enhance the international competitiveness of a country. Hu further mentions that mastering information and networking technology and possessing highly skilled human resources pave the way to realising economic, social, and technological development and participating in international internet governance matters (Y. Hu, 2016).

Noting that as control and competitiveness of a country in cyberspace have become a key measure to evaluate its comprehensive national power and international competitiveness, Xie Xinzhou, dean of the Peking University School of New Media, asserts that building a cyber superpower is a key condition to build China as a powerful modern socialist country. He identifies four criteria to evaluate whether a country is a cyber superpower or not. First is *technical attributes*, such as proficiency in core technologies, level of informatisation, development of information infrastructure, and status and influence in international cyber governance. Second is *tool attributes*, such as data and information resources which shape soft power and competitiveness. *Economic attributes* form the third criterion as the digital economy plays an important role in accelerating economic development, improving productivity, creating new markets and industries, and achieving inclusive and sustainable development. Fourth is *ideological and cultural attributes*, based on the contribution a country makes to the progress of human civilisation, given the profound impact of cyberspace on human thought and culture (Xie, 2018).

Reflecting on the question "what is considered a cyber superpower?", Wang Yukai, professor at the Central Party School and a member of the fourth National Informatization Expert Advisory Committee, identified a few characteristics of a cyber superpower. These include having a world-class information infrastructure, a clear cyberspace strategy, clout in the international community, adequate cybersecurity capabilities, and the ability to occupy the commanding heights (Y. Wang, 2021). Geng Zhongyuan, professor at Zhejiang University of Finance and Economics, enlists three elements that could help advance the goal of building China into a cyber superpower. The first element comprises data, networks, and information infrastructure, and their integration with the manufacturing sector. Physical and cultural aspects of cyberspace form the second element, and the third element includes governance aspects such as cybersecurity, protecting the interests of the public, safeguarding national sovereignty, ensuring rule of law, and reforming global cyber governance (Geng, 2021).

Zheng Bijian, former executive vice president of the Central Party School, describes cyber power as the grand strategy of China's modernisation in the new phase of development and finds China progressing from a major cyber power to a cyber superpower. Keeping the third decade of the 21st century as the target of this goal, Zheng stresses on "six major forces" driven by cyberspace. These forces are – improving productivity (using core technologies and emerging technologies), cybersecurity and deterrence capabilities, cultural power, governance (regulations, digital governance system, and modernisation of the governance system), innovation (digital technology as the driving force), and competition (B. Zheng, 2021).

On the notion of China as a cyber superpower, Li Yan, deputy director of the Institute of Cyber Security at China Institutes of Contemporary International Relations, delves into China's standpoint on "building a community of common future in cyberspace" representing the interests of developing countries and designating China as a reformer of the existing global cyberspace/internet governance system (Li, 2019). Cai Cuihong, professor at the Center for American Studies at Fudan University, explains that the cyber superpower status for China means self-sufficiency in cyber capabilities and does not equate to China imposing its own beliefs and doctrines upon other countries in the international system. Arguing that the difference of perspectives between China and the Western countries on cybersecurity in general stems from China's distinctive national conditions, Cai pronounces cybersecurity to be a social governance problem for China with direct bearing on its national security (Cai, 2015).

As far as the disposition of Chinese political leadership towards cyber power is concerned, while speaking at various forums Xi Jinping has time and again reiterated the importance of building China into a cyber superpower. Table 3.1 collates highlights of the key speeches of Xi Jinping where he has mentioned or elaborated on the objective of building China into a cyber superpower. Since taking over the lead of the Central Leading Group for Cybersecurity and Informatization, Xi Jinping has consistently stressed upon cyber power to be a national priority for China to reach its true economic, societal, and military potential (*China Daily*, 2014a).

While describing the need to develop information technologies and the security of the internet as "two wings of a bird and two wheels of an engine," Xi Jinping accentuates the fact that development and security work hand in glove – which fundamentally is the abstract of leaderships' view on cyber power (*China Daily*, 2014a). As a cyber superpower, China realises its long-term goals of economic and social development through informatisation, expands China's information networks well beyond its territorial borders, and retains the absolute authority to control these networks and the information therein.

**TABLE 3.1** Highlights of Xi Jinping's key speeches on cyber superpower

| Year | Occasion | Highlights |
|------|----------|------------|
| 2014 | First meeting of the Central Leading Group for Cybersecurity and Informatization | • Called on for efforts to build China into a cyber superpower<br>• Described internet development and security as the "two wings of a bird and two wheels of an engine"<br>• Noted that "no Internet safety means no national security"<br>• Identified the building blocks of cyber power – indigenous technology, comprehensive information services, prosperous cyber cultures, infrastructure, human resources, and international cooperation |
| 2015 | Opening ceremony of the second edition of the World Internet Conference | • Called cyber surveillance, attacks, and terrorism as a global scourge<br>• Called on the international community to work together to foster a peaceful, secure, open, and cooperative cyberspace<br>• Spoke of principles to be upheld to transform the global internet governance system – respect for cyber sovereignty, maintaining peace and security, promoting openness and cooperation, and cultivating good order<br>• Introduced five proposals to work together – accelerated development of global internet infrastructure, an online platform for cultural exchange, innovative development of cyber economy, cybersecurity, and equity and justice in the internet governance system |
| 2016 | Group Study Session of the Political Bureau of the CPC Central Committee | • Proposed six "accelerations" to catapult China as a cyber superpower:<br>  • Indigenous innovation in networking and information technology<br>  • Higher contribution of the digital economy to China's economic growth<br>  • Enhance cyber defence capabilities<br>  • Improve capability for the management of cyberspace<br>  • Extensive use of information technology in social governance<br>  • Enhance China's discursive power in international rule-making for cyberspace |

(Continued)

**TABLE 3.1** (Continued)

| Year | Occasion | Highlights |
|------|----------|------------|
| 2018 | National Cybersecurity and Informatization Work Conference | • Outlined the areas for future work on informatisation and cybersecurity:<br>  • Strengthening online propaganda and orienting public opinion<br>  • Safeguarding cybersecurity<br>  • Promoting innovation in core technology areas of informatisation<br>  • Allowing informatisation to realise its full potential in economic and social development<br>  • Strengthening military–civil fusion in informatisation and cybersecurity<br>  • Active participation in international cyber governance discussions and discourse<br>  • Advancing towards the goal of cyber superpower through indigenous innovation |

Compiled by the author.

In response to the changes brought about by cyberspace to the national security strategies, defence policies, and military force restructuring in other parts of the world, especially the US, China released (a public version of) its military strategy in 2015. For the first time in a military document of such significance, China declared that "cyberspace and outer space have become new commanding heights in strategic competition among all parties" (State Council, 2015b). Noting that the strategic competition in cyberspace has turned fierce and countries are deploying cyber military forces, the strategy sought to expedite the development of China's own cyber force. And towards the end of 2015, China established Strategic Support Force consolidating the cyber warfare and intelligence-gathering apparatus of the PLA.

China's desire or the intent to use cyberspace as an instrument of state power to extend its influence globally and achieve the envisioned goals of development, economic growth, social prosperity, and modernisation of the armed forces is quite explicit. Speaking at the National Cybersecurity and Informatization Work Conference in 2018, Xi Jinping again drew attention to the significance of new ideas, viewpoints, and theses, and theoretical and applied innovation in building China into a cyber superpower (China Copyright and Media, 2018). Researchers and scholars from CNCERT/CC, China Institutes of Contemporary International Relations, and China Center for Information Industry Development further deliberated on the idea recommending how could this be achieved with a focus on the development of core internet technologies, driving reforms in cyberspace governance, and making breakthroughs in emerging technologies (Q. Liu, 2018).

China's resolve to dominate cyberspace or to occupy the so-called "commanding heights" in cyberspace is quite evident from the advocacy for the objective by the highest echelons of political leadership (Sharma, 2016). While building the strategic thinking and putting in place the desired institutional frameworks to meet that end, China has undertaken a host of actions – be it massive state-led investments to accelerate research and development in the high-technology sector, provisioning of a *Cybersecurity Law*, toughened control on information, tabling of a forward-looking *National Cyberspace Security Strategy*, an outward-looking *International Strategy of Cooperation on Cyberspace*, or the World Internet Conference which attracts industry leaders and thousands of technology entrepreneurs and analysts from all across the globe.

### National cyberspace security strategy

Cybersecurity made it to China's national security calculus with the enactment of *National Security Law* in 2015. Article 25 of the law seeks to "enhance network and information security in general, security of the key infrastructure and information systems, dissuade criminal activity, and most importantly, maintain cyberspace sovereignty and security and development interests of China in cyberspace" (National Security Law of the People's Republic of China, 2017). This essentially was a declaration that cyberspace is very much integral to China's national interests, and the *National Cyberspace Security Strategy* released by the CAC later in 2016 further fortified this assertion. The strategy remains to be the mainstay of China's endeavours in the direction of cybersecurity ever since then.

Envisioning a peaceful, secure, open, cooperative, and orderly cyberspace, the strategy reaffirms China's prevalent positions and propositions on the further development of cyberspace and its security. In terms of strategic importance, the strategy places cyberspace at par with the domains of land, sea, air, and space. It makes a note of the emerging threats from the cyber domain to political stability, economy, and social harmony in the form of foreign interference in internal affairs, undermining of political systems, subversion of regimes, and cyber terrorism and crime. The strategy is equally wary of the international competition arising from the desire of states to control the strategic resources of cyberspace and influence norms building, and even from their pursuit of cyber deterrence strategies (CAC, 2016). The strategy sets these five objectives to uphold and ensure peace:

- restraining arms race and conflicts
- enhancing security

- promoting openness in information technology standards, policies, and markets
- strengthening cooperation in the areas of cyber terrorism, cybercrime, and internet governance
- engendering order through domestic and international legal frameworks and development of norms

The strategy also endorses the following four primary principles:

- respect for sovereignty in cyberspace (the right to independently choose the path of development, governance, and public policy)
- peaceful use of cyberspace (in accordance with principles of the *UN Charter*, inclusiveness, and mutual trust)
- governance of cyberspace according to the law (order and protection of privacy and intellectual property rights)
- balancing cybersecurity with development

The document further outlines the following strategic tasks:

- defending sovereignty in cyberspace by all measures and thwarting threats of subversion to the regime
- safeguarding national security
- protecting critical information infrastructure
- dissuading cyber terrorism and crime
- ameliorating network governance through cybersecurity laws and regulations and implementing the *Internet Plus Action Plan*
- strengthening international cooperation in cyberspace by means of reform of the global internet governance system, formulation of international norms for cyberspace, and international treaties

The strategy echoes the apprehensions of Chinese Government against the backdrop of perceived threat of external interference in its internal affairs, possibly in the form of inciting social unrest and subverting the regime or massive cyber-enabled surveillance and espionage. The strategy is also a proclamation that China's interests now extend into the cyber domain and China is well within its right to defend its national security and interests leveraging all the available means. The strategy also professes peace, openness, and cooperation urging others to refrain from engaging in cyber hegemony, interfering in the internal affairs of other countries, and instigating an arms race in cyberspace.

Amongst the host of tenets promulgated in the strategy, "cyber sovereignty" clearly stands out. At multiple instances, the strategy asserts that cyber sovereignty has become an important part of national sovereignty and deems it to be inviolable. The principle of sovereignty in cyberspace is discussed in detail in the later part of the chapter. After a strategy in place, the next step in the quest to build China into a cyber superpower was to bring in a legal framework to secure China's growing interests in cyberspace. And to that end, the *Cybersecurity Law* came into force on 01 June 2017 after two years of deliberations and public consultations.

## Cybersecurity law

The 2017 *Cybersecurity Law* is China's first comprehensive privacy and security regulation for cyberspace. It is basically an evolution of the numerous existent rules and regulations related to computer, network, and cyber security into a macro-level legal framework which now assimilates internet security, information security, communications security, network security, computer security, and the security of industrial control systems installed in the critical infrastructure establishments. Article 1 of the law speaks of safeguarding cyberspace sovereignty and national security, and protecting the rights and interests of citizens and other organisations in China. Addressing most of the concerns pertaining to national security mentioned in the *Cyberspace Security Strategy*, Article 12 of the law provisions that individuals and organisations "must not use the network to engage in activities endangering national security, national honour and interests, inciting subversion of national sovereignty, the overturn of the socialist system, inciting separatism, undermining national unity, advocating terrorism or extremism, inciting ethnic hatred and ethnic discrimination" (2016 Cybersecurity Law, 2016; Creemers et al., 2017).

Article 24 of the law instructs network operators to furnish information on the real identity of the users. The inability to trace the origin of a cyber-attack, or to identify the real perpetrators of an attack or an act of crime on the internet is one of China's longstanding sources of resentment with the present architecture of the internet. The Article further supports research and development of technologies which can establish or confirm the electronic identity of the users over the internet with reciprocity. Enforcing data localisation, Article 37 of the law makes provision for retaining personal information and other important data related to critical information infrastructure to be stored locally within the borders of China (2016 Cybersecurity Law, 2016; Creemers et al., 2017).

China attaches great importance to the security of critical information infrastructure against attacks, intrusions, interference, and destruction given their wide-ranging impact on the national security, national economy, and the livelihood of the people. An entire section (Articles 31–39) of the *Cybersecurity Law* is dedicated to the security of critical information infrastructure. The law empowers the Government to supervise or investigate cybersecurity processes and initiate legal action if the enterprises or the management concerned are not compliant with the provisions of the law (2016 Cybersecurity Law, 2016; Creemers et al., 2017). With the growing importance of data and the desire to control its flow to safeguard its own interests, China in recent times has strengthened the legal framework for the security of data.

### Data security law and personal information protection law

Like many governments in other parts of the world, the Chinese Government has also identified data as a key resource for its socio-economic development. With the growing salience of data and digital technologies in every aspect of the economy, the political leadership in China has sought to building the requisite legal and regulatory frameworks for data protection and securing the digital economy. The Fourth Plenary Session of the 19th Central Committee of the CPC, held in 2019, characterised data as a factor of production, alongside land, labour, capital, and technology (China Internet Information Center, 2019; Kamensky & Slawson, 2019). This further echoed in the April 2020 guideline on improving the market-based allocation of production factors issued by the CPC Central Committee and the State Council (State Council, 2020). Data-driven innovation and the associated technologies were the focal point of the 14th Five-Year Plan. China's *Data Security Law* (National People's Congress, 2021a) and the *Personal Information Protection Law* (China Briefing, 2021; National People's Congress, 2021b) came into force in quick succession towards the end of 2021. These two pieces of legislation further specify the requirements of data localisation, data export, and data protection that were first promulgated in the *Cybersecurity Law*.

In addition to regulating data processing and ensuring data security, one of the purposes stated in Article 1 of the *Data Security Law* is to safeguard the sovereignty, security, and development interests of China. Article 21 of the Law classifies data related to national security, critical aspects of the economy, and personal data of the Chinese citizens as "core data" which attracts stricter regulatory oversight. Article 35 requires organisations and individuals to share the data having national security implications with public security and national security bodies. The Law applies to all data activities in China and it also has extraterritorial application if the data activities are deemed to have a bearing on China's national security and public interests.

The *Personal Information Protection Law* specifies the scope of personal information, clarifies the legal basis for the processing of such information, specifies the obligations and responsibilities of data processors, and also lays down the requirements for data localisation and cross-border transfer of personal information. Article 43 of the Law provisions reciprocal measures if any country or region takes discriminatory prohibitive, restrictive, or other such measures against China in respect of the protection of personal information.

Control of data and its flows, and extraterritorial powers over the data market also translate into control over Chinese technology companies which have eventually become massive data processors, have global ambitions, and could leverage foreign markets to bypass the domestically imposed restrictions. They would need to tread more carefully in their cybersecurity practices and handling of data. There are growing concerns over the use of provisions of data or cybersecurity laws as a pretext to exert state control over technology giants. For instance, in July 2021, the Chinese ride-hailing company Didi Chuxing was subject to a cybersecurity investigation by CAC under the Cybersecurity Review Measures soon after it was listed on the New York Stock Exchange. The company was even stopped from registering new users till the investigation was on over the misuse of customers' personal information (*Global Times*, 2021; Z. Lee, 2021; Reuters, 2021). Later, the updated Cybersecurity Review Measures, which came into effect in February 2022, made it mandatory for online platform operators holding the personal information of more than 1 million users to apply for a cybersecurity review with the Cybersecurity Review Office of CAC before their public listing on foreign markets (China Law Translate, 2022).

Recognising that data is the lynchpin of digital economy, the three laws aim to assure protection of data and privacy in China, which is essentially in line with developments in other parts of the world. These laws not just conform China's data protection and privacy practices to international standards, but also form the legal basis of its international engagement on data security issues, which of late has gained pace. However, the restrictions China intends to place on the free flow of information and the rights of the citizens online stand in contradiction with the founding principles and ethos of the internet. Although exercising these measures ensures regime security and helps consolidating power, but the extensive oversight of the Chinese Government on the origin, flow, and consumption of information ranging from media to culture attracts criticism worldwide.

### Controls and censorship

The internet has always been an open platform where people cutting across cultural, physical, and political boundaries could communicate and build social connections and virtual communities. Emanating from open societies, freedom of expression and thought has been the founding ethos of the internet. Internet freedom – including freedom of expression and access to information – has contrary perceptions in the democratic and authoritarian forms of government as it differently affects their cultural and political settings. Predicting the impact of transnational communications in stimulating social interdependence among societies in their 1989 book, Keohane and Nye argued that authoritarian states are likely to control telecommunications and social transactions or interactions which they consider disruptive for the stability of the regime and resort to censoring and curtailing these communications (Keohane & Nye, 1989: 4, 228). Despite the pluralistic characteristics of the internet and its ability to provide public space for billions of people and enable diversified exchange of information and opinion, unrestricted freedom and access to information on it is also seen as a potent threat.

China has for long been an opponent of the inherent values and ethos of the internet. Internet restricts the control of the Government or the CPC on the free flow of information and content. The CPC perceives the internet, at large, to be a potential threat to the political stability of the one-party state. It also undermines CPC's time-tested methods of social and political control. The internet could arguably be deemed as the first thing or matter the CPC was unable to control since coming to power with the establishment of the People's Republic of China in 1949 (Bi, 2001). By the time commercial internet services began in China, the political turmoil ensuing Tiananmen Square protests of 1989 had already led the CPC to reaffirm its control on information through stringent regulations for publishing or broadcasting to curb freedom of information and freedom of the press in China (Hao et al., 1996). The then Minister of Posts and Telecommunication Wu Jichuan had categorically mentioned in 1995 that linking (China) with the internet does not necessarily mean absolute freedom of information (Jiang, 2010).

Hachigian in a 2001 article had anticipated that the shift in flow of communications and access to information would have potential consequences for the CPC rule once the internet penetrates deep into the Chinese society (Hachigian, 2001). A 2002 RAND Corporation monograph observed that the internet actually enabled local efforts of dissidence in China to come to the fore in national and global discussions which allowed dissidents to communicate with each other, with the dissident community in exile, and the supporters through e-mail, websites, web-based magazines, and chat rooms (Chase and Mulvenon, 2002). Wary of the perils of the internet, the CPC-led Government wasted no time in strengthening the existing censorship and control mechanisms to meet the requirements of the information age and resorted to a series of legal and technical measures.

A slew of laws, regulations, and guidelines now control every aspect of the flow of information on the internet in China. The first of the legal measures to regulate internet content dates back to 1997 in the form of *Measures for Security Protection of the International Networking of Computer Information Networks* which enforced licensing and approval requirements

(Interim Regulations on the Management of International Networking of Computer Information, 1997). It has been amended several times or fortified with new regulations as per contemporary requirements. The *State Secrecy Protection Regulations for Computer Information Systems on the Internet* in 2000, for instance, enforced control on information appearing on Chinese websites in the pretext of protection of state secrets (State Secrecy Protection Regulations for Computer Information Systems on the Internet, 2000). A 2017 regulation requires users to register their real names with mobile service providers and on social media platforms. Amending the previous News Regulations, the 2017 *Regulations on Administration of Internet News Information Service* brought online news and information services as well under the fold of regulations (Ip et al., 2017).

By and large, these regulations have defined the boundaries of acceptable and unacceptable content in the view of the CPC. Regulations are further complemented by self-censorship in the industry, such as the *Public Pledge of Self-Regulation and Professional Ethics for China's Internet Industry* promulgated in 2002 which consisted of 31 articles on ethical behaviour expected of internet companies operating in China (*China Daily*, 2002). Coming into effect in March 2020, the *Regulations on the Ecological Governance of Online Information Content* placed sweeping restrictions on online content producers (CAC, 2019). Owing to the vast scope and extent of laws and regulations on censorship, a number of governmental bodies or agencies are involved in their administration and implementation.

The General Administration of Press and Publication performs a host of functions from drafting and enforcing prior restraint regulations to granting publication licenses, and approval of applications for information services websites to content monitoring. The body is also authorised to screen, censor, and ban any publication whether in print or online. The State Administration of Radio, Film and Television controls the entire broadcast content, be it over television, radio, or the internet. The MIIT regulates the internet service providers and controls licensing for internet information services. One of the responsibilities of the State Council Information Office is to administer the operations of news websites in China. The MPS is responsible for content filtering and monitoring over the internet (CECC, n.d.). The Central Propaganda Department of the CPC monitors content to ensure that the published content is consistent with its political agenda.

China has deployed one of the world's most advanced technological means to control access to information, censor content, and monitor user activities on the internet. Owing to the reasons discussed earlier, the need for a technology solution to closely monitor the internet was felt quite early on. And therefore, the MPS initiated the Golden Shield Project way back in 1998 vying for control on information originating and flowing within China. The project – implemented in 2003 – uses IP address blocking, IP address misdirection, and packet filtering. Moreover, in order to filter and block unwanted content from outside of China, another set of technical measures for internet traffic monitoring were put in place – metaphorically known as the "Great Firewall of China" (Goldsmith & Wu, 2006). This system uses Domain Name System blocking and Uniform Resource Locator (web address) blocking or redirection to restrict the access for internet users in China to the blacklisted websites or the websites whose address contains blacklisted words. The system also monitors the content of the webpage for unapproved keywords or phrases and drops the connection if it detects any of those in the webpage. The National Computer Network and Information Security Management Center under the CAC is known to be responsible for the development of censorship tools for the Great Firewall of China.

Some of the technologies originating from China's internet censorship and control programme have even been subject to sharp criticism because of their global ramifications. The prime example is WLAN Authentication and Privacy Infrastructure (WAPI) technology, which the Government mandated in 2003 to be deployed in all wireless devices sold in China (Gao, 2008: 152–153). WAPI was designed to allow only authenticated users on the network and it used a China-specific encryption standard which caused controversy because it was seen as a technical trade barrier. Though WAPI was never accepted as a standard and it was scrapped later, but it stands as a reminder of the fact that Chinese Government could try all possible means to meet its objective of information control on the internet.

China's wide-scale censorship programme has even forced American technology giants to compromise on the principle of internet freedom while operating in the lucrative Chinese market, which they generally boast of while operating in other countries. Microsoft, Yahoo, and Google have been criticised for participating in the self-censorship programme mandated by the Chinese Government through the *Public Pledge of Self-Regulation and Professional Ethics for China's Internet Industry*. To abide by this so-called pledge, Microsoft allegedly censored its blog tool called Spaces (BBC, 2005, 2010). Yahoo also reportedly censored search results within China and it has even been accused of supplying information on bloggers to the Chinese authorities which later led to their conviction (BBC, 2010; SCMP, 2002).

Interestingly Google had a Chinese-language version of its search engine as early as 2000, but based in the US it was not subject to censorship. Due to technical reasons, Google moved it to China in 2006, agreeing to abide by the self-regulation pledge; though it later stopped censoring search results and pulled out of China in 2010 (Lau, 2010). Examining these three cases, Dann and Haddow (2008) argue that these leading technology companies have aided censorship in China, and in doing so, they enabled the Government to violate the right of Chinese citizens to freedom of information.

Since Xi Jinping took over as the General Secretary of the CPC Central Committee in 2012 and eventually the reigns of cybersecurity, the internet censorship in China has arguably turned fiercer. The memories of pro-democracy agitations across North Africa and West Asia during 2010–2011 – commonly known as Arab Spring – were still fresh. The internet was the enabling medium for Arab Spring, and with Tiananmen Square protests of 1989 in hindsight, China remains utterly circumspect of the use of internet in political and pro-democracy agitations. A series of events since 2013 indicate that Government's control on the information and content accessible to Chinese citizens over the internet has tightened in a two-pronged approach which uses both technology and legal measures (BBC, n.d.). Social media and micro-blogging platforms have proliferated in every corner of the world. China, from 2014 onwards, has adopted extremely strong measures to curb online content under the so-called "cleansing cyberspace" operation to rid cyberspace of "rumours" and "slanderous content" (Xinhua, 2014b).

In a series of crackdowns, the CAC has removed billions of posts, suspended millions of forums, blogs, and social media accounts; blocked thousands of websites; and shut down many of the live streaming apps and online entertainment and news accounts as part of this massive "clean-up" campaign (Xinhua, 2015a, 2017c; X. Zhou, 2017). The editors of news portals have been made fully responsible and accountable for the content, production, and news on their websites (Choi, 2016). In his speech at the 2016 Cybersecurity and Informatization Work Conference, Xi Jinping categorically pointed out the perils of the internet to stir subversion and religious extremism and propagate separatism (China Copyright and Media, 2016b).

Measures to block anticensorship tools were reported from China ahead of the 19th National Congress of the CPC in 2017. The end-to-end encrypted personal messaging application WhatsApp also faced a partial ban and the Government cracked down on the Virtual Private Networks (VPNs) and other tools used to circumvent the Great Firewall. VPNs are the only resort to access restricted websites and search engines for research activities (Haas, 2017). The telecommunication carriers were directed to block the access to VPNs in July 2017 (SCMP, 2017). Apple was also forced to drop VPN apps from iStore (Cadell, 2017). The crackdown on tools used to circumvent censorship reportedly continued in the run-up to the 20th National Congress of the CPC in 2022 (Haldane & Shen, 2022).

All things considered, the CPC finds a rigorous censorship regime essential to maintain its supremacy and deliberately links censorship to the political stability of China. By virtue of its design, the internet enables the free flow of information and it severely limits the control of the state on the flow of information among people. Internet freedom is therefore presented as anathema to the values of the CPC and the Chinese Government. Regulations enforced through a myriad of agencies stifle freedom of expression and freedom of access to information in order to eradicate views contrary to the CPC's political thought and found to be critical of the Government.

With these measures in place, China has challenged the conventional wisdom that opening up to the internet eventually loosens control of the government on information. China has, in fact, succeeded in reaping the economic benefits of the internet, or cyberspace, without compromising the Government's control on information and freedom of expression in this realm. China intends to draw the legitimacy for its suppression of free flow of information and freedom of expression and speech from the concept of internet or cyber sovereignty. Sovereignty in cyberspace bestows the Chinese Government all the rights and powers to regulate the cyber domain within its political borders as it deems fit and allows the Government ample space to refute the criticism of its draconian censorship and information control measures.

### China's views on cyber sovereignty

Sovereignty for a state, as Waltz has put it succinctly, means the freedom "to decide for itself, how it will cope with its internal and external problems" (Waltz, 1979: 96). Sovereign states devise their own strategies and make their own decisions to meet their needs and desires. China's understanding of sovereignty in cyberspace is by and large an extension of this very connotation of sovereignty in a territorial context. It underpins China's assertion that the governance of cyberspace should be the sole province of governments. The concept of sovereignty in cyberspace came into the limelight when it was found mentioned in the 2010 white paper *The Internet in China*. The white paper, an official government document, noted that "within Chinese territory the Internet is under the jurisdiction of Chinese sovereignty" and the "Internet sovereignty of China should be respected and protected."

The two issues that apparently shaped China's conception of cyber sovereignty are the control of the US government on internet resources and the insecurities arising from interference by foreign countries, often termed as "cyber hegemony" (C. Cai, 2018; S. Li, 2017; Ministry of Foreign Affairs, 2017; H. Xu, 2006). Chinese writings and media reports suggest that China's proactive engagement in the global discourse on cyber governance picked pace in the aftermath of Snowden revelations in 2013 (C. Cai, 2018; X. Fang & Hu, 2014; *Global Times*, 2013a, 2013b, 2014; Qu, 2018). Edward Snowden, a sub-contractor with the US National Security Agency (NSA), disclosed massive cyber espionage and surveillance activities of the US intelligence community targeting political leaders in foreign countries, including mainland China and Hong Kong. The revelations disclosed that the NSA had hacked Tsinghua University too, which houses one of the six network backbones that route internet traffic in China (Singer & Freidman, 2014).

The revelations came under heavy criticism in China and supposedly altered China's perspectives on cyber governance and cybersecurity at large, also fuelling Government's push for cyber sovereignty which eventually came to be seen as a centrepiece of China's cyber policy and its position on international cyber governance.

In line with the Chinese assertion, Lu Wei, the then head of the State Internet Information Office and later Director of the CAC, saw cyber sovereignty as an extension of national sovereignty in cyberspace, akin to how it extended to the sea and airspace earlier. Lu argued for sovereignty to be central to China's view of cyberspace and advocated that it should form the basis for international cooperation (W. Lu, 2016; Segal, 2013). In 2014, during the inaugural edition of the World Internet Conference, China attempted to insert a point on internet sovereignty into the Wuzhen Declaration, which attracted wide criticism on the text of the declaration and also on the way the document was circulated to the attendees (Gady, 2015; Shu, 2014). The next year, the concept of internet sovereignty made it to the 2015 *National Security Law*. Speaking in 2015 at the opening ceremony of the second edition of the World Internet Conference, Xi Jinping invoked the principle of sovereign equality, enshrined in the *UN Charter*, to profess respect for sovereignty in cyberspace. Upholding the view that sovereign equality encompasses all aspects of interstate relations including cyberspace, Xi Jinping called on states to "respect the right of individual countries to independently choose their own path of cyber development, model of cyber regulation and Internet public policies, and participate in international cyberspace governance on an equal footing" (Xi, 2015).

The *Cyberspace Security Strategy* further elaborated on China's interpretation of this concept, categorically mentioning that the infringement of sovereignty in cyberspace will not be tolerated. Reiterating Xi Jinping's statement at the World Internet Conference, the Strategy expounded on the right of the states to formulate laws and regulations for cyberspace in accordance with their respective national imperatives, manage their cyberspace, and prevent and punish any threat to their national security and national interests (CAC, 2016). China has been a flag-bearer of this idea of sovereignty in cyberspace at multiple forums, so much so that it is one of the core principles of China's *International Strategy of Cooperation on Cyberspace*, released in 2017. In fact, the best elaboration of the concept of cyber sovereignty in a Chinese policy document is found in this Strategy, and it states that

> as a basic norm in contemporary international relations, the principle of sovereignty enshrined in the UN Charter covers all aspects of state-to-state relations, which also includes cyberspace. Countries should respect each other's right to choose their own path of cyber development, model

of cyber regulation and Internet public policies, and participate in international cyberspace governance on an equal footing.

*(Ministry of Foreign Affairs, 2017)*

Concomitant to the Government's efforts surrounding cyber sovereignty, the concept has featured considerably in the writings of Chinese scholars and high-ranking Government officials. These writings help gaining a granular understanding of this concept in the context of China. With regard to the profound changes brought by cyberspace to the political, economic, cultural, and social environment, Hu Yuning argues that cyberspace has altered the centrality of state in the international system and it has had a strong impact on the traditional understanding of sovereignty (Y. Hu, 2016). Contrasting the differences between American and Chinese notions of sovereignty in cyberspace, Jiang Min contends that the former looks at cyberspace as a single unit which is sovereign in its own right and takes a user-centric and rights-based approach to its management. While the latter views it from the perspective of territorial sovereignty and finds a state-centred approach to be a better fit (M. Jiang, 2010).

Noting that the computer networks of a country are rightfully part of its territory, Fang Binxing argues that cyberspace formed on the physical facilities of these networks belongs to the national territory, and hence a country can rightfully exercise national sovereignty over cyberspace (*People's Daily*, 2014). Explaining the scope of cyber sovereignty, Wang Jun includes network facilities in the national territory, network service providers, and users of these services within the sovereign jurisdiction (*People's Daily*, 2014). Lang Ping views data centers, network service providers, submarine cables, international standard-setting bodies, ICT supply chains, workforce, technological innovation, etc., as the areas crucial to the maintenance of cyber sovereignty (*People's Daily*, 2014).

Adherence to the principle of cyber sovereignty, as per An (2016), allows a country to better exercise its jurisdiction within its own territory and maintain independence in handling its cyber affairs, building the corresponding infrastructure, and curbing cybercrime. Zhang Li explains that the emphasis laid on cyberspace sovereignty in China's *National Cyberspace Security Strategy* is rooted in the desire to be able to pursue cyber policies in accordance with China's national conditions without any interference (CAC, 2017a). Du Zhichao and Nan Yuxia contend that the internet cannot completely free itself from the control of sovereignty. They argue that the challenges thrown open by the information age do not really undermine the sovereignty of the state as the response to these actually warrants the intervention of the state and the corresponding national rules and regulations extend national sovereignty to cyberspace (Du & Yuxia, 2014). Echoing the same notion of cyber sovereignty, they deduce that this concept mainly includes four aspects – cyber jurisdiction, cyberspace independence, equal sharing of cyber resources, and cyber self-defence. The last one here refers to the right of the state to take necessary measures to protect itself from attacks originating outside its territory and does not exclude the possibility of a military response in cyberspace.

In a research paper, Cai Cuihong elucidates the main reasons behind China's advocacy of cyber sovereignty. The first one has roots in the history and stems from China's colonial experience in the 19th and 20th centuries and its concern arising out of the alleged Western interference in Taiwan, Tibet, and Xinjiang. Cyber sovereignty therefore protects China from Western influence and becomes the means to secure governance rights. The second reason, according to Cai, is China's strong belief in the irreplaceable role of the state in cyber governance, owing to the political authority the government has in terms of the ability to muster resources, meet essential needs, make and implement policies and regulations, and ensure national security (C. Cai, 2018). The third reason is anchored in China's apprehensions over the stronghold of the Western countries on global cyber governance processes. Safeguarding state sovereignty for China also engenders equal participation of all governments in policy- making, irrespective of their levels of internet development. The fourth reason, as per Cai, is China's recognition of the fact that American stronghold, termed as hegemony, over the internet is widely attributed to its national and technological power, and these in general are fundamental to a states' dominant position in global governance systems.

Denoting cyber sovereignty as indivisible and inviolable, Li Shao explains the imperatives of cyber sovereignty in the context of ideological security. Li underlines the digital age risks of ideological infiltration and ethnic and cultural hatred incited by foreign hostile forces with the emergence of social media and other digital platforms in his attempt to justify that cyber sovereignty helps prevent violation of the mainstream value system (S. Li, 2017). Also touching upon cyber hegemony (the use of information technology to restrict the free use of information by others for economic, political, and military interests), Li contends that China should embrace cyber sovereignty in order to ensure cybersecurity and maintain ideological stability, and continue to promulgate the concept internationally.

Based on a historical analysis of cyber sovereignty in the Chinese discourse, Katharin Tai and Yuan Yi Zhu conclude that this concept which was initially used at the domestic level to associate with different policy goals before making its way to the international statements has largely remained undefined (Tai & Zhu, 2022). They observe that China's conception of cyber sovereignty should be seen as a function of historical perception of sovereignty as it has long been a source of political legitimacy, which very well predates the founding of the People's Republic of China.

Since it first appeared in the 2010 white paper of the Chinese Government, cyber sovereignty has consciously been made the mainstay of China's international engagement. It continues to feature in the cyber policy and strategy documents and finds a frequent mention in the statements of China's political leadership. Advancing the principle of cyber sovereignty basically kills two birds with one stone. It affords China a legitimate cause to exercise authority and control on the technical and behavioural aspects of the cyberspace within its jurisdictional boundaries and simultaneously allows China to ingrain its own values into cyber governance, which historically has had a deep Western influence.

## International perspectives on China's cyber power

China's actions in cyberspace have engendered concerns too, and the cyber threat from China in the wider geopolitical milieu reverberates in the Western analysis – be it the media, the intelligence community, leading cybersecurity firms, or the influential policy think-tanks. Chinese leadership's call to converge national efforts towards cyber power stirred a debate in strategic circles internationally on what to make of it as China's cyber power has perceptions abound.

In a policy paper evaluating China's cyber power, Greg Austin contends that the scholarly efforts to analyse the relational power dynamics of China's willingness to exercise power in the cyber domain in the context of theoretical tenets of power in international relations, or its contours in the information age, have been limited (Austin, 2016). The existing literature is based on the interpretation of leadership statements and the widely known instances of China's alleged engagement in cyber espionage or cyber operations against foreign countries. In the quest for how China thinks about cyber power and to decipher the political aspirations of cyber power from the key policy announcements and phrases used by the leadership while looking at cyberspace as an instrument of power, Simon Hansen underscores four key themes that emerge out. The first one revolves around maintaining social stability and the control on public opinion, and the second pertains to sustained economic growth to which the legitimacy of the CPC hinges on. Third sees China's international engagement on cybersecurity to be proactive, advancing its agenda, and shaping the discourse, and the fourth reveals that cyberspace fits precisely into China's broader great power ambitions (Hansen, 2014).

Greg Austin further points out the apparent inconsistencies China's leaders render in the very meaning of the term cyber power – sometimes the emphasis is on the foundational aspects of economy, scientific, technical, or military resources, while other times it is described as China's ability to persuade or force other actors in cyberspace. He finds their disposition towards the accumulation of power resources, which also shapes the vision of cyber power as the one seeking to consolidate the attributes of cyber power. On the point of assessment of China's cyber power, he enunciates that a better approach could be a detailed analysis of how China exercises its power in cyberspace.

In a book-length study titled *China's Cyber Power*, Nigel Inkster analyses cyber incidents to shed some light on the way China exercises its power in cyberspace to build a realistic understanding of China's cyber power. Reflecting on the alleged large-scale cyber espionage operations attributed to China, its capabilities in the military domain, and the policies and strategies which have global implications, he concludes that China will not shy away from exercising cyber power to seek to intimidate and coerce weaker adversaries. He cautions that "China's use of cyber power will not be restricted to achieve tactical effects in the battlefield," but be used *in extenso* to disable a powerful adversary (Inkster, 2015). In the meanwhile, China's strategy will seek to shape international structures and rules on cyber governance and security in a way that effectively erodes the supremacy of potential adversaries.

Analysing China's cyber power against the backdrop of America's national security in the military context, Jayson M. Spade concludes China has demonstrated that it is a strong cyber power if looked at within the framework of his definition of cyber power. This definition, as mentioned in the previous chapter, is the "ability of a nation-state to establish control and exert influence within and through cyberspace" (Spade, 2012).

Cyber power in the context of China first appeared as a political statement, which certainly had varying interpretations and nuances. Scholarly understanding of China's cyber power and of the concept of cyber power within China has expanded as a reasonable body of work has examined the implications of China's cyber power and the thought process within China on cyber power in general. Analysts from leading policy think-tanks in the US, Australia, and the UK have looked at China's cyber power mainly from a military, political, or security angle to draw implications. In contrast, Chinese scholars present an inward-looking view of China's cyber power based on what could be termed as pacifist values, basically portraying that the end-goal of cyber power is to make China self-sufficient in the cyber domain. In the writings of Chinese scholars and analysts, the comparison with the cyber capabilities of the US is quite prominent, and the developments such as the creation of the US Cyber Command in 2010, its international strategy for cyberspace, and Snowden revelations are invoked frequently questioning the intentions of the US in cyberspace.

## Discussion

The national informatisation and cybersecurity effort have received profound attention from the political leadership in China, and hence the institutions built to govern these functions have eventually been consolidated and brought under the direct supervision of the top leadership. Over the last three decades, China has built a comprehensive governance regime to accelerate and manage the integration of internet and information and communications technologies across the functions of governance, economy, and society. China has simultaneously built and strengthened the policy and regulatory framework spanning digital economy, cybersecurity, online content, and data security.

With reference to the cyber power model, evidence from this chapter suggests that China has built most of the *Capacities* listed as part of *National Cyber Policy*. China has a national cyber strategy in place and rolled out focused policy and legal measures, and it has built and empowered the apex agencies to ensure coordination among the various ministries and bodies tasked with informatisation or cybersecurity work. As far as the historical evidence of using cyber as an instrument of power is concerned, lending from some of the recent analyses (Austin et al., 2022; CISA, 2022; Vavra, 2020; Williams, 2021), it is safe to conclude that China has not shied away from using cyber as an instrument of power.

In terms of *Capabilities*, cybersecurity in China is now pursued as a national priority, more so as the political leadership has made the intent and resolve to build China into a cyber superpower abundantly clear. The cybersecurity initiative has profound support of the leadership, to the extent that it is directly spearheaded by the top leadership. The apex bodies, Central Cyberspace Affairs Commission or Cyberspace Administration of China, are supervised and driven by the top political leadership, clearly indicating their deep interests or disposition towards cyber affairs. The authoritative powers vested in these apex bodies assure coordination among various ministries, technical agencies, and power-epicentres, thereby paving the way for effective implementation of the tenets of cyber strategy and the corresponding policy measures.

Coming on to the tenets underpinning the objective of building China into a cyber superpower, there is no denying that China has pursued these goals quite aggressively. The tenets that could be placed under the ambit of *National Cyber Policy* are strengthening cybersecurity, digital economy, and CPC's control over information and leadership over cybersecurity work. As part of China's cybersecurity effort – which is projected as a precondition to development – the strategy, legal, and regulatory measures have kept pace with the deepening interests of China in cyberspace. The creation of CNCERT/CC and Central Leading Group for Cybersecurity and Informatization, the development of *National Cyberspace Security Strategy*, *State Informatization Development Strategy*, and the provisioning of *Cybersecurity Law*, *Data Security Law* and *Personal Information Protection Law*, in addition to a slew of regulations spanning encryption, critical infrastructure protection, internet services, intellectual property rights, electronic signatures, and crime, in aggregate have strengthened the overall cybersecurity posture. Put together, they have provided the requisite grounding and strategic direction to China's cybersecurity initiative and paved the way for the effective implementation of technical cybersecurity measures.

However, the shortage of skilled professionals in cybersecurity roles has time and again been flagged as a concern, denoting that this issue remains a major impediment (CAC, 2017b; China Copyright and Media, 2016b; Y. Hu, 2016; L. Xu, 2015). One of the articles from 2018 had estimated it to be between 7,00,000 and 1.4 million, and noted that due to organisational constraints it gets increasingly difficult to recruit and retain professionals (Z. Lu, 2018). The regional digital divide in China and the challenges with the digital transformation of traditional industries are also identified as lacunae (Xie, 2018). The 2017 ICT Development Index of the International Telecommunication Union had ranked China 80th among 176 countries (ITU, 2017). However, China's 2021–2025 Informatization Plan claims a leading position for China in the development of information infrastructure with the world's largest optical fibre and 4G network, and lead in the commercial use of 5G (Creemers, Dorwart, et al., 2022). The Plan also noted the reducing disparities in rural informatisation. A 2021 report from the World Economic Forum analysing 140 countries by their digital competitiveness over the last three years ranked China the highest within the G20 countries (Meissner, 2021).

Owing to decades of directed policy formulation to propel informatisation, digital economy has emerged as a prime driver of China's economic growth. In terms of value, China's digital economy now stands as the second largest in the world. With the implementation of long-term plans such as the *Internet Plus Action Plan*, there is a greater push for the integration of digital economy with the real economy and transformation of traditional industries with the help of new-age digital technologies. Digitalisation is also regarded as an instrument to increase productivity and create new markets and industry segments. Digital transformation of the manufacturing sector in China is assessed to be progressing steadily with the growing adoption of digital technologies broadly in process control as well as in management and administration functions (NDRC, 2022). Digital economy has also received priority in the long-term economic development planning and it now features prominently in the Five-Year Plans.

Realising the economic benefits of data and balancing it with the national security imperatives, China has stepped up the legislative and regulatory response to assure the protection of data and personal information and govern the processing, storage, use, transfer, and cross-border flow of data. A strong data protection framework incentivises investments in data-intensive businesses and encourages competition and innovation. China's data protection framework – enabled by *Data Security Law* and *Personal Information Protection Law* – is anticipated to form the foundation of China's next phase of economic growth. These laws together with the *Cybersecurity Law* make China's cybersecurity and data protection practices match with those of the developed economies and form the legal basis of its international engagement on data security issues. Some of the provisions in these laws enabling public security and national security bodies' access to data, whether residing in China or outside, have fuelled the ongoing concerns around the emphasis on government access to private-sector data in China. Foreign companies based in China, who need to comply with these regulations, are treading with caution. Moreover, the provisions in laws for data localisation under specific circumstances help China address the concerns over foreign intelligence gathering and give impetus to the growth of cloud industry in China.

While ensuring that the enormous socio-economic benefits of cyberspace are realised for the Chinese citizens, the CPC regime has by and large succeeded in retaining its control on information and freedom of expression in this domain. A mix of sweeping measures and state-of-the-art technological means to monitor internet traffic and manage internet content help CPC enforce a rigorous censorship regime, which is seen as essential to maintaining the supremacy of the CPC and the political stability of China. The risks of foreign interference and surveillance, subversion of regime, separatism, and cyber terrorism and crime emanating from the cyber domain are characterised as threats to the political stability, economy, and social harmony of China warranting stringent censorship and information control measures. Rather than opening up to the internet which enables freedom of expression and information, the CPC regime has not only subsumed it under the vast censorship apparatus but also leveraged it to shape public opinion.

In addition to CPC's absolute control over information, its strong leadership over informatisation and cybersecurity efforts is seen as the fundamental requirement to build China into a cyber superpower. With the growing importance of cyberspace for China, both in terms of economy and security, cyber and digital affairs have witnessed centralisation of authority. The decision to upgrade Central Leading Group for Cybersecurity and Informatization as the Central Cyberspace Affairs Commission in 2018 consolidated CPC's control over the development and regulation of cyberspace in accordance with its priorities and goals. The determined efforts of CPC towards consolidation of power over the critical aspects of cyberspace and the extensive supervision on the origin, flow, and consumption of information in this domain have made China subject to international scepticism.

China's actions in cyberspace and the resolve to occupy the commanding heights of cyberspace or building China into a cyber superpower could be interpreted in several ways. Notwithstanding the economic benefits it has reaped from cyberspace, China has remained vigilant of the threats to its political and social stability and the intentions of other states, right from the onset of the internet and the ensuing phenomenon of informatisation to contemporary cyber affairs. Concerns over the leading position of the US in many aspects and its longstanding stronghold on global cyber governance are abundantly clear from the scholarly writings and political statements. These are often invoked along with the Snowden revelations to justify China's stringent control and censorship measures.

To ensure security under geopolitical circumstances, it becomes necessary for China to define national borders or boundaries for this virtual domain of cyberspace. And the desire to do so hinges upon the principle of sovereignty in cyberspace. China views sovereignty in cyberspace from the perspective of territorial sovereignty and contends that the role of the governments in cyber governance is irreplaceable. China views cyberspace as another domain of human existence, and the juxtaposition of the principles of territoriality and sovereignty gives the Chinese Government the legitimacy to control the developmental, economic, and security aspects of cyberspace.

The concept of cyber power with reference to China has two main connotations. First is inward-looking, and cyber power status for China in this case essentially means self-sufficiency in cyber capabilities, the ability to exert control on cyberspace based on its own ideological values, enforcing its own vision of order in cyberspace, and pursuing developmental interests and cyber governance within its territorial boundaries. Cyber power enables China to force global companies to bend their practices and principles while operating within its borders. Cyber power here influences the behaviour of technology giants who generally are at loggerheads with the governments in other parts of the world on matters of privacy and civil liberties. The other connotation of China's cyber power is outward-looking, and this stems from China's intent to challenge the prevalent global cyber governance practices and change the very identity of cyberspace within its borders rather than moulding its political views or the practices of censorship and control according to what is normal in cyberspace. Cyber power also allows China to ingrain its own values into the governance model and technology of the internet which has evolved with a deep influence of the West and libertarian values.

The two strategic purposes quite evident are the enhancement of security and the willingness to play a decisive role in the future of cyberspace. Security revolves around maintaining political stability and social harmony, immunity from foreign interference, subversion, and curbing crime, terrorism, and separatism. China realised the risks of the internet quite early on and initiated the Golden Shield Project and the so-called Great Firewall of China with the motives of exerting control on access to information, censoring content, and monitoring user activities closely on the internet. The strategy, laws, and regulations have been categorically clear on this matter.

Security imperatives to a large extent drive China's desire to control the free flow of information and suppress internet freedom, and the legitimacy to do so is derived from its own conception of sovereignty in cyberspace. Placing threats from cyberspace among the sorts of terrorism and climate change assigns a sense of urgency to pursue security in cyberspace more resolutely.

China also realises that national power is fundamental to a state's dominant position in global governance systems. And by that measure, cyber power should be fundamental to a state's dominant position in global cyber governance. Cyber power in the context of foreign policy and diplomacy could again lead to many interpretations, but at the fundamental level it fulfils China's desire to reform and ingrain its own values into the prevalent global cyber governance practices and set the agenda for the future of cyber governance and cybersecurity. The next chapter discusses how this agenda is pursued as part of China's proactive cyber diplomacy.

## Note

1 It included one supercomputer centre and three campus-based networks: China Academy of Sciences Network, Tsinghua University Network, and Peking University Network.

# 4
# CHINA'S CYBER DIPLOMACY

## Going global with China's version of cyber governance

A draft resolution by the Russian Federation in the First Committee of the United Nations General Assembly in 1998 brought the subject of information security on to the UN agenda. Since then, governments have actively engaged at the UN towards building norms for responsible state behaviour in cyberspace. There has been a clear-cut divide between the two competing approaches for the governance of cyberspace – one sticks to the existing model where multistakeholder bodies make all the decisions and governments have a limited role to play, while the other seeks to alter this model to be replaced with a multilateral approach where the governments, represented equally such as at the UN, make the decisions and all other actors play a consultative role. The diplomatic efforts have therefore been a tug-of-war between these two diametrically opposite approaches as the proponents of both have strived to ingrain their vision into the governance mechanism of cyberspace.

China has been quite vocal amidst this growing politicisation of cyber governance. The chapter examines how China strives to bolster its leadership on the pertinent issue of cyber governance in international and regional organisations and other groupings, and seeks to extend its normative influence. The chapter expands on China's international engagement on the internet or cyber governance and attempts to interpret its key positions and critique the multistakeholder approach, looking at the evolution of the process of norms development over the years. The chapter then discusses how China's proactive diplomatic engagement has promoted its position at various platforms, beginning with the case of the *International Code of Conduct for Information Security*, and then looking at the role of the World

DOI: 10.4324/9781003473510-4

Internet Conference in this quest, and China's plan of action articulated in the *International Strategy of Cooperation on Cyberspace*. Towards the end, the chapter dissects the technology dimension of China's Belt and Road Initiative and highlights the recent initiatives for digital currency and global data security.

## Cyber norms and China's cyber diplomacy

The internet has been a unique experiment, not just as a technology but also as a governance model. Since the very beginning, volunteering individuals and groups have fulfilled the critical roles of technology and protocol development and management of its resources, be its IP addresses or the Domain Name System. The whole process has been inclusive, open, and international as the reach of the network spread to different parts of the world. However, as commercial interests grew and security considerations became paramount, the governance mechanism of the internet drew attention of the governments.

The term "internet governance" came into existence in the 1980s with reference to the technical management functions of the core resources of the internet, such as protocols, IP addresses, domain names, and root servers. Brought into use by the technical community responsible for the upkeep of the internet, "internet governance" mostly meant governance "of" the internet, or in other words, the governance of the network infrastructure (Chapelle, 2007). These functions were performed by individuals or self-organised groups of individuals. For instance, the responsibilities of domain name system management and allocation of IP address blocks from the early 1970s to the early 1990s were executed by Jon Postel who was working at the University of Southern California (Snyder et al., 2016).

The Internet Assigned Numbers Authority (IANA), which was created in 1988 during the transition from ARPANET to the internet, managed these functions until 1998 when the newly established Internet Corporation for Assigned Names and Numbers (ICANN) took over IANA functions from the University of Southern California. With representation from the private sector, technical community, internet users, and civil society in the decision-making, and keeping governments' representation at bay, the ICANN was a multistakeholder organisation. To represent governments' interests, the UN member states were invited to form a Governmental Advisory Committee (GAC) for advice, but it was non-binding on the ICANN board.

China had some engagement with ICANN in the initial phase. In 1999, Chen Yin, a deputy bureau director in the former Ministry of Information Industry represented China at the GAC. China ceased sending representatives to GAC meetings in 2001 owing to ICANN's acceptance of Taiwan in the GAC and its anxieties over the disproportionate power of American corporations in some of the functions related to the management of internet resources (Hong, 2016). Although the Chinese Government abstained from attending the GAC until 2009, but the interactions between ICANN and other actors in China did not come to a halt.

China was back to ICANN GAC in June 2009 and some concessions were extended, such as renaming Taiwan as "Chinese Taipei" and an accelerated process to create internationalised top-level domain names as well as the opening of a new set of Generic top-level domains. Translating into expedited approval and allocation of new Chinese country code top-level domains to the CNNIC and also country code top-level domains in Mandarin, this reform was viewed as appeasement to keep states like China and Russia happy with the ICANN regime (Mueller, 2011: 183–184). The international discourse on internet governance however had undergone a sea change between 2001 and 2009 as it was now hotly debated at various platforms. Internet governance by now had emerged as a public policy issue, having commercial, cultural, and social implications to which the free flow of information and freedom of expression were inherent.

The subject of internet governance came to the fore as states began debating at the World Summit on the Information Society (WSIS) – convened under the auspices of the UN over two phases in 2003 (Geneva) and 2005 (Tunis). In the run-up to the first phase of the WSIS, the control of the US Government on ICANN came under criticism, and China with the support of the developing countries (Group of 77) tried building the case for an international internet treaty and the establishment of an intergovernmental internet organisation vying for government's role in decision-making related to the development of the internet.

China argued for governmental control on the decisions pertaining to the management of internet resources instead of the private sector, which was at odds with the American and the European approach favouring the leadership of private sector (Kleinwächter, 2007: 55–56). China's desire to alter the prevailing internet governance system stemmed from its concerns over the unilateral control the US Government maintained on the DNS though ICANN. The Chinese Government therefore made every possible effort to bring the governance of the DNS under an international organisation such as the ITU where it was granted an equal role in the decision-making.

To that end, China's cyber diplomacy centred its critique on the uneven distribution of internet resources and the root servers, and US Government's control on IANA functions by virtue of the contract between ICANN and the US Department of Commerce National Telecommunications and Information Administration (NTIA) to perform these functions (ICANN, 2000). China's objections also stemmed from the very character of the ICANN, which to date remains to be a non-state actor after all, outside of the control and oversight of states as far as the policymaking and governance of the internet is concerned (Mueller, 2011: 182). Notwithstanding the differences, the recognition of the prominent role of non-state actors in the governance of the internet was common to both the opposing views – the contention was primarily over the leadership role.

To arrive at a common understanding of the scope of internet governance and roles and responsibilities of the stakeholders and to prepare the ground for negotiations in the second phase of the WSIS, the UN Secretary-General was requested to establish a Working Group on Internet Governance (WGIG). It came up with a working definition of internet governance as, "the development and application by Governments, the private sector and civil society, in their respective roles, of shared principles, norms, rules, decision-making procedures, and programmes that shape the evolution and use of the Internet" (WGIG, 2005b). WGIG also recommended the creation of the Internet Governance Forum (IGF), but there was no agreement on the role of the US government in the management of the internet. In its comments to the WGIG in 2005, China underscored "the lack of participations and rights of developing, least developed countries and United Nations in the decision-making process regarding the global Internet policies" and suggested that "sovereign governments and governmental organizations should play leading roles under the United Nations' framework while guaranteeing the broad participation of all the other stakeholders" (WGIG, 2005a).

The second phase of the WSIS ended up with a consensus on some basic principles of internet governance and the establishment of the IGF – a multi-stakeholder policy dialogue for discussions on public policy issues amongst others, with representation from the private sector, governments, technical and academic communities, inter-governmental organisations, and media (IGF, 2015a, 2015b; ITU, 2005). The Tunis Agenda brought about a consensus that states should not interfere in decisions regarding another country's country-code top-level domain, and recognised that "all governments should have an equal role and responsibility for international Internet governance and for ensuring the stability, security and continuity of the Internet" (ITU, 2005). The governments critical of the US Government's control over ICANN and the DNS viewed it as a success. However, to China's disappointment, the WSIS could not bring about a change in the control the US had over the functions of ICANN. Moreover, the IGF, though nominally under the auspices of the UN, was also designed as a multistakeholder forum affording equal status to the participating governments, private sector enterprises, and the technical and academic communities – another platform which was not in conformity with China's preference for an intergovernmental organisation.

The mandate of the IGF, set out for five years initially, was renewed for five years in 2011 (UNGA, 2011a) and for another ten years in 2015 (UNGA, 2015b). China opposed the renewal of the mandate of the IGF in

2010 (Mueller, 2011: 184), but once it was renewed, China and the Group of 77 tried to make IGF intergovernmental and bring directly under the control of the UN system (Parliament of UK, 2010). China attempted to include the word "multilateral" when the mandate was up for renewal in 2015 (Ermert, 2015). During the WSIS process and afterwards, China's cyber diplomatic efforts have aggressively pushed the multilateral approach to the governance of the internet, seeking to bring it under the aegis of the UN. This effort was supported in no small measure by Chinese analysts and internet policy commentators who wrote on the dominant position of the US in technological standards, intellectual property on technology, and the DNS – sometimes calling it "cyber hegemony" or "cyber dominance" (C. Jiang, 2010, cited in Harold et al., 2016) and even suggesting the transformation of ICANN into an international organisation (L. Jiang et al., 2013, cited in Harold et al., 2016).

As China's cyber diplomacy turned assertive towards the end of the first decade of the century, the 2010 white paper *The Internet in China* gave these efforts a direction coherent with China's domestic policy positions (State Council, 2010). The white paper reiterated China's position that "the role of the UN should be given full scope in international Internet administration" and supported "the establishment of an authoritative and just international Internet administration organization under the UN system." The World Conference on International Telecommunications in 2012 (WCIT-12) – where the International Telecommunications Regulations were being renegotiated first time since 1988 – turned out to be another battleground as heated discussions were held on whether these regulations should be extended to the internet or not.

A proposal for the work of the conference submitted to WCIT-12 – which surfaced as a leaked document – aimed to redefine the internet with extensive government controls and supervision. One of the provisions in the proposal stated that

> Member States shall have the sovereign right to establish and implement public policy, including international policy, on matters of Internet governance, and to regulate the national Internet segment, as well as the activities within their territory of operating agencies providing Internet access or carrying Internet traffic.
>
> *(WCITLeaks, 2012)*

This was jointly proposed by Russia, United Arab Emirates, China, Saudi Arabia, Algeria, Sudan, and Egypt and seen by others as an attempt to shift internet governance away from ICANN to the UN system placing the powers and responsibilities of internet governance under the jurisdiction of the ITU (Min, 2013).

The proposal was withdrawn and the final text of the revised regulations however did not contain any specific provisions on the internet, albeit "internet" appeared under one of the non-binding appendices calling for efforts to "foster an enabling environment for the greater growth of the internet" (ITU, 2012). An amendment to the preamble of the regulations on the "right of access of Member States to access international telecommunications services" was regarded as an attempt to legitimise state control over the internet. The treaty failed to achieve consensus as only 89 member states signed the treaty and 55 member states, including the US, Canada, Australia, the UK, and several European countries refused to sign the revised version of the treaty (Ackerman, 2012; EDRi, 2012; The Conversation, 2012).

Ahead of WCIT-12, there was a push back on the very idea of bringing internet governance under the fold of the ITU. In an opinion piece, Vinton Cerf (one of the pioneers of the internet) elucidated why such a regulation jeopardises the idea of the internet (Cerf, 2012). He argued that each of the ITU member states gets equal voting rights irrespective of their record on fundamental rights and a simple majority can trigger changes. Moreover, the negotiations are also held among the governments, with very limited access for civil society or non-state actors. Vinton Cerf maintained that the internet prospered because it grew organically as a result of collaboration among civil society, academia, private sector, and voluntary standards bodies on the matters of development, operations, and governance out of the oversights of any government, and because of its very design, the ITU will be a barrier to civil society participation. The Internet Society also opposed such a move and in its comment to the WCIT preparations noted that "Internet is built on multistakeholder cooperation that includes an important role for governments, but similarly engages the private sector and civil society, through a bottom-up, inclusive process, consistent with the Geneva Declaration of Principles" (Internet Society, 2012).

A major shift in this debate came with the Snowden revelations in 2013, which changed the whole outlook of many countries on the issue of security over the internet. The US was subject to sharp criticism over the massive surveillance programme as it came to the knowledge of the public that the US and its Five-Eyes Alliance were involved in a massive pan-global espionage and surveillance operation over the internet. China's interpretation of the situation was that the US and its allies are exploiting their dominant position in information and communication technologies and China's cyber diplomacy exploited this heavily to advance its own agenda and vision for internet governance. In the aftermath of the Snowden revelations, the pressure on the US escalated further to transition IANA functions to a multistakeholder body. The US Department of Commerce announced its intent to do so in 2014 and completed the process in September 2016 (Internet Society, n.d.-a).

In the norms development space by then, substantial progress had been made at the UN as the Group of Governmental Experts (GGE) had arrived at consensus on some key principles in their 2013 report. The report upheld that "the international law, in particular the UN Charter is applicable to the cyber-sphere, and recognised state sovereignty in its conduct of ICT-related activities" (UNGA, 2013). China considered this to be consistent with its stated position on cyber sovereignty. China was one of the first movers at the UN to initiate discussions on norms, although it was under the theme of information security. China has participated in all the six UN GGEs from 2004 to 2021 as traditionally the permanent members of the UN Security Council have had a seat on all UN GGEs (GIP, n.d.).

In December 2018, the UN General Assembly established two new processes – a GGE, and an Open-Ended Working Group (OEWG) which was an outcome of Russia-sponsored resolution with the support of China. Unlike UN GGE which comprises 25 select member states, participation in the OEWG process is open to all interested UN member states. Collaborating with the member states of the Shanghai Cooperation Organisation (SCO), China has twice (in 2011 and 2015) proposed an *International Code of Conduct for Information Security* at the UN General Assembly. The UN system has been the centre point of China's norm entrepreneurship efforts.

Norm entrepreneurs are the individuals, organisations, governments, or a group of any of these, who seek to establish norms in a particular field. Norms are not synonymous to legally-binding agreements or instruments, and as Finnemore and Hollis have noted, they do not come into being by fiat or desire, nor are they imposed in a vacuum. Norms therefore "grow out of specific contexts and manifest through social processes and interactions among particular groups of actors" (Finnemore & Hollis, 2016: 427). Normative power helps states serve their national interest using normative instruments, which essentially is the ability to attract other actors to join the state's vision of what the "norm" is in a specific field, and in international relations it emanates from the aspiration to influence the world order (Tikk-Ringas, 2017). Moreover, succeeding in the endeavour of norm-making requires a methodical strategy and activism which works out at multiple levels and platforms (Finnemore & Hollis, 2016: 447).

China's norm-making efforts are spread over the UN system, the SCO, and its bilateral relations. The Chinese Government is the primary norm entrepreneur here, and the quest to garner support of the other like-minded states and legitimacy for China's vision of cyber sovereignty is apparent in China's diplomatic efforts over the last two decades. Being critical of the disproportionate allocation of internet resources and representation in internet governance, China often purportedly claims voicing the concerns of the developing world. China argues that the lack of sufficient resources and technology expertise severely constrains the representation of the developing countries at multistakeholder bodies for internet governance, and therefore an intergovernmental organisation such as the ITU may better serve their national interests. An intergovernmental organisation for the governance of the internet, or a multilateral governance model, has been the cornerstone of China's cyber diplomacy for all these years along with the concept of cyber sovereignty. A group of countries have aligned with this normative position of China on the issue of internet or cyber governance – which runs diametrically opposite to the approach endorsed by the US and European countries – indicating the possible rise in China's normative power.

The revised outline of China's *State Informatization Development Strategy* had mentioned active participation in global governance and enhancement of China's international influence and discursive power as one of the goals (China Copyright and Media, 2016a). At the 19th National Congress of the CPC, Xi Jinping spoke of leveraging Chinese wisdom and Chinese approach to solve the problems facing mankind (Xinhua, 2017i). China's cyber diplomacy, whether through new ideas such the *Code of Conduct* or alternative approaches such as the OEWG, wholeheartedly seeks to increase the appeal of China's vision for cyberspace among developing countries and building partnerships or groupings of like-minded states that subscribe to its vision.

As a norm entrepreneur, China's cyber diplomatic efforts are on the lookout for avenues to promote its intergovernmental or multilateral vision for cyberspace and embed the principle of cyber sovereignty in the global cyber governance mechanism. In this quest, the SCO has acted as the incubator of the *International Code of Conduct for Information Security*, the World Internet Conference is trying to institutionalise China's outreach to the global technology community, and the ICT dimension of the Belt and Road Initiative seeks to propagate China's technology and standards to the different parts of the world. The forthcoming sections discuss these three carriers of China's vision for cyberspace and its *International Strategy of Cooperation on Cyberspace* which binds the cyber diplomatic efforts.

## International Code of Conduct for Information Security

Seeking a prominent global role in cyber governance and enhanced cooperation on security issues in cyberspace, China has attached great importance to its cyber diplomatic efforts. The 2010 white paper *The Internet in China* underscored the imperatives of regional and international cooperation on issues related to cyberspace. It mentioned the Association of Southeast Asian Nations (ASEAN), SCO, and the UN as the focal points of China's diplomatic efforts. China's desire to shape international discourse on cyber issues in line with its own vision and security interests is a longstanding one. For the very same purpose, China has leveraged SCO as a staging ground to put its views forward to the international community. The proposal of a draft

*International Code of Conduct for Information Security (Code of Conduct)* to the UN General Assembly in 2011, moved together with Russia and two other member states of the SCO, was one of the first ambitious attempts in the direction of shaping norms for responsible state behaviour in cyberspace.

Outlining the identification of rights and responsibilities of the states in information space as one of the purposes and international stability and security as the objective, the *Code of Conduct* listed 11 voluntary pledges for the signatories. It broadly entailed

> respect for the sovereignty, territorial integrity and political independence of all states, non-use of ICTs to carry out hostile activities or acts of aggression and attempts to curb dissemination of information which incites terrorism, secessionism, extremism, or undermines other political, economic and social stability of others.
>
> *(UNGA, 2011b)*

The *Code of Conduct* did underscore the prime concerns of its sponsors and called in for a multilateral approach to the management of the internet. The *Code of Conduct* however did not really succeed in garnering support of other countries at the UN (CCDCOE, 2015).

A revised draft *Code of Conduct* was proposed to the UN General Assembly in 2015, this time with the support of all the founding member states of the SCO – China, Russia, Kazakhstan, Kyrgyzstan, Tajikistan, and Uzbekistan. The ground principles of the revised *Code of Conduct* and its content did not drastically depart from that of the previous version, though it purportedly ironed out the divergent views. The states voluntarily subscribing to the *Code of Conduct* would

> pledge to comply with the *Charter of the United Nations* and universally recognised norms governing international relations; not to use ICTs to interfere in the internal affairs of other states; endeavour to ensure the supply chain security of ICT goods and services; respect rights and freedoms in the information space but subject to certain restrictions such as national security and public order; refrain from the threat or use of force; and promote the establishment of multilateral, transparent and democratic international Internet governance mechanisms and confidence-building measures among others.
>
> *(UNGA, 2015a)*

In the span of four years – between the initial and the revised *Code of Conduct* – a few events triggered a major shift in the international discourse on cybersecurity (or information security) which also had an influence on international cyber diplomacy, in general, and the *Code of Conduct* in particular. Snowden revelations in June 2013 changed the whole paradigm of states' perception of cyber threats and cybersecurity. By then, the UN GGE (established in 2011) had also submitted its consensus report and it upheld that the international law, in particular the UN Charter, is applicable to cyberspace (UNGA, 2013). The sovereign right of states on the governance of the internet had been debated extensively at the WCIT-12 with China and Russia advocating for more government control, while the US and European countries standing by the multistakeholder model of internet governance. In the interregnum, both Russia and China underwent leadership changes. Xi Jinping took over the reins of the Government in 2013 and the lead of cyber affairs in early 2014, bringing cybersecurity directly under the ambit of his office and instituting some stringent measures as discussed in the previous chapter.

The updated version of the draft *Code of Conduct* reflected the changes brought about by these events. It was in conformity with the recommendations of the UN GGE report, especially because the report had recognised state sovereignty in the conduct of ICT-related activities and it had been a pressing issue for the member states of SCO. The revised *Code of Conduct* came up with new sections on the role of states in internet governance and the need for confidence-building measures, which further brought it in synchronisation with the recommendation of the UN GGE consensus report. A code of conduct promising an equitable role for all the states in internet governance and preventing the use of ICTs and communication networks for interference in internal affairs was likely to generate interest among states who were seeking security in this increasingly contested domain. A unique experiment in its own way, the *Code of Conduct* was an undertaking to provide an alternative approach and to alter the discourse on the normative behaviour of states in cyberspace. Since Russia and China often associate participation in the internet governance process with dominance in cyberspace, the *Code of Conduct* essentially sought to make this process more equitable and offset the dominance of the states like US.

Another aspect of the *Code of Conduct* worth mentioning is its origins and placement at the SCO, as it has been an outcome of norm entrepreneurship within the framework of this regional organisation. The SCO was established in 2001 with the objectives of "strengthening mutual trust among the member states, fostering cooperation in trade, economy, research, technology and culture, and maintaining security and stability in the region" (SCO, n.d.). After convergence on the plan of action related to international information security in 2007, the *Agreement on Cooperation in Ensuring International Information Security* between the member states was concluded in 2009 bringing cybersecurity and cyber norms under the fold of SCO. The Agreement enshrined the common vision of SCO member states for the management and the governance of the internet, and it categorically identified information weapons, terrorism, cybercrime, and the use of dominant position by states to the detriment of the interests and security of others as prime threats (SCO, 2009). The draft *Code of Conduct* proposed in 2011 was therefore born out of this 2009 agreement, putting forward the ideas of the SCO member states on information security to the international arena. The member states fight against cyber terrorism, separatism, and extremism under the Regional Anti-Terrorist Structure, and they hold regular joint-exercises as part of this initiative (Xinhua, 2019e).

Though the SCO member states share some common threats, the perspectives of the SCO on cybersecurity and cyber governance tend to reflect the views of its dominant members – China and Russia. The SCO has been serving as the staging ground for these two member states to push their perspectives and principles, especially those pertaining to cyber sovereignty and regime stability, to the international community and the UN enveloped in the legitimacy afforded by a regional organisation. The SCO's conceptualisation of information security encompasses control on content and information over the internet writ large. States are therefore likely to leverage their influence in regional organisations to propagate novel practices, or alter the existing ones, in conformity with their ideas and principles for cyber governance. Norms building for cyber and information security remains to be a highly contested space in the international arena.

Against this backdrop, the apparent objectives of China's cyber diplomatic efforts are to build a coalition of like-minded states to propagate the multilateral approach to cyber governance and make the principle of cyber sovereignty visible and alluring to the international community. The SCO, being a multilateral platform itself, serves the former objective very well as seen in the case of the *Code of Conduct* where China forged partnerships with the member states. For the latter, and to extend its normative influence in global cyber governance, China in 2014 unveiled a new instrument – the World Internet Conference. From the dais of this annual flagship event, the Chinese Government continues to assert respect for sovereignty in cyberspace.

## World Internet Conference

The idea of a conclave to bring global internet technology leaders to China and showcase both its emerging high-technology sector and the vision for the internet took the shape of what is now known as the World Internet Conference. Another purpose this high visibility event was supposed to serve is to give thrust to China's model for cyber governance as an alternative to the prevailing West-centric system. It is held in the town of Wuzhen – therefore also known as Wuzhen Summit – annually by the CAC and Zhejiang Provincial People's Government. With prominent figures of the technology industry from nearly 100 countries in attendance (World Internet Conference, n.d.), at the time of conception, this conference was seen as China's arrival on to the world stage of technology – the first of its kind and magnitude in China, and arguably in the world.

The World Internet Conference attracts international technology leaders, heads of big technology companies, non-governmental organisations, government officials, and academicians who share technology breakthroughs and exchange ideas on global internet governance (World Internet Conference, 2015). At the conference, China's own technology giants such as Alibaba Group, Baidu, Tencent, Xiaomi, Huawei, etc., share the platform with their global competitors like Qualcomm, IBM, Microsoft, and Google (Xinhua, 2016e).

At the first edition of the conference in 2014, when the memories of Snowden revelations were still fresh, Xi Jinping in his remotely delivered speech called on states to work together to contain the abuse of ICTs and oppose cyber surveillance and cyber-attacks. Conveying to the world the high priority attached to this conference, Xi Jinping attended and delivered his speech in person at the second edition and even pushed China's viewpoint of a multilateral approach to internet governance.

In his speech, Xi Jinping reiterated "respect for cyber sovereignty, peace and security, openness and cooperation, and good order" to make five propositions corresponding to the building of global internet infrastructure, development of cyber economy, security and order in cyberspace, and an equitable and just internet governance system. Knowing that the event has high international visibility, the speech was crafted to expound China's take on key principles (Xi, 2015). One of the points "multilateral approach with multi-party participation" in China's view meant consultation among all parties and players be they governments, international organisations, internet companies, technology communities, non-government institutions, or individual citizens, but the governments were to remain the principal actor. It also brought out the intrinsic connection China establishes between this approach and the principle of sovereignty in cyberspace – enshrined in the *Charter of the United Nations*, and essentially boils down to the "right of individual states to independently choose their own path of development and regulation for cyberspace and related public policies." The speech made it clear that foreign companies are very much welcome to China as long as they abide by China's laws – pointing towards China's across-the-board regulations for control and censorship, which were discussed in the previous chapter.

Speaking at the sixth iteration of the World Internet Conference in 2019, Wang Lei, Coordinator for China's Cyber Affairs, boasted of the relevance of cyber sovereignty in the light of the March 2019 terrorist attack in Christchurch which triggered the Christchurch Call[1] – an endeavour to bring states together to prevent the use of online services to disseminate terrorist and violent extremist content (Christchurch Call, n.d.; L. Wang, 2019). He also noted the call for a ban on interference in electoral processes through social media and other electronic means, expressing satisfaction that states are now coming to realise that cyber terrorism and cybercrime are common challenges. The platform of the World Internet Conference was leveraged to affirm that China's version of internet governance fits better in the contemporary security environment.

In spite of the ardent support of Chinese Government to the World Internet Conference and an aggressive outreach, China's multilateral approach has by and large failed to gain much traction among states in other parts of the world (K. Fang, 2015). The reach and influence of the World Internet Conference seem to be limited to the SCO member states, especially the ones that were part of the *International Code of Conduct for Information Security*. However, the World Internet Conference continues to be used to exhibit China's growing prowess in cutting-edge technology such as artificial intelligence, 5G, and the internet of things by placing discussions on these themes in the conference agenda. The World Internet Conference has given China its own platform to promote a competing vision for the future of the internet.

The conference also stands as a testament to China's proactive cyber diplomacy, seeking to set an agenda for cyber governance and cybersecurity, and shape the international discourse on the subject. It serves as the vehicle to extend China's normative influence in international cyber governance. Although the leadership's disposition for the multilateral approach to cyber governance was quite clear when Xi Jinping spoke from the podium of the World Internet Conference in 2015, but the mention of cyber sovereignty as an organising principle of cyber governance did ignite a debate. To promote its own brand of cyber governance and pursue the strategic goal of building China into a cyber superpower, the Chinese Government needed a plan of action for its diplomatic efforts which resonates with these principles, and it took the shape of an international strategy for cyberspace.

## International Strategy of Cooperation on Cyberspace

Jointly issued by the Ministry of Foreign Affairs and the CAC in 2017, the *International Strategy of Cooperation on Cyberspace* elaborated on China's approach to international cyber affairs packaged in six strategic goals and nine action points (Ministry of Foreign Affairs, 2017). The prime motivation behind this endeavour was to give the principles of cyber governance espoused over the years by China a solid grounding and a concrete shape. These principles by then were largely restricted to political statements. The Strategy reaffirms China's propositions on cyber governance and cybersecurity to guide its foreign policy and diplomatic efforts, also elucidating on the thought process behind these propositions and China's position on international cyber issues. At the fundamental level, the Strategy interlocks with China's domestic cyberspace security strategy, foreign policy goals, digital economy ambitions, and the wider geopolitical imperatives.

The basic principles of the Strategy remain the same (peace, sovereignty, and shared governance and benefits) as reiterated earlier at multiple forums, but the principle of sovereignty formed the core premise of the document. It called cyberspace a new domain of state sovereignty and upheld the central role of the UN in building international consensus on the issues of divergence. The strategic goals outlined in the Strategy emanate from these principles, and the goals include – safeguarding sovereignty and national security, developing a system of international rules governing cyberspace, promoting fair internet governance, protecting rights and interests of citizens, promoting cooperation, and building platforms for cyber cultural exchange. In aggregate, these objectives aim to building international consensus on sovereignty in cyberspace, govern the flow of information with respect to national security needs, expand the scope and expanse of digital economy, tether development with security, and look for an enhanced defence capability in cyberspace to safeguard sovereignty (Ministry of Foreign Affairs, 2017).

The Strategy set the tone for a new approach against the backdrop of unbalanced development, inadequate rules, inequitable order, acts of hostility, and aggression in cyberspace. Being wary of the perils of external influence and China's vulnerability to foreign-aided dissent and political unrest, the Strategy solicits states to refrain from "cyber hegemony or interference in other countries' internal affairs, or engage in, condone or support cyber activities that could undermine the national security of others" (Ministry of Foreign Affairs, 2017). The Strategy upheld sovereignty in cyberspace essential for China's freedom to exercise jurisdiction over its own ICT infrastructure and safeguard the rights and interests of its citizens in cyberspace.

Recognising China's exposure to the risks from supply chain contamination and backdoors in imported ICT products, particularly in the aftermath of Snowden revelations, the Strategy distinctly pointed out the need to restrict states from leveraging their advantageous position in technology to undermine the security of ICT products and services supply chains of other states. The Strategy denoted militarisation and building up deterrence in cyberspace to be a hindrance to international security and strategic mutual trust. China's own military strategy and force restructuring however defy this proclamation.

Diplomacy is an effective tool to propagate and reinforce China's position on cyberspace affairs at the international stage. The key highlight of the Strategy therefore are the nine points in the "plan of action" which conjointly have steered China's cyber diplomacy over the last few years and would continue to do so in the years to come. The nine points are elaborated in Table 4.1. At the very basic, China's diplomatic efforts strive to garner support for its version of cyber governance from like-minded states across bilateral and multilateral platforms, and addresses its prime concerns related to what is termed as "arms race in cyberspace" – pointing towards the US and the countries placed at a better position in cyberspace.

On the matter of norms of responsible state behaviour in cyberspace, China gives itself a pat on the back citing the *Code of Conduct* developed together with SCO member states, and for extending support to the UN GGE process. The uphill task for China's cyber diplomacy is to convert China's version of norms into universally accepted ones, and to that end, it would need to foster partnerships. This places the World Internet Conference high on the diplomatic agenda. As per the *International Strategy of Cooperation on Cyberspace*, some of the regional organisations and groupings found to be of interest in this quest in addition to SCO are – BRICS, the ASEAN Regional Forum, the Forum on China–Africa Cooperation, the China–Arab States Cooperation Forum, and the Asia–Pacific Economic Cooperation Forum. Some of these platforms with which the Strategy seeks to forge close engagement already have ongoing initiatives on countering cyber terrorism and cybercrime.

To further strengthen China's identity as a reformer of institutions, one of the action points in the Strategy states "institutional reform of the UN Internet Governance Forum so as to strengthen its decision-making capacity and make it open and transparent in functioning and procedures" (Ministry of Foreign Affairs, 2017). And stemming from China's longstanding resentment, one of the diplomatic tasks listed in the Strategy is to "participate in international discussions on fair distribution and management of critical Internet resources and promote the reform of the ICANN, ensuring greater openness and transparency in its decision-making and operation" (Ministry of Foreign Affairs, 2017).

With an eye on the imperatives of digital economy, the Strategy seeks to expand China's role in cybersecurity capacity building and technology transfer leveraging the high growth in its domestic ICT industry. This task is vital to build China's image as a technology provider and infrastructure builder. The subtle mention in the Strategy of cyber cultures points towards enhancing China's cultural influence, or in other words, its soft power. Another action point bearing strategic importance is the symbiotic relationship between China's cyber diplomacy and the Government's flagship Belt and Road Initiative. The Strategy speaks of extending full support to the Chinese internet enterprises and those from the manufacturing, financial services, and ICT sectors to go global, become internationally competitive, and expand their global supply chains.

**TABLE 4.1** Highlights of the plan of action under the International Strategy of Cooperation on Cyberspace

| Main points | Highlights of the plan of action | Remarks |
|---|---|---|
| Peace and stability in cyberspace | • Threats should be addressed through dialogue and consultation, and countries should work together to curb the abuse of ICTs and prevent arms race in cyberspace.<br>• Explore how international law could be applied to cyberspace; to build mutual trust and prevent cyber conflicts. | • Peace and stability in cyberspace remain to be the core tenets of UN GEE norms and of every mechanism on cyber cooperation.<br>• China is wary of the competition from technologically advanced countries and plans to use norms to dissuade them from harming China's interests in cyberspace. The Strategy therefore mentions of preventing arms race and cyber conflicts. |
| Rule-based order in cyberspace | • The role of the UN in formulating international rules for cyberspace is central. China is committed to participate in the UN GGE process and other UN mechanisms.<br>• Seeks to enhance international dialogue and to gain support for the *International Code of Conduct for Information Security (Code of Conduct)*. | • "Rule-based order" does not find a mention in the UN GEE norms or reports, but China has used it extensively since 2014. Its use denotes cyberspace to be an unruly domain that needs control and regulation – a justification for stringent measures for censorship and control.<br>• *Code of Conduct* is China's prime norm-making exercise whose wider acceptance is essential for its success and China's image as norm entrepreneur. |
| Partnership in cyberspace | • Expand dialogue mechanisms and bilateral foreign policy exchange on cyber issues (the World Internet Conference and other international/bilateral forums will be leveraged).<br>• Seeks to promote cooperation among member states of SCO, BRICS, and other regional organisations and groupings on cyber issues and digital economy. | • The World Internet Conference is the cornerstone of China's outreach to countries and private enterprises to make its propositions (mainly multilateralism and sovereignty) attractive and accepted as the foundations for cyber governance.<br>• China has leveraged SCO to its advantage to push norms in the form of *Code of Conduct* to the UNGA. China plans to engaging with other groupings especially BRICS to make its vision for cyberspace acceptable among the prominent developing economies. |

*(Continued)*

**TABLE 4.1** (Continued)

| Main points | Highlights of the plan of action | Remarks |
|---|---|---|
| Reform of the global internet governance system | • Presses on the need for institutional reform of the IGF (making member election and report submission open and transparent) and ICANN (making it a truly independent international institution and ensuring openness and transparency). | • It is not clear what China means by reform of the IGF. <br> • Although China engages with ICANN, but continues to be critical of it. It is unclear how China plans to reform this system on which governments do not have much control. |
| International cooperation on cyber terrorism and cyber crimes | • Seeks to build norms to address cyber terrorism and work towards international convention on combating cyber terrorism. Seeks to promote discussion on a global legal instrument. <br> • Will continue engagement with ARF and BRICS, and establish bilateral mechanisms on these two issues. | • Cybercrime and terrorism are truly transnational issues which need cooperation at multiple platforms. <br> • Moreover, since there is no legal instrument yet to tackle these issues and China attempts to fill the void. It is also because China considers itself to be a victim of cybercrime and terrorism. |
| Protection of citizens' rights and interests including privacy | • Calls for establishing principles to protect privacy in cyberspace and measures to curb infringement of privacy using cyber means. <br> • Plans to facilitate cooperation between the Government and businesses to safeguard privacy in cyberspace. | • China has enacted laws for data security and personal data protection. China has also initiated the Global Initiative on Data Security which attempts to champion norms related to data security. <br> • China invokes privacy protection mainly with reference to the threat from foreign interference or espionage, and not from the point of view of Government-led online content and behaviour monitoring. |

(Continued)

**TABLE 4.1** (Continued)

| Main points | Highlights of the plan of action | Remarks |
|---|---|---|
| Digital economy and sharing of digital dividends | • Implement the 2030 agenda of sustainable development; promote digital inclusion, trust, and security in internet applications; and build capacity in developing countries.<br>• Protect intellectual property rights; oppose trade protectionism; and foster cooperation in network communication, mobile internet, the internet of things, and big data.<br>• With respect to Belt and Road Initiative, plans to encourage and support Chinese ICT companies in going global. | • Aligning with the agenda of sustainable development to bridge digital divide establishes China as infrastructure builder.<br>• Digital economy is now one of the prime drivers of China's economic growth.<br>• China has earlier benefitted from trade protectionism, but with rising prowess in ICTs, it now opposes protectionist measures.<br>• China is leveraging Belt and Road Initiative to facilitate Chinese ICT companies going global and harness markets in middle- and low-income countries with high growth potential in IT and ICT sectors. |
| Global information infrastructure development and protection | • Promote information infrastructure connectivity and protection of critical information infrastructure and data; and promote cooperation in the areas of early warning, emergency response, technology innovation, and standards. | • Building information infrastructure is a major challenge before developing economies owing to technology and financial constraints. China plans to help them by leveraging domestic capacity.<br>• Closer interaction in security areas paves the way for deeper technology ties and acceptance of national technology standards. |
| Exchange of cyber cultures | • Enhance cultural exchange and learning about different cultures leveraging cyberspace; and facilitate operations of Chinese companies overseas. | • With the increase in digital content consumption and its impact on society, this point becomes essential for China to enhance its soft power and cultural affinity in other societies. |

Compiled by the author with inputs from the International Strategy of Cooperation on Cyberspace (Ministry of Foreign Affairs, 2017).

The *International Strategy of Cooperation on Cyberspace* intends to foster digital connectivity with the countries part of the Belt and Road Initiative and to expand information infrastructure in their respective jurisdictions, what could metaphorically be called as the Digital Silk Road – the digital side of the Belt and Road Initiative. China's advancements in ICTs, telecommunications, and digital emerging technologies, discussed in the next chapter, further complement this objective. The Strategy is essentially a reflection of China's expectations from its international engagement on cyber issues. It puts forth China's intent to set the agenda for cyber governance and cybersecurity quite succinctly. The interlocking or integration of the Strategy with China's *National Cyberspace Security Strategy* and other national initiatives, and with the Digital Silk Road puts some of the action points into practice.

## Digital Silk Road

In 2013 China unveiled the transcontinental multibillion-dollar investment initiative for infrastructure development and economic integration with countries along the historic Silk Road route. Dubbed "One Belt One Road" then, it emerged out of two interrelated ideas Xi Jinping floated during his visit to Central Asia and Southeast Asia in 2013. He spoke about "building the Silk Road Economic Belt and the 21st Century Maritime Silk Road" encompassing overland corridors and a maritime shipping route panning across the continents of Asia, Europe, and Africa, and connecting the economic zones of East Asia and Europe (Xinhua, 2015b). It later came to be known as the Belt and Road Initiative (BRI), and an official outline for the BRI was released in 2015 jointly by the National Development and Reform Commission (NDRC), the Ministry of Foreign Affairs, and the Ministry of Commerce.

Focused on emerging markets, the BRI intended to increase connectivity between the Asian, European, and African continents as a means to accentuate trade flows and spur economic growth and development. According to an estimate by the consulting firm PricewaterhouseCoopers, the initiative has the potential to mobilise up to USD 1 trillion as outbound state funding for activities over the ten-year period from 2017 (PwC, 2016: 4). From 2013 to December 2022, China's cumulative engagement amounted around USD 950 billion in countries part of the BRI, and till March 2022 it had signed cooperation agreements with 149 countries and 30 international organisations (UN Peace and Development Trust Fund, 2022; C. N. Wang, 2023). Amongst others, energy, transportation (railways, highways, and ports), and real estate have comparatively received a larger share of investments as part of the BRI, and they together account for around 75 per cent of the total investments (Nedopil, 2020).

Since the very beginning, the BRI has received utmost political attention and the projects under its auspices have been executed with a high priority. Soon after the idea was promulgated in 2013, the Leading Group for Promoting the Belt and Road Initiative was established in 2014 as an administrative office under the NDRC to oversee and coordinate the implementation of BRI projects. Many ministries and institutions have been employed to execute the various functions of BRI. The State Council, for instance, provides the blue print and guidance for the BRI. The Ministry of Commerce facilitates and tracks the investments made and projects executed by Chinese enterprises in BRI countries, while the Ministry of Foreign Affairs provides diplomatic support and coordinates flagship events of BRI such as the Belt and Road Forum. Other institutions responsible for funding and execution of projects include People's Bank of China, commercial banks, state owned enterprises, and private companies.

In addition to policy coordination, trade, financial integration, and people-to-people exchanges, facilitating connectivity is one of the five priorities for the BRI. Digital connectivity and information infrastructure fit very well into this priority area, setting the stage for China's Digital Silk Road initiative. It was initially introduced as "Information Silk Road" in the 2015 outline of the BRI, in the context of improving connectivity through cross-border optical fibre cables and other communications networks. The outline spoke of expediting networks, transcontinental submarine optical fibre cable projects, and spatial (satellite) information corridors to the countries along the BRI (NDRC, 2015). As a subset of the BRI to enhance digital connectivity, Digital Silk Road has complementarities with other infrastructure development projects of the BRI, such as smart ports, smart cities, and shipping. Not surprisingly, the initiative finds a higher degree of interlocking with China's domestic industrialisation and informatisation plans and strategies.

The *Made in China 2025* plan in 2015 had already embodied a strategy for the manufacturing sector to go abroad, promote international industrial cooperation, and implement the two segments of the "One Belt, One Road" initiative beginning with neighbouring countries. The Government's flagship digital economy initiative *Internet Plus Action Plan* supported Chinese internet-based companies with expertise in manufacturing, finance, and ICTs to increase their presence in the global markets, in accordance with the "One Belt, One Road" initiative (K. Li, 2015). Speaking of increased cohesion between China's development plans and technological standards and the countries along the route of BRI, the 13th Five-Year Plan inched the Digital Silk Road closer to China's economic planning. The ICT cooperation proceeded with the vision of building transnational communication networks.

Giving these ideas more grounding, the revised outline of the *State Informatization Development Strategy* in 2016 extended support to the "One Belt, One Road" initiative. With reference to network interconnection with neighbouring countries and beyond, it directed the implementation of China-ASEAN Information Harbor and a Digital Silk Road to link up countries and regions in the Pacific, Central and Eastern Europe, West and North Africa, Southeast Asia, Central Asia, and South Asia (China Copyright and Media, 2016a). The *National Cyberspace Security Strategy* in 2016 also promulgated the construction of digital infrastructure in developing countries, also supplementing the BRI. The *Special Plan on Advancing Cooperation of Science and Technology Innovation in the Belt and Road Construction* of the Ministry of Science and Technology in 2016 extended the scope of the initiative beyond digital infrastructure development to joint efforts in the field of ICTs. It included developing applications for cloud computing, the internet of things, smart cities, building technology for information security, mobile-based payment systems, and the deployment of next-generation mobile telecommunication systems (Belt and Road Portal, 2016).

While addressing the opening ceremony of the first Belt and Road Forum for International Cooperation in mid-2017, Xi Jinping spoke about cooperation in the frontier areas of technology such as artificial intelligence, nanotechnology, quantum computing, big data, and cloud computing to build "Digital Silk Road of the twenty-first century" (Huang, 2019). In late 2017, the Digital Silk Road came to the limelight when the *Belt and Road Digital Economy International Cooperation Initiative* was rolled out at the fourth edition of the World Internet Conference with China, Egypt, Serbia, Thailand, Turkey, Laos, Saudi Arabia, and United Arab Emirates agreeing to cooperate on digital economy and building a Digital Silk Road (Guo, 2017). Though large-scale physical infrastructure projects have traditionally been the focal point of the BRI at large, digital infrastructure development projects have begun receiving much more attention in recent times. The second Belt and Road Forum for International Cooperation in 2019 also held a sub-forum on the Digital Silk Road, which highlights the thrust the Chinese Government began giving to this initiative. The 14th Five-Year Plan also intends to continue building the Digital Silk Road and providing digital assistance in the form of technology, equipment, and services to less developed countries.

A framework developed by Fudan University segregates the concept, objectives, and activities of the Digital Silk Road into – digital infrastructure (telecommunications), trade (e-commerce, supply chain, logistics), finance (online payment, financial services, regional financial institutions), people's hearts (traditional and social media, online education, cultural exchange), and policy (digital governance, cybersecurity, data sharing) (Dekker et al., 2020). At the functional level, the Digital Silk Road is basically a broad set of policies to facilitate the construction and financing of ICT infrastructure that supports the objectives of the BRI strategy. It leverages the technological advances made by the Chinese private sector enterprises in digital networks, networking devices, telecommunication equipment, mobile applications, security equipment, and other applications of big data, cloud computing, the internet of things, and artificial intelligence.

In terms of implementation, the Digital Silk Road entails projects ranging from the construction of networking infrastructure to telecommunication networks and carrier services, and from over-the-top services to e-commerce and satellite (BeiDou) information/navigation services (Silk Road Briefing, 2020). Over the years, the initiative has graduated from merely laying down optical fibre cables and provisioning networking equipment to the integration of next-generation technology solutions and 4G/5G telecommunication networks.

The Digital Silk Road projects could be classified into three to four broad categories, which are interrelated and tend to complement each other. The first is digital and telecommunication infrastructure, which may include the provisioning of undersea and terrestrial telecommunication cables, ICT infrastructure to broaden internet access, smart cities, and data centres (Eurasia Group, 2020). Some of these projects though predate the Digital Silk Road initiative. Since the early 2000s, leading Chinese networking and telecommunication equipment manufacturers such as Huawei and ZTE Corporation have been laying optical fibre cables and building the internet infrastructure and latest-generation telecommunication networks in Southeast Asia, West Asia, Africa, and Latin America (Guan, n.d.). These two companies already have had a long-standing presence in the developing countries including in countries part of the BRI, and they have a critical role to play in the upcoming roll-out of the 5G mobile services in some of these countries (Segal, 2020). Being part of the Digital Silk Road, the expertise of Chinese telecommunication service providers such as China Unicom in telecommunication network management and services further complements these projects (Belt and Road News, 2019).

The second category of Digital Silk Road projects encompasses the installation of data centres, cloud services, and smart city solutions. The smart city solutions also include electronic surveillance and public security systems based on artificial intelligence. Built on the foundations of these telecommunication networks and digital infrastructure is the third category of projects which includes over-the-top services, e-commerce, cloud services, and financial technology (Eurasia Group, 2020). In the long term, the Digital Silk Road has the potential to serve as a vehicle for China to push its own technology as a viable and practical alternative to the existing ones. This initiative is being supported in no small measure by an assertive cyber diplomatic practice.

At the strategic level, the Digital Silk Road meets several objectives for China ranging from offsetting domestic manufacturing overcapacity and enabling the global expansion of Chinese enterprises to the wider acceptance of China's technology standards and propagation of its vision for internet governance (P. Cai, 2017; Hong, 2018: 2685; PwC, 2016). The issue of manufacturing overcapacity had surfaced around 2013 when the MIIT instructed 1,400 companies across 19 industries to cut production (Y. Zheng, 2013). One of the ways for Chinese companies to cut production in China is by developing projects overseas, and BRI is one of the such modalities. This has also found a reference in an article by Hu Huaibang, former Chairman of the China Development Bank, where he mentioned addressing the issue of industrial overcapacity by transferring some of the facilities to the countries along the BRI (H. Hu, 2018).

Sharing the geopolitical and geo-economic aims of BRI, the Digital Silk Road augments China's claim on technology leadership and portrays it as a technology provider or digital infrastructure builder, especially among the price-sensitive developing economies. A befitting example here could be Myanmar, where less than one per cent of the population had access to broadband internet in 2012 (Chan, 2019; Chan & Rawat, 2019). China is currently known to be working with Myanmar to launch 5G services by 2025, which could be a leapfrog development for the country's telecommunication infrastructure (Nitta, 2019). The transformational role of digital technologies in economic growth is widely acknowledged, and empowering digital infrastructure and basic connectivity in developing countries is an important foreign policy tool for China to be regarded as infrastructure builder. And precisely for the same reason, the Digital Silk Road interlocks so well with China's domestic developmental strategies and initiatives.

In a bid to augment the acceptance of the Digital Silk Road initiative, China has further aligned it with the 2030 Sustainable Development Goals of the UN. Goal 9 – industry, innovation, and infrastructure – seeks to bridge the digital divide as more than four billion people, 90 per cent of whom are from developing economies, are yet to have access to the internet (UNDP, n.d.). Speaking at the opening ceremony of the first Belt and Road Forum for International Cooperation in 2017, the UN Secretary-General António Guterres had urged China to align BRI with the 2030 Agenda for Sustainable Development – arguing that they both seek to deepen connectivity in infrastructure, trade, finance, policies, and people despite being different in their nature and scope (Guterres, 2017). Earlier, at the 2015 World Internet Conference, the then ITU Secretary-General Zhao Houlin had also advocated for closer cooperation between the ITU and BRI (called as One Belt, One Road at that time) to bridge the digital divide between developed and developing economies (*China Daily*, 2015).

As a result, the ITU signed a memorandum of understanding with MIIT during the first Belt and Road Forum for International Cooperation in 2017 to expand ICT infrastructure in close to 60 countries (X. Liu, 2019). Further bringing the BRI and the 2030 Agenda for Sustainable Development closer, the Export-Import Bank of China signed an agreement with the ITU to address the digital divide issue and meet the 2030 Sustainable Development Goals through BRI at the second Belt and Road Forum for International Cooperation in 2019 (Ministry of Foreign Affairs, 2019). Anchoring the Digital Silk Road in the developmental agenda gives it the much-required legitimacy as China expands projects under this initiative, especially 5G mobile services, into other countries along the BRI. Moreover, as some of the BRI projects have been executed as part of China's foreign aid to developing and underdeveloped countries, China is quite likely to use this modality to develop digital infrastructure as part of the Digital Silk Road in some of these countries.

Another aspect that neatly aligns with the Digital Silk Road Initiative – beyond pushing China's technology and equipment into countries part of the BRI – is China's quest for wider acceptability of its technology and engineering standards. Standardised processes and specifications ensure the interoperability of technology. It is a widely held view that China's deep involvement in the development of digital infrastructure and next-generation telecommunication networks across the BRI countries could be leveraged to push China-made technology standards (P. Cai, 2017; Eurasia Group, 2020; Giovannini, 2020; Gong & Li, 2019). The *Made in China 2025* plan also sought to "accelerate the internationalization of Chinese standards," while the Standardization Administration of China also seeks to enhance standards cooperation and integration with BRI countries through the exchange and sharing of standards information (Ministry of Foreign Affairs, 2019). By 2019, China had already signed 85 standardisation cooperation agreements with 49 countries (NDRC, 2019). International acceptance of China's standards and playing a greater role in setting the international technology standards have become an increasingly important factor in China's claim to leadership in next-generation technology. Some of the key aspects of emerging technologies and standards have further been discussed in the next chapter.

Although the Digital Silk Road was conceived to supplement the BRI, but given the existing technological competition fuelled by China's advancements in next-generation technology research and development, it has acquired a central place in the initiative and in China's cyber diplomacy as well. At the time of conception, the Digital Silk Road had clear economic imperatives as it was anticipated to boost the growth of digital economy in China as well as in the countries that are part of the BRI. As this initiative graduated from merely laying optical fibre cables and deploying networks to the large-scale integration of business and governance solutions and rolling out customer-centric services built on top of the infrastructure, it could serve purposes well beyond economic considerations.

Through the Digital Silk Road, China seeks to position its technology – backed by conducive financing modalities – as an affordable option as more and more developing countries with poor digital infrastructure scramble to reap the benefits of digital economy. Along with the infrastructure, these countries also intend to roll-out online governance services and deploy advanced technology for security and surveillance, not to mention their rally to deploy 5G mobile services. Backed by an unparalleled technology research and development capability and equipment manufacturing capacity, China's cyber diplomacy not only intends to exploit this opportunity but also aligns the Digital Silk Road with the 2030 Sustainable Development Goals and the ITU has given this ambition the much-needed legitimacy under the guise of bridging the digital divide. It also cements China's position as a technology provider and growth enabler, both of which serve soft power purposes.

Promulgating the idea of a digital currency in mid-2020, China made its intention very clear to build an alternative to the prevalent systems which do not align with its interests. The idea has all the potential to bypass the existing US-dominated global payments and settlement system. China is well positioned to leverage the growing digital connectivity as part of the Digital Silk Road and the deepening trade ties and economic engagement with the BRI countries to push its strategic objective of internationalising the Renminbi. The digital version of the Renminbi is anticipated to first come into operation with the countries along the BRI.

## Digital Renminbi (RMB)

The People's Bank of China (PBoC) began pilot trials of a digital currency in mid-2020, beginning with Shanghai, Shenzhen, and four other cities (The People's Bank of China, 2020). With this, China became the first country in the world to partially digitise its existing monetary base or the cash in circulation. The PBoC began working on the idea of a digital currency in 2014 with the project dubbed "DC/EP" (acronym for Digital Currency/ Electronic Payments) (*Financial Times*, 2020). As part of this initiative, a Digital Currency Research Institute was established in 2017 followed by a pilot programme in December 2019. The DC/EP project is based on blockchain technology, and the digital RMB is basically an electronic version of the official currency – a digital legal tender backed by the Chinese Government and pegged 1:1 with the RMB. The project also implements the Government's *FinTech*[2] *Development Plan (2019–2021)*. The circulation of the digital RMB and its settlement is bound to be integrated with the conventional banking system, to be managed by the PBoC. The international dimension of the digital RMB is to be interpreted against the backdrop of China's discontentment with the dominance of the USD as the global reserve currency, and its desire for RMB to be accepted as an international currency.

The USD holds a dominant position as an investment and a reserve currency in the prevalent international monetary system. Data from the

International Monetary Fund suggests that the USD accounted for around 61 per cent of all central bank foreign exchange reserves in 2019, with RMB at less than 2 per cent (IMF, n.d.). Moreover, close to 47 per cent of the global payments and 88 per cent of foreign exchange trading is executed in USD (Frankel, 2019). Cognisant of this disproportionate share of the USD in comparison to other currencies, China and Russia in 2009 had called for "a new reserve currency" to replace the USD (Beam, 2009).

The US also maintains dominance over the Society for Worldwide Interbank Financial Telecommunication system – better known as the SWIFT system. It is a global financial messaging service which enables cross-border payments and is used by around 11,000 institutions from all across the world (SWIFT, n.d.). China often contends that the US has dominance on the decision-making of the SWIFT owing to its majority in the board of the organisation. Since the US has used the SWIFT system in the past to enforce economic sanctions against Iran and Cuba (Harper, 2018; A. Zhang, 2019), China remains wary of the potential US sanctions against its companies which could exclude them from a settlement system in which the US maintains such dominance.

The DC/EP project and the ensuing digital RMB allows China to build an alternative to this arrangement. Moreover, an RMB-based trade settlement system is further understood to reduce dependence on the USD in trade and financial transactions (Shirai, 2019). However, it is the internationalisation of RMB that China aspires to achieve from digital RMB, aiming to engender a stable international monetary environment for its economic development (Lai, 2015). An internationalised currency affords the issuing country and its domestic enterprises and financial institutions some advantages in terms of limiting exchange rate risks and reducing capital costs while operating in international financial markets. It also allows the governments to finance a part of, or, the entire fiscal deficit by issuing debt in international markets.

China's push for internationalisation of RMB therefore stems from both economic factors and geopolitical considerations as Chinese companies are increasingly facing backlash in the US and other parts of the world. Huawei, for instance, is already subject to the entity list of the US Department of Commerce – effectively banning its business with American enterprises. China has progressed with the DC/EP over the last six years. In 2023, digital RMB is available for use in 26 cities and 17 provinces across China, and the transactions using digital RMB touched 1.8 trillion yuan (USD 249 billion) at the end of June 2023. The circulation of digital RMB however accounted for only 0.16 per cent of cash in circulation in China (Wee, 2023). China is also part of international trials involving the cross-border use of digital currencies backed by central banks to settle trade (BOFIT, 2023).

As China's economic cohesion with the BRI countries grows, China is most likely to extend the DC/EP to these countries over an RMB-based trade settlement system. A Deutsche Bank report had termed the DC/EP as a "soft or hard power tool as it can potentially erode the primacy of the USD in the global financial market if the companies adopt digital RMB for their cross-border transactions" (Deutsche Bank, 2020). A digital RMB may work as a soft power tool in the BRI countries, but it simultaneously epitomises China's desire to build alternate systems if the existing ones do not fulfil its economic ambitions or tend to undermine its security interests.

## Global Initiative on Data Security

The Global Initiative on Data Security could be seen as China's attempt to provide thought leadership and take a lead in setting global rules for data security. In September 2020, speaking at an international conference on digital opportunities for cooperation and development, Foreign Minister Wang Yi unveiled the Global Initiative on Data Security (FMPRC, 2020c) – an eight-part framework for global digital governance (FMPRC, 2020a). It is worth mentioning here that Article 11 of the *Data Security Law* and Article 12 of the *Personal Information Protection Law* speak about carrying out international cooperation on issues related to data security governance and personal information protection, and participating in the formulation of international rules and standards on these.

In a nutshell, the initiative calls on states to secure the global ICT supply chains, refrain from ICT activities that undermine other states' national security, not to request domestic companies to store data generated and obtained overseas in their own territory, and respect the sovereignty, jurisdiction, and governance of data of other states. It also mentions that ICT products and services providers should not install backdoors in their products and services, and providers should timely notify the users of serious vulnerabilities found in their products. In addition to governments, the initiative invites international organisations, ICT companies, technology communities, civil society organisations, and individuals to support these efforts (FMPRC, 2020b).

The initiative was announced amid the growing mistrust of Chinese ICT companies and social media apps globally owing to security concerns. At that time, the US had taken firm steps to restrict Chinese companies from doing business in the US describing them as national security threats. Additionally, in August 2020, the US Department of State had announced the Clean Network Initiative – a coalition of trusted partners comprising governments and telecommunication companies formed to keep the so-called "untrusted" IT vendors "which are required to comply with directives of the Chinese Communist Party" away from their country's telecommunication services, 5G networks, cloud infrastructure, and mobile application ecosystems (US Department of State, 2020).

The Global Initiative on Data Security was China's pushback against the US's campaign targeting Chinese companies on security grounds. In this regard, Wang Yi stated that "a certain country keeps making groundless accusations against others in the name of clean network" (Xinhua, 2020a). Calling the Clean Network Initiative discriminatory, exclusive, and politicised "dirty network," Lu Chuanying, the Secretary-General of the Research Center for the International Governance of Cyberspace at Shanghai Institutes for International Studies, denoted it as a threat to the stability and development of cyberspace (C. Lu, 2020). The fact that the Global Initiative on Data Security was announced just days before the first High-Level Digital Dialogue between the EU and China (European Commission, 2020), it was seen as an attempt to address the prevailing security concerns about Chinese telecommunication equipment manufacturers and internet companies given the importance of European market for China.

Calling the US's backlash on Chinese telecommunication equipment manufacturers and internet companies a unilateral action, the Global Initiative on Data Security sought to project China as a defender of multilateralism. Give the lack of global consensus on data security, the initiative could also be seen as a norm entrepreneurship attempt to claim global leadership on an issue gradually gaining prominence. The initiative was not path-breaking and the text mainly drew from the language China had repeatedly used at previous occasions. It reflected China's stated vision on data security, such as localisation requirements and respect for sovereignty, and its concerns. China had been voicing these positions at international forums and the initiative was an attempt to precipitate these ideas and take the lead in defining global rules for data security. In order to make these ideas compelling, China had simultaneously progressed in putting in place a domestic regulatory regime for data security.

## Discussion

The multistakeholder body ICANN is the epitome of cyberspace empowering non-state actors as its powers on the governance of internet resources rival those of the states. Such an arrangement threatening the traditional dynamics of power and challenging the primacy of the state reverberates in China's incessant attempts to alter this order into a multilateral one where states have the sole authority on decision-making on matters related to cyberspace. China's views on sovereignty in cyberspace, arising out of the desire to exert authority on cyberspace within its territorial borders, and its vision for cyberspace juxtaposes the top-down decision-making power of the governments to a territorial conception of cyberspace. From the same understanding stems its security dilemma, as the dominance of the US in cyber governance has for long been China's primary concern. Until the transfer of IANA functions to ICANN in 2016, China had been extremely vocal in its criticism of the unilateral control the US maintained on the DNS through ICANN and expressed its anxieties over China's internet resources – deemed to be a national resource – being controlled by others.

Cyber sovereignty, which is the organising principle of cyber governance for China, forms the very premise of China's cyber diplomacy. To practice sovereignty in cyberspace, China needs a multilateral approach to its governance, preferably under the aegis of the UN where it enjoys equal rights in the decision-making as a member state and non-state actors perform only a consultative role. Beginning with the WSIS two decades ago, China's cyber diplomatic efforts have sought to propagate this vision and gather wider international support and acceptance of the principle to legitimise it. China's cyber diplomacy strives to bolster China's leadership on cyber governance in regional organisations and among the groupings of developing countries in order to extend its normative influence, or in other words, its discursive power. It is useful to recall that in the run-up to the first phase of the WSIS, China had teamed up with G77 countries to push for an international internet treaty and the establishment of an intergovernmental internet organization.

China's voicing of concerns over cyber governance purportedly on behalf of the developing countries is again a bid to increase the appeal of China's vision and approach among the developing countries which sometimes lack the resources and expertise to play a constructive role in the multistakeholder bodies. The *International Code of Conduct for Information Security* and the World Internet Conference became the modalities to extend China's vision in the international arena, while the *International Strategy of Cooperation on Cyberspace* gave the existing principles a coherent shape and provided a plan of action for the cyber diplomatic efforts. Implementing the plan of action, the Digital Silk Road is an attempt to extend the reach of China's technology, and technology standards thereof, while a digital Renminbi reflects China's inclination to explore alternative systems and approaches to serve its national interests. As a norm entrepreneur, China's efforts are spread over regional organisations, the UN system, and the World Internet Conference – a multistakeholder platform that China has built for itself to enhance its normative power.

With reference to the cyber power model, evidence from this chapter suggests that China possesses the *Capacities* listed as part of *Cyber Diplomacy*. China has an international strategy for cyberspace in place, which tethers the ideas and principles China has for the future of cyberspace with a clear plan of action. China's intent to play an influential role in cyber governance and its reform is loud and clear, whether stated in its strategy documents or articulated in the form of speeches such as the one at the opening ceremony of the second World Internet Conference, or the 36th collective study session of the Central Political Bureau, or even including reform of cyber governance as part of "six accelerations." China's incessant attempts to bring the governance of the DNS under an international organisation such as the ITU also reflect its resolve. Moreover, the *Code of Conduct* and the proposal at the WCIT-12 are some examples of China's cyber diplomatic activism seeking to forge partnerships with like-minded countries on issues of common interest and leveraging them to meet its interests.

In terms of *Capabilities*, China has built some but there are certain gaps which limit its ability to exert influence. Leveraging the SCO to propagate its ideas and priorities for cyber governance and strengthening normative power underscores China's influence in regional organisations. The capability that stands out is the ability of China to synergise its *International Strategy of Cooperation on Cyberspace* with the national strategies and policies, such as the *National Cyberspace Security Strategy*, *State Informatization Development Strategy*, Five-Year Plans, and other flagship national development and industrialisation initiatives of the Government. The Digital Silk Road initiative also finds deep integration with China's domestic economic and industrial development strategies and initiatives. Most importantly, evidence suggests that China has had a limited influence in the existing cyber governance processes despite pursuing it aggressively as a key tenet of the objective of building China into a cyber superpower.

In line with China's increasing assertiveness to gain influence over global governance institutions, its cyber diplomatic efforts have sought to extend China's normative influence in international cyber governance. To that end, whether through new ideas such as the *Code of Conduct* or alternative approaches such as the OEWG, China's cyber diplomacy wholeheartedly seeks to increase the appeal of China's vision for cyberspace among developing countries and build partnerships or groupings of like-minded nations subscribing to this vision. Seeking to bolster China's leadership on cyber governance issues, its cyber diplomatic efforts span the UN system, regional organisations, and prominently the SCO, the groupings of developing countries, and its bilateral relations.

The World Internet Conference has afforded China its own platform to promote a competing vision for the future of cyberspace. It also stands as a testament to China's proactive cyber diplomacy, seeking to set an agenda for cyber governance and cybersecurity and shape the international discourse on this subject. The conference serves as a vehicle to extend China's normative influence in international cyber governance. These efforts reflect China's intent to set the agenda for cyber governance which actually serves the purposes of shaping international debates on the subject and propagate its own ideas or norms for the governance of cyberspace. Most noticeable is China's desire to provide an alternative to the Western approach, be it sovereignty in cyberspace or a multilateral approach to cyber governance which have been the cornerstone of China's cyber diplomacy for all these years. A small group of countries have aligned with this position of China on the issue of cyber governance.

The *International Strategy of Cooperation on Cyberspace* seeks to expand China's role in global cybersecurity capacity building and technology transfer, leveraging high growth in the domestic ICT industry. To that end, initiatives like the Digital Silk Road project China's image as a technology provider and digital infrastructure builder that enables connectivity and empowers digital economy in developing countries. Further alignment with the 2030 Sustainable Development Goals and tethering with the digital divide issue provides Digital Silk Road the necessary legitimacy and ascends its acceptance in other parts of the world. Moreover, once extended to the BRI countries, technology is anticipated to embody China's principles on the governance of ICT and cyberspace along with China-made technology standards. In the long run, the Digital Silk Road could potentially serve as a vehicle to push Chinese technology as a viable and practical alternative to the existing ones. With China's growing economic interaction with BRI countries, digital RMB is quite likely to be extended to these countries for settling cross-border transactions. This is in line with China's desire to build alternate systems if the existing ones do not align with its economic ambitions or undermine its security interests.

Despite such an aggressive cyber diplomatic effort, China's influence in global cyber governance remains to be limited and it has rather not succeeded in bringing any significant changes so far. For instance, the prominent model for cyber governance remains to be multistakeholder, despite China's efforts to bring it under an international organisation. China's successive attempts to bring the governance functions of the internet under the UN or the ITU, whether during the WSIS or later at the WCIT-12, have also failed to bring about any substantive changes. China's attempt to push for an international internet treaty and the establishment of an Intergovernmental Internet Organization in the run-up to the first phase of the WSIS was unsuccessful. Another attempt to make the IGF intergovernmental and bring it directly under the control of the UN in 2015 also did not succeed.

As far as the *International Code of Conduct for Information Security* is concerned, it has by and large failed to gather much traction among states in other parts of the world beyond the SCO. There have been few takers of it at the UN. Moreover, even the high-level representation at the much-hyped World Internet Conference is limited to the member states of the SCO. The Global Initiative on Data Security – a recent attempt of China to claim global leadership on data security issues – has not received much support either. China has limited influence on the global internet governance platforms and it has not yet demonstrated significant ability to establish new institutions for cyber governance. Although China has leveraged the existing ones such as the ITU and the SCO to propagate its own ideas on norms and governance of cyberspace.

The diplomatic initiatives discussed in the chapter are anchored in China's interpretation of the geopolitical realities of cyberspace, and they work primarily towards consolidating and gaining a dominant position on the issues of prime importance in cyberspace. A dominant position translates into control on the governance functions of cyberspace, which in China's view, is achievable only in a multilateral arrangement. In China's view, sovereign right or control is necessary not just to maintain autonomy in the management of cyberspace within its territorial borders, but also to legitimise the technology and regulations it has put in place to address the security concerns in cyberspace.

A dominant position in cyberspace is China's pathway to international acceptability of its perceptions, principles, and practices of cyber governance. It essentially allows China a greater say in the decision-making related to the development and governance of cyberspace and provides the space to mould them according to its own economic and geopolitical interests. Cyber diplomacy, to that end, plays a critical role in extending the international reach and influence of the ideas China espouses and strengthens its discursive and normative power, or in other words, the power over opinion. One of the aims of China's cyber diplomacy is also to augment China's soft power – be it in the form of agenda-setting, making its vision of cyber governance attractive, increase its acceptance through persuasion and image projection, and through the process of standards-development.

The writings of Chinese scholars and analysts and speeches of political leaders quite often relate the dominance of the US on internet governance with its leadership in the intellectual property and technology standards of the underlying architecture of the internet. China's aspiration for a dominant position in global cyber governance therefore gives the impetus to enhance the global competitiveness of its domestic research and development base and the industry, especially in the emerging technologies space. The next chapter looks at the technology dimension of China's cyber power, expanding on artificial intelligence, next-generation networks, and quantum information sciences. China claims a leading position in some of these emerging digital technologies.

## Notes

1 Led by France and New Zealand, Christchurch Call is supported by 51 countries and some of the leading technology companies.
2 FinTech is the acronym for Financial Technology.

# 5
# EMERGING DIGITAL TECHNOLOGIES
## China's great leap forward

Innovation in the technology sphere holds great value propositions for developed and developing countries alike. Since the establishment of the People's Republic of China, the advancement of science and technology (S&T) and the development of industry have found resonance in the key policy documents, be it government white papers, reports at the National Congress of the CPC, or the Five-Year Plans. China devised centrally managed S&T and industrial development plans to shuttle financial and human resources towards high-technology sectors identified as crucial for its socio-economic growth and national security. Given the unprecedented focus on informatisation in China's economic and social development, the ICT sector has long been the focal point. The *National Medium to Long-term Plan for the Development of Science and Technology* (MLP), for instance, had identified next-generation internet, broadband mobile telecommunication, high-performance computing, integrated circuits, and intelligent information processing as core technology areas in the information industry. It also placed quantum regulation studies among four major scientific research programmes (State Council, 2006).

The *State Informatization Development Strategy* envisions a leading position for China in next-generation networks and seeks building a competitive advantage in the areas of cloud computing, big data, smart manufacturing, and the internet of things. Technology research, development, and standardisation of 5G mobile telecommunications are also recognised as a strategic objective in the strategy. Enlisting digitalisation, networking, and informatisation of the manufacturing industry as a strategic goal, the *Made in China 2025* plan lays emphasis on 5G mobile telecommunications, quantum computing, intelligent manufacturing, and industrial internet of

DOI: 10.4324/9781003473510-5

things and big data applications (State Council, 2015a). Among the emerging digital technologies, emphasis is apparent on artificial intelligence (AI), big data, quantum information sciences, the internet of things, high-performance computing, and next-generation networks (Ministry of Science and Technology, 2006, 2012; State Council, 2016).

For further analysis in the context of advancements in emerging digital technologies, the chapter delves into the progress China has made in next-generation networks, which includes the China Next-Generation Internet initiative, 5G mobile communications, and Network 2030. Thereafter, the chapter takes up quantum information sciences and artificial intelligence, but it begins with shedding light on why China has devoted much attention to technology standards.

## Strategic relevance of technology standards

Speaking during his inspection visit to the electron–positron collider facility in 1988, Deng Xiaoping said that "it has always been, and will always be, necessary for China to develop its own high technology so that it can take its place in this field" (Deng, 1988). He attributed China's international standing to the progress it had made in the strategic weapons and space programmes. China's political and technology leaders have closely associated high technology with economic development and national power, and pursued it as a national priority. Regarding the competition among states for the elements of national power, the promulgators of China's National High-Technology Research and Development Program (863 Program) categorically linked high technology with state power and international standing – highlighting the strategic relevance of high technology for China's long-term economic development (Feigenbaum, 2003: 189).

Correlating high technology with state power and international standing, Shi Changxu, an academician of the Chinese Academy of Science, argued that high technology is the most important amongst all the elements that comprise national power, for which states compete in their international relations (Feigenbaum, 2003: 189). Scientific research fulfils China's needs for national prestige by supporting defence technology and industrial technology, and serves the long-term goal of regaining what China considers to be its rightful place in the international system (Sigurdson, 1980). As a result, research and technological development in high-technology sectors has received profound support from China's political leadership, and the task was implemented aggressively through state-led S&T plans and research programmes. With the onset of information technology, China's leaders began contemplating on gaining an advantageous position, calling it as seizing the "high ground" or "commanding heights" in this competition.

Jiang Zemin in his book *On the Development of China's Information Technology Industry* pressed on the need for China to "control the high ground of industrial development" and concentrate efforts and available resources in the areas of microelectronics (design and manufacturing of ICs), high-performance computing (super computer, network computing, quantum computing, AI), software, and networks (next-generation network technologies, broadband mobile wireless communications, network and information security) (Z. Jiang, 2009: 35–49).

Development of ICTs is a research-intensive endeavour, and companies and research institutions need to make heavy investments in R&D to stay ahead of the competitors and succeed in the market. Patents incentivise these investments in research activities and promote innovation as they reward R&D by protecting the rights of the innovators. The commercial and economic incentives of innovation have always propelled R&D activities and it gained further importance with globalisation as companies began expanding beyond their national borders. This phenomenon also gave rise to the need for standardisation, which basically provides uniformity so that products have global acceptance and application.

Standards facilitate trade and transfer of technology despite being developed in different countries, and removing these technical barriers to trade leads to market expansion, creating new markets, and as a result fuelling economic growth (*NPES Standards Bluebook*, 2005). Standards are essential for technologies to gain wide adoption and expand in the global markets (WIPO, n.d.). Standards ensure interoperability of products and services, their safety, reliability and quality, improve cost efficiency through economies of scale, and promote innovation as they set off participation, competition, and collaboration to create the best solution possible (Qualcomm, 2020).

Standards play an important role in the ICT industry as the products consist of a variety of devices and components which are developed and manufactured by different companies, but they need to connect and work with each other. Standards set forth the specifications and requirements for processes, devices, and systems. It is because of standards that Wi-Fi, Bluetooth, mobile phones, and telecommunications provide ubiquitous connectivity to the users be it in any part of the world. In technology fields like that of ICT, standards are essential for interconnection and interoperability when the technology developers, integrators, and service providers are scattered across the globe.

Standardisation – the process of setting globally acceptable standards – has historically been voluntary, consensus based, and collaborative. It requires concerted efforts of standard-setting organisations, national standards development organisations, industry associations, research organisations, and private sector enterprises. However, standardisation in the ICT and telecommunications industry has eventually become extremely competitive. Companies and research institutions involved in cutting-edge technology R&D compete with their global counterparts to get their patented technology accepted and incorporated into a standard so that it becomes a Standards Essential Patent (SEP). Companies have a strong commercial interest in influencing the requirements of the standard to be aligned with their patented technology as this provides them monetary benefits in the form of licensing fees. Standard-setting organisations however prevent entities from holding-up patents, and the participants are generally required to license SEPs on "Fair, Reasonable and Non-Discriminatory" or "Reasonable and Non-Discriminatory" terms to other players in the market (Farrell et al., 2007: 603).

For a country, the leading position of its companies and research organisations in the ownership of intellectual property translates into global technology leadership. It is a testament to the national R&D capabilities and capacities, industrialisation levels, human resources, and the maturity of the innovation ecosystem. Historically, it is industrialised countries that have dominated standardisation. Countries are now using standards as an industrial policy tool to advance their national interests in the different domains of technology, and it is quite evident in the case of ICTs (Biddle et al., 2012: 180). Technology standardisation, which traces its origins to the phenomena of globalisation and trade liberalisation, is increasingly turning into an arena for commercial gains and geopolitical tussles. Once characterised by international cooperation, it is increasingly turning into a domain of contestation and dominance. The quest for influence on standard-setting organisations and the race to set the standards render them to be another theatre of great power politics.

Cognisant of the strategic importance of standards, China has taken several initiatives to ascend its position in the global competition for standards, and ICT is one of the key areas of attention. Coming out of China, standards such as Time Division-Synchronous Code Division Multiple Access (TD-SCDMA) for mobile telecommunications and WLAN Authentication and Privacy Infrastructure (WAPI) for wireless networks attracted wide attention. The 2018 *Artificial Intelligence Standardization White Paper* of China notes that standards have become an important indicator to gauge the technology development levels of countries, and the engagement of a country in standards development is a key lever to not just promote industry innovation but also to seize the "commanding heights of industry competition" (CESI, 2018: 33). Owning intellectual property in the form of patents and activism in standard-setting bodies is integral to China's "Go out" policy, which was announced at the turn of the century and guides China's integration with the international system and facilitates the global expansion of Chinese enterprises. Standards feature prominently in *Made in China 2025* – the national strategic plan for the modernisation of China's manufacturing sector.

A 2013 analysis of technology standards in China found that Chinese standards by then had failed to gain market support beyond China, and even within China they had a limited success. It also noted that the prominent standards coming out of China, such as the TD-SCDMA, have a significant share of foreign intellectual property (Breznitz and Murphree, 2013: 2). Arguing that the ability of a country to set international standards has an impact on its trade and technology landscape, a 2020 *Global Times* article noted that a few of the 160 members of the International Organization for Standardization (ISO) have defined about 95 per cent of the ISO standards, and China's share is a meagre 0.7 per cent (*Global Times*, 2020).

A 2019 report by the Swedish Institute of International Affairs observed that China considers technology standardisation as a tool to enhance its international influence (Björk, 2019). In the arena of technology standardisation, which is now charged with geopolitical competition, China seeks a position commensurate with its rising global status. China began working on the *China Standards 2035* plan in 2018 to cement this objective and provide a national action plan to play a leading role in setting international standards in technology areas like AI, the internet of things, 5G, blockchain, big data, and integrated circuits (Bruyère and Picarsic., 2020: 19). Standards in these areas are yet to be defined and China sees this as an opportunity (Y. Liu, 2018). China is already integrating its standardisation processes with the BRI countries and some of the international and regional standardisation organisations (China Market Regulation News, 2020). China is known to have signed a memorandum of understanding on technology standardisation with 49 BRI countries (NDRC, 2019).

A leading position in technology standards serves multiple goals for China. It has direct economic benefits as ownership of standards by Chinese companies could save them from royalty obligations. Chinese enterprises could further expand their presence in the global markets and even compete with their Western counterparts in the established markets. Indigenous innovation reduces China's dependence on foreign intellectual property in high technology, and a lead position of Chinese companies in international standard-setting organisations precipitates China's technology leadership. This could elevate China's status in the international system and help gain the so-called "commanding heights" or a "rightful place". China's engagement with international standard-setting organisations has consequently increased, and so have China's efforts to internationalise its national technical standards, for example, through the Digital Silk Road.

The outcomes that China anticipates from the *China Standards 2035* plan or its standardisation efforts, in general, hinge upon the "leapfrog" advancements it aspires to make in the realm of emerging technologies. China understands that this endeavour will rest on the foundations of its R&D capacity and capability, the competitiveness of its industry, and the maturity of its innovation ecosystem. China's advancements in emerging technologies have gained global attention, and some of the prominent areas where it has made a mark, such as quantum, next-generation networks, and AI, are discussed in detail in the forthcoming sections.

## Next-generation networks

The technology underpinning communications networks moves at a fast pace. New requirements in terms of bandwidth, security, performance, mobility, and quality-of-service continue to drive research in the quest for next-generation networks, be it the internet or mobile communications. These networks have undergone major transformation if compared to the envisaged utility and scope at the time of their conception. Mobile communications system, for example, has evolved from supporting only voice services in the case of first- and second-generation systems to providing broadband internet access in the fourth generation (4G) which enables high-definition multimedia content streaming and a host of other data-intensive applications.

In the case of the internet, the widely used standard – Internet Protocol version 4 (IPv4) – was deployed way back in 1983 and it uses 32-bit addressing which can support a maximum of 4.3 billion devices. At the time of deployment of IPv4, the number of addresses it could support was thought to be way more than enough. But the exponential growth in the numbers of personal computers, smartphones, and now the internet of things devices is propelling the need to find alternatives or workarounds which can meet the requirements of the future.

The impending shortage of address space was recognised as early as the late 1980s, and this triggered an evaluation and design process. The IETF had initiated the development of a new protocol in 1993 – now known as Internet Protocol version 6 (IPv6). After deliberations in IETF working groups and extensive testing and refinements, the IPv6 was included in an IETF draft standard way back in 1998, but it was ratified as an internet standard only in 2017 (Deering and Hinden, 1998, 2017). It uses a 128-bit address which can support approximately 340 trillion-trillion ($2^{128}$) unique IP addresses (Internet Society, n.d.-b). The research on the future design of the internet is an evolutionary process, and it continues to make headway in all parts of the world. There are two broad approaches to address the technical challenges with IPv4. One is to retain the existing architecture of the internet which has constraints pertaining to backward compatibility and implementation. The second approach is to design an entirely new architecture which does not have these constrains.

With an emphasis on both these approaches, China set off its research endeavour into the next generation of internet and mobile communication networks by the late 1990s. China's resentment with the present state of the internet mainly arises from the issues of scalability, performance, security, quality of service, and network management and control. On the issue of IP addresses, China often contends that the US controls 74 per cent of the four billion IPv4 addresses, and allocation to China is just equal to what is allocated to the University of California alone (B. Liu, 2004), despite being home to close to a billion internet users.

In terms of strategic planning, the MLP had identified next-generation networks – encompassing broadband mobile telecommunication and next-generation internet – as one of the areas under the priority topic Major Next-Generation Internet Technologies and Services. The revised outline of the *State Informatization Development Strategy* envisions consolidating a globally leading position in next-generation mobile telecommunications and internet, and vigorous participation of Chinese entities in the formulation of international standards. The 12th Five-Year Plan had recognised next-generation mobile communications and the internet as strategic emerging sectors which are key to China's plan for building a modern nationwide information infrastructure. The 13th Five-Year Plan further gave thrust to research in 5G mobile networks and the next-generation internet. The 14th Five-Year Plan also commits to accelerate the large-scale deployment of 5G networks and sets eye on the technology for 6G networks. The China Next-Generation Internet project and the plan for a complete transition to IPv6 by 2025 have received a major push, while Chinese telecommunication equipment manufacturers have made great strides in the technology of 5G mobile networks. Of late, China has proposed and is aggressively pursuing the idea of Network 2030 in a bid to overhaul the very architecture of the internet.

### China Next-Generation Internet

The foundations of innovation in internet-related technologies in China were laid way back in the late 1990s with the Next-Generation High Credibility Network initiative for research and development of next-generation internet. Researchers at China Education and Research Network (CERNET) built an IPv6 test bed in 1998. With the support of the National Natural Science Foundation of China (NSFC), the first next-generation internet pilot network was completed in 2001, and in 2003 the National Development and Reform Commission (NDRC) approved and began the implementation of China Next-Generation Internet (CNGI) project after securing go-ahead from the State Council.

Spearheaded by NDRC, CNGI was a joint endeavour of the Chinese Academy of Engineering, the Ministry of Science and Technology, the former Ministry of Information Industry, the Ministry of Education, the Office of the Informatization Leading Group, and the Chinese Academy of

Sciences, supported in no small measure by the major internet service providers and leading networking equipment manufacturers (CNGI, 2010). The project accelerated research on networking technologies in China and led to CERNET2 (jointly developed by the network centre of the CERNET with 25 universities), which came into existence in 2004 and it was reportedly the world's largest next-generation internet demonstration network based entirely on IPv6 backbone (Gu & Liu, 2005). CERNET2 formed the test bed for next-generation internet research allowing researchers to gain valuable experience with IPv6.

The IPv6 network built under the framework of the CNGI project is composed of six backbone networks built by China Telecom, China Unicom, China Mobile, China Netcom/CAS, CERNET, and China Railcom (China Telecom, n.d.). As part of this network, two IPv6 internet exchanges – CNGI-6IX in Beijing and CNGI-SHIX in Shanghai – were established to connect IPv6 backbone networks in China with each other as well as with IPv6 networks in other parts of the world (Y. Liu et al., 2013). The primary objective of the CNGI initiative is to promote research and development and deployment of key internet technologies in China, which includes IPv6. CNGI facilitates an early transition to a network based entirely on the IPv6 standard and the Chinese Government attaches great importance to this initiative as it lays the foundation of wide-scale integration of China's traditional industries – from manufacturing to agriculture – with the internet.

China's IPv6 capability has witnessed a sharp rise from 2018 onwards (APNIC, 2023b), attributed to the strong emphasis the Government has laid upon the large-scale deployment of IPv6. The *Action Plan for Promoting Large-scale Deployment of Internet Protocol Version 6*, published in 2017, sets detailed targets and steps to achieve full transition to IPv6 by 2025 – building the world's largest commercial IPv6 network in terms of users and traffic (State Council, 2017a). In a phased manner, it plans to complete the transition for commercial websites and applications, government extranet websites, data centres, content distribution networks, cloud service platforms, radio and television networks, and 5G networks and services. The Action Plan targeted to surpass 500 million active IPv6 users towards the end of 2020 accounting for more than 50 per cent of internet users in China. But at the time of writing it stood at around 31 per cent, significantly trailing India (78.5 per cent), the US (57.5 per cent), Germany (63 per cent), and Japan (53 per cent) (APNIC, 2023a).

Another key concern China raises quite often is related to the security aspect of the internet, which is nestled in its fundamental design principles. Packet forwarding on the internet, by design, is based on the destination IP address and hence IP address of the source is not validated. This feature makes it easy to spoof the source IP address concealing the real identity of the sender, and it is heavily exploited to perpetrate malicious activities and cyber-attacks. In view of this, Article 24 of China's *Cybersecurity Law* also mentions a network identity credibility strategy and stresses the need for R&D into electronic identity authentication technologies.

In order to overcome this limitation in the next-generation internet, researchers at Tsinghua University proposed Source Address Validation Architecture (SAVA) and implemented it in CERNET2. It was presented at an IEEE conference in 2007 and subsequently proposed as a Request for Comments to the IETF in 2008 (Bi et al., 2008; J. Wu et al., 2007). SAVA ensures that every packet received and forwarded in the network holds an authenticated source IP address, which means that the IP address is authorised by an internet address authorisation organisation and the entity sending the packet is authorised to use that IP address. This renders packets traceable to the source IP address and the location and ownership of the IP address verifiable – making it easy to get to the origins of malicious activities and misbehaving hosts on the network. And since the packets with an unauthenticated source address are not forwarded in the network, launching an attack becomes increasingly difficult. An IETF working group (named Source Address Validation Improvements) was established in 2008 to take the idea forward and standardise mechanisms that prevent nodes attached to the same IP link from spoofing each other's IP addresses (IETF, 2011).

For China, these efforts at the end of the day aspire to resolve the IP address space limitations and security conundrums that arise out of the fundamental design features of the internet. The ability to trace-back the source IP address could go a long way in cracking down on malicious activities on the internet. But this ability also affords more control to the governments and hence it has the potential to erode anonymity which is one of the founding features of the internet. The technology enabling source address validation also aids the goal of the Chinese Government to exert authority and control on users' behaviour over the internet, which is an arduous task in the present configuration. China, left out of the design and development process of the present generation of the internet, expresses its resentment with the internet and alleges that the Western countries have a deep influence on the technology and the founding philosophy of the internet.

With CNGI, China envisions an internet built to fulfil its economic goals and more important, aligned to its ideological inclinations. One of the rationales behind the CNGI project was to seize the opportunity to develop the next generation of the internet, realising that China fell behind many countries in the development of prevalent generation of the internet (CNGI, 2010). For China, CNGI heralds its arrival as a key player in the global pursuit of technological improvements in the internet and assures a greater say in the design, development, and the technology of the next generation of the internet. In another priority area of next-generation networks, that is broadband mobile communications, China has succeeded in turning the tables in the global telecommunications market. Chinese telecommunication equipment manufacturers have succeeded in making their mark in the industry with the onset of 5G wireless technology, giving tough competition in 5G patents and standards.

## 5G mobile telecommunication system

Successive generations of mobile telecommunication systems have drastically increased the data speed – from a mere 384 kbps in the case of 2G, it went up to 1 Gbps with the deployment of 4G. The next generation of mobile standards, 5G, is unleashing new applications and services leveraging significantly improved speed, network performance, and reliability (ITU, 2018: 1). Along with high data rate, 5G reduces latency in the network, saves energy, and enables massive device connectivity. The deployment of 5G encompasses three sets of use cases: *Enhanced Mobile Broadband* for scenarios that require high data rate over a wide area or in densely populated areas; *Massive Machine Type Communications* for densely placed IP-connected devices having varying requirements of quality of service; and *Ultra Reliable Low Latency Communications* for communications in mission-critical applications such as self-driving vehicles and remote surgeries. The International Mobile Telecommunication 2020 (IMT-2020 Standard) has set the macro-level requirements for 5G.

By 2026, 5G is expected to account for more than 50 per cent of the total mobile data (Ericsson, 2020: 13). The contribution of 5G technologies to the global economy over the next 15 years is estimated to be around USD 2.2 trillion (GSMA, 2019: 4). The direct impact of 5G on a wide range of technologies and industrial sectors is what enhances its strategic importance. The technology underpins the communication needs of the internet of things in smart cities and smart manufacturing, autonomous vehicles, and remote surgeries and telemedicine in healthcare. 5G can enable military communications in extremely high-frequency band, which is known to have a very low probability of interception, detection, and jamming (Defense Science Board, 2019: 6). It can also enhance battlefield awareness with real-time transmission of imagery, videos, maps, and support the operations of autonomous vehicles leveraging improved data rates and lower latency. China's rise as a leading technology player in telecommunications with the emergence of 5G has been a matter of scrutiny in different parts of the world, and China, nevertheless, is sparing no effort to lay claim to leadership in wireless broadband technology.

Beginning with the production of automated telephone switches in 1957, the manufacturing of telecommunication equipment in China has come of age (Harwit, 2007: 315). In the pre-reform era, being a high-technology sector R&D and industrialisation in telecommunications had a heavy military influence and the PLA continued to invest resources in this sector even during reforms. Under the Great Dragon Group, the Zhengzhou Institute of Information Engineering of the PLA in 1991 jointly developed an indigenous digital switch named HJD-04 (X. Shen, 1999). And to commercialise this switch, a company with the name Great Dragon Information Technology was established in 1994 as a state-owned enterprise. The Datang Telecom Technology Co. Ltd. (DTT) was founded by China Academy of Telecommunications Technology (CATT) in 1998. These companies, along with the private enterprises Huawei and ZTE Corporation,[1] have advanced telecommunications research in China and contributed significantly to the development of next-generation mobile networks.

A research project entitled Digital Mobile Communications Technology (GSM) – sponsored by the former State Planning Commission and the former Ministry of Posts and Telecommunication – kicked-off China's R&D endeavour for the development of telecommunication standards in the year 1992 (Pitt & Xu, 2002: 132). Correlating indigenous innovation in telecommunications with the national security of China formed the premise for the Government to aggressively push this endeavour. The flagship National High Technology Research and Development Program (863 Program) made a substantial contribution to this objective. In 1997, the ITU called for technical proposals to the IMT-2000 mobile telecommunications standard, or the 3G. In response, CATT/DTT proposed Time Division-Synchronous Code Division Multiple Access (TD-SCDMA)[2] as China's 3G standard in 1998, and in 2000 it was accepted as one of the 3G standards (Whalley et al., 2009).

Development of SCDMA was one of the research priorities during the Ninth Five-Year Plan. The Government extended financial support of RMB 700 million (around USD 85 million) in 2003 for further development of the standard (Xudong, 2014: 602). During the successive 10th and 11th Five-Year Plans, China commercialised TD-SCDMA and simultaneously advanced R&D in the next-generation mobile telecommunications as a national priority. China later proposed TD-LTE Advanced as a candidate for the 4G Standard and rolled-out 4G services in China based on this home-grown standard (Shanzhi Chen et al., 2014: 172).

On the policy front, the MLP enlisted next-generation broadband mobile telecommunication as one of the 16 major special projects (State Council, 2006). The 13th Five-Year Plan also identified 5G mobile communications as one of the areas for innovation in next-generation technology industries and prioritised its research and the development of commercial applications (State Council, 2016). The new outline of the *National Informatization Development Strategy* had set research, development, standardisation, and industrialisation of 5G technology as one of the strategic objectives, and it even envisaged a globally leading position for China in 5G. The 14th Five-Year Plan seeks to accelerate the large-scale deployment of 5G networks. The *Made in China 2025* plan also targets to make major breakthroughs in 5G technology areas such as core routing, switching, optical transmission, and network architecture (US Chamber of Commerce, 2017: 67). The MIIT, jointly with NDRC and MoST, founded the IMT-2020 (5G) Promotion Group in 2013 to facilitate commercial adoption of the technology in China (Lo & Lee, 2018: 6). The research, development, standardisation, and industrialisation of 5G technology in China were pursued as a national priority.

In the history of mobile telecommunication standards, the European companies were at the forefront of 2G in the 1990s, then the Japanese companies dominated the 3G standard in the early 2000s, and followed by American companies leading 4G standard in the early 2010s. China saw 5G as pivotal to consolidate its leading position in telecommunications, rather than playing catch-up with the technology. The ascend of China from the sidelines of the standard-setting processes for 3G and 4G to a central position in the case of 5G could be seen as a harbinger of its growing influence in the global technology ecosystem.

Various analytic firms have published reports on the rankings of companies engaged in the 5G standard-setting process, looking at the data from patent applications and granted patents relevant to the 5G standard (based on publicly available declarations made to standards bodies). These reports are heavily publicised by the Chinese media, in a way to support its claim of leadership in mobile communications technology. A report of the patent analytics firm IPlytics analysing data till January 2020 found that Huawei holds the largest portfolio of declared 5G patents (Pohlmann & Philipp, 2020). A 2020 report by GreyB also found Huawei to be leading with the most declared 5G patents (Hassan & Kumar, 2020). Financial Analysis firm Finbold with data till February 2020 found Huawei to be the frontrunner in patenting 5G technology. It attributed 3,147 patents to Huawei, followed by Samsung and ZTE Corporation (Devanesan, 2020). Another IPlytics report looking at data till April 2022 found that Huawei has declared most 5G patents, followed by Qualcomm, Samsung, LG, Nokia, Ericsson, and ZTE (Pohlmann & Buggenhagen, 2022).

The accuracy, representation of data, and methodology adopted in such patent analysis reports have however remained questionable. Drawing conclusions and ranking companies based entirely on the numbers of patent applications or technical contributions to standard-setting bodies is arguably not the right metric to determine technology leadership or innovation capacity (Bird&Bird, n.d.). Determining the value and impact of the patents is also not a straightforward task in the technology realm (Moorhead, 2020), and it further compounds in the case of 5G given its crossover with other industries such as manufacturing, automotive, and healthcare. This could also mean that not all 5G patents are relevant.

As far as the deployment of 5G is concerned, China is one of the first countries to rollout commercial 5G services. It launched 5G services across 50 cities in November 2019, and now China has the largest 5G network and user base in the world. Till May 2023, China had deployed a total of 2.84 million 5G mobile base stations (Xinhua, 2023b).

There is no denial of the fact that from 3G to 5G, the number of patent applications made by Chinese companies has increased and so have their technical contributions to standard-setting bodies. This could also be attributed to the investments made by Chinese companies in R&D capacity not just within China but worldwide. Huawei, for instance, has invested in 18 R&D facilities across eight European countries and ZTE Corporation has 13 facilities within and outside China (Embassy of PRC in India, n.d.; Huawei, 2015). The race to 5G, which involves research publications, pilot runs, spectrum allocation, and standards development, has not left geopolitics untouched. Although enormous economic potential is one of the key driving factors behind the competition, leadership in 5G also indicates technological superiority in the research, development, and deployment of next-generation networks.

Since the genesis of the 3G standard, R&D in next-generation mobile telecommunications has been pursued in China as a national priority. It serves three wider objectives. Enhanced R&D capacity in this field tightens China's hold on indigenously built core technologies, which offsets its security concerns regarding technology of foreign origin. Moreover, R&D is the bedrock of innovation and a notable intellectual property (patents and SEPs) portfolio assures better monetisation opportunities for the innovators, which in turn enhances their revenue, stimulates industrialisation, and gives rise to immense economic avenues. The third objective it serves for China is to aggregate its technological power as this industry has traditionally been dominated by American, European, and Japanese companies. China's lead in 5G patents, standards, and market share denotes China's position at the forefront of technological advancements and dexterity in their commercialisation.

Communications technology is the bedrock of cyberspace, and mobile communications in particular has gained strategic importance in the face of the unprecedented surge in demand for data and mobility. A stronghold on intellectual property rights in this field certainly indicates technology leadership, and China saw 5G as a chance to make it to the elite list of countries that are at the cutting-edge of communications technology. It also gives China an upper hand in exporting 5G equipment, particularly to the countries part of its Belt and Road Initiative bolstering the Digital Silk Road initiative. Looking beyond the horizon with its Network 2030 initiative, China continues to advance research endeavours pushing for changes in the underlying architecture of the internet.

## Network 2030

China unveiled the futuristic idea of Network 2030 at the third annual ITU IMT-2020/5G Workshop in 2018. Richard Li, Chief Scientist of Future Networks at *Futurewei Technologies* (R&D arm of Huawei located in the US), presented this idea. Network 2030 is dubbed to be revolutionary in the sense that it intends to replace the very architecture that has underpinned the internet for half a century now. Its genesis lies in the technical limitations the internet might have in the face of futuristic applications such as holographic telepresence, industrial internet, tactile internet, smart cities, remote healthcare, and autonomous vehicles. Keeping an eye on network capabilities beyond the 5G era, Network 2030 builds the case for "New IP" which could support high-precision services like remote surgery and intelligent transportation by improving latency and data rate (R. Li, 2018). At the 2018 workshop, a new Focus Group on Network 2030 was established within Study Group-13 (SG-13) of the ITU.

Since 2018, Huawei has aggressively pursued this idea in order to garner wide support and to take it forward at the ITU. Huawei's Future Networks Team prepared a white paper for SG-13 of ITU-T which discussed the gap between the technological advancements anticipated a few years ahead and the protocols of the internet (Future Networks, 2017). The white paper argued that the internet of today based on a best-effort delivery approach will fall short in meeting the demands of bandwidth, latency, and quality of service as the applications advance. It sparked off a debate questioning the resilience of IP architecture and incumbent infrastructures in the face of future applications which will have precise specifications related to latency, bandwidth, end-to-end service assurance, and end-to-end security. The paper entitled *New Internet Protocol for the Network 2030* provoked thinking on a new suite of network protocols for IMT 2020 (5G) and the future application scenarios as a progression of network infrastructure capabilities such as (micro) low latency, security by trust, protocol efficiency, and routing technologies.

The ITU-T SG-13 established a focus group on technologies for network 2030 ("FG NET-2030") in July 2018 to investigate the capabilities of networks, future network architecture, requirements, use cases, and enabling mechanisms for communication demands of emerging applications from new industry verticals for the year 2030 and beyond. FG NET-2030 is mandated to identify the gaps in the existing technologies and standards for fixed data communication networks towards Network 2030 and formulate the vision, requirements, and architecture thereof. Richard Li chairs FG NET-2030, and it has representation from the leading equipment manufacturers, service providers, and research institutions in the telecommunications domain from the US, Russia, China, Japan, the Republic of Korea, the UK, Belgium, Brazil, and Canada.

Since its establishment, FG NET-2030 has published one white paper, one deliverable document, four technical reports, and two technical specifications (architecture framework and terms and definitions) (FG NET-2030, n.d.). Laying down the groundwork, the white paper examined three characteristics relevant to the networks in 2030 – the emergence of new verticals, the development of new communication services, and the advent of new network infrastructures dispersed terrestrially, over the air, and in space. The deliverable document analysed technical gaps and performance targets for new services and capabilities, while the technical specification documents delved into architecture framework, and terms and definitions for Network 2030. The technical reports assessed key network requirements for 12 use cases,[3] identified issues and technologies that are not addressed in the current work on network and communication services with respect to Network 2030, and documented Network 2030 demonstrations of New IP related to computing power network, self-generated intent-based system, and internet-scale holographic-type communications.

At the September 2019 meeting of the Telecommunication Standardization Advisory Group (TSAG), a group of Chinese companies (Huawei, China Mobile, China Unicom) and the MIIT, in reference to the continuing work in FG NET-2030, proposed to initiate a strategic transformation of ITU-T over the next study period. Recognising the growing integration of telecommunication networks with the internet, the proposal document, called *Contribution 83*, reiterated three key challenges before the current network – inability to meet the requirements of performance and structure in the future as it is basically designed only for telephones and computers, and insufficiency in the case of diverse networks such as space-terrestrial network, internet of things network, and industrial network; the risk of splintering ("islands" of networks) as more and more unilateral and temporary technologies are deployed; and inadequacy in security and trust (ITU-T TSAG, 2019a).

The proposal strongly recommended ITU-T to "shoulder the responsibility of a top-down design for the future network, initiate a long-term plan for future network research and spearhead global research and development for the same" and most importantly, to "consider designing a new information and communications network with new protocol system" that could meet the demands of the future (ITU-T TSAG, 2019a). Huawei followed up with a tutorial elaborating on the challenges and requirements of future networks (such as integrated space–terrestrial networks, end-to-end requirements for intrinsic security, heterogeneous networks, deterministic forwarding) and possible research directions pertaining to New IP, new trustworthy model, user-defined customised request for networks, and new transport technologies (ITU-T TSAG, 2019c).

Although this effort received support of the industry and research institutions from across the globe, it has simultaneously been subject to sharp criticism, especially from the Internet Society and IETF. An Internet Society discussion paper refuted the very requirement of a New IP arguing that the internet was fundamentally designed to interconnect different types of networks, and the wireless, wire-line, and satellite networks have been considered in the development of the prevalent TCP/IP since beginning (Sharp, 2020). One of the core design goals in the evolution of the internet over the last four decades has been to allow communication over multiple and heterogeneous technologies, thereby avoiding the formation of "islands" of networks.

The paper reminds that new services, applications, and protocols are already being developed and deployed in many areas, and deterministic networking being one of them is presently under consideration at IEEE, IETF, 3GPP, and ITU-T SG15. And other areas identified by FG NET-2030 such as network coding, source routing, service-oriented routing, and network computing are also under investigation at the Internet Research Task Force. The paper concludes that overlapping work is duplicative and costly, and developing a new protocol system runs the risk of creating multiple non-interoperable networks which basically is "self-defeating" (Sharp, 2020).

In its response to the TSAG liaison statement on the *New IP, Shaping Future Network* proposal, the IETF resisted the need for a monolithic New IP designed using the top-down approach and called it harmful as it risks creating network islands, impairing interconnection, and jeopardising interoperability. The IETF countered most of the issues listed in the proposal. On the issue of latency, IETF pointed out that its work in this area dates to the 1990s and spans the development of technologies like integrated services, resource reservation protocol, multiprotocol label switching, and active queue management. Other areas under research at IETF include terrestrial and satellite networks integration, transport layer security, and deterministic networking (Cooper, 2020). Considering its experience and the progress made collectively so far, IETF expressed confidence in meeting the performance goals with extensions of the current IP stack. In its response, IETF categorically said that any requirement for the extension or modification to IETF technologies must be discussed with the IETF at the first place. It requested the ITU-T "not to accept any such proposals in the future before the IETF has held a discussion on them" (Cooper, 2020).

Europe's regional internet registry Réseaux IP Européens Network Coordination Centre (RIPE NCC) also echoed similar concerns in its response to TSAG on the proposal. It asserted that continuing evolution of the technical standards and governance models for the internet should take place from within the organisations and structures that invented the internet and supported its development over the last five decades (Hogewoning, 2020). RIPE NCC contested departure from the traditional "bottom-up" approach to decision-making, and called the technical rationale presented in the proposal as flawed and found the alternate designs to be unrealistic. Objecting to this course of action, RIPE NCC also affirmed that the work pertaining to the evolution of the IP stack and the associated technical standards should be left to the IETF and recommended the TSAG not to pursue any work items related to the proposal, or even on the IP stack per se, under the ambit of the ITU (Hogewoning, 2020).

Voluntary groups of individuals have been the vanguard of the evolution of internet – right from mere an experiment to a ubiquitous technology interconnecting heterogeneous networks and underpinning a myriad of applications. The multistakeholder approach to internet governance is a hallmark of the evolution process of internet infrastructure, technologies, standards, and the governance of its resources. With Network 2030, and the subsequent formation of FG NET-2030 and the proposal for New IP, China intends to alter the architecture of the internet. It is nevertheless clear that the idea itself is antagonistic to the fundamental values of internet such as openness, transparency, and user centricity.

The resolve to change the course of technology, such as replacing TCP/IP with New IP, and alter the governance structure of the internet represents China's aspirations to develop alternatives aligning with its economic and security needs. China, so far, has mustered the support of a handful, yet prominent, enterprises and research institutions to steer this idea forward. China's ability to muster wide support for this idea would also signify its traction within the technology community as a leader, thus cementing its position as a dominant player in the domain of advanced technologies.

As discussed in the previous chapter, China has always endorsed a multilateral approach to internet governance, and its pursuit of the idea of Network 2030 at the ITU is in furtherance of this conviction which runs counter to the Western preference for a multistakeholder approach. By way of comparison, decision-making in IETF is based on rough consensus and rests entirely on technical grounds, while ITU being an intergovernmental organisation remains susceptible to political influences and diplomatic manoeuvring. If China succeeds in carrying this idea forward at ITU-T leading to the development of the New IP standard, it will pave the way for China to shape the future of the internet.

China never had a say in the architectural and technological development of the internet, which was largely spearheaded by technologists from the Western countries who engrossed liberal values and ethos in the technology of the internet and the processes which govern its evolution. China's security concerns arise from the present architecture and schematics of the internet, while its resentment with the disproportionate allocation of resources is seen as an impediment to its economic growth. Also in the telecommunications sector, China has historically played a peripheral role which was mainly concentrated around the manufacturing of equipment built with foreign intellectual property.

However, the evidence presented in this section suggests that China has succeeded in turning the tide. It is now in a position to have a larger say in the technologies and standards for the next-generation of communication networks, reaping the benefits of reforms in its domestic R&D infrastructure initiated five decades ago. Riding this wave, China has also surprised the global scientific community with experimental breakthroughs in quantum sciences and technology which have significant implications for the disciplines of computing and cryptography.

## Quantum information sciences and technology

The evolution of underlying technology pertaining to the fundamental phenomena of "superposition" and "entanglement" in quantum mechanics has advanced the discipline from laboratories to real-world applications in computing and cryptography. Encryption algorithms are the cornerstone of secure digital communications, be it personal information, military and government secrets, sensitive business information, or financial transactions. Overcoming the computational barriers of digital computers, quantum computers can break encryption algorithms built on the principles of mathematical complexity such as integer factorisation or the discrete log problem (NIST, 2016). Quantum computers can solve the integer factorisation problem efficiently using Shor's algorithm, and they can even break Diffie–Hellman or elliptic curve Diffie–Hellman key exchange protocols which are prevalent algorithms and used widely.

In cryptography, secure key distribution has been one of the fundamental problems given the limitations in practical implementation. In 1984, Charles H. Bennett and Gilles Brassard proposed to generate random key using polarised photons (quantum property of light) and distribute it over a quantum channel. This key was supposed to be used for secure communication over public networks. Later established as BB84, the protocol proposed a practical mechanism for quantum-key distribution using a quantum channel to transmit random bits between the users. This eventually led to successful key distribution through the mediums of optical fibre, air, and space. The ability to detect any instance of eavesdropping in the channel is what makes quantum communications secure.

After years of research scientists have succeeded in overcoming the technology limitations to quantum computing and cryptography, both of which are strategically significant for the security of digital communications in the future. Quantum information sciences have remained one of the priority technology areas for China and the subject has attracted sustained funding and support of the Government. The revelations made by Edward Snowden about the massive espionage programme of the US – which also targeted China – gave impetus to the objective of securing the Government, CPC, and military establishment from foreign surveillance. With substantial support of the political leadership, Chinese scientists have succeeded in carving a niche for China in this endeavour at the cutting-edge of science and technology. More than scientific feats, leap-frog advances have "strategic significance for China" (Lin et al., 2016), steering it ahead in high-technology areas and inching further towards the goal of becoming a cyber superpower.

Quantum computing and communications were one of the focus areas for fundamental research in China as early as the Tenth Five-Year Plan. Owing to distinctive applications in the security of digital communications and military operations, the subject drew the attention of the scientific and political leadership (X. Chen, 2009; China Economic Net, 2012; Y. Liu, 2011; Wen, 2011). In the implementation of the 11th Five-Year Plan, the MoST, NSFC, and CAS initiated various projects on quantum control and quantum communications. The NSFC and CAS announced and initiated another set of projects during the 12th Five-Year Plan. The NDRC also initiated the Beijing–Shanghai Quantum Secure Communication Backbone project to build a quantum key distribution channel between Beijing and Shanghai (Q. Zhang et al., 2019). The 13th Five-Year Plan continued to build the momentum on quantum research. The 14th Five-Year Plan committed to taking forward cutting-edge research in this area as well as the deployment of the technologies developed so far for quantum computing and quantum communications.

Research on quantum information sciences in China began around 1998 when the NSFC convened the Xiangshan Science Forum for quantum information. The Key Laboratory of Quantum Information was established in 2001 at the University of Science and Technology of China (USTC) in Hefei through the National Basic Research Program (973 Program) to conduct basic and applied research on quantum communications and quantum computing (USTC, n.d.). Since its establishment, the key laboratory had many path-breaking scientific accomplishments in quantum-key distribution to its credit, and it has evolved into a leading research hub for quantum information sciences not just in China but globally.

In 2004, the key laboratory had succeeded in establishing a long-distance (around 125 km), point-to-point, optical fibre-based quantum communication link between Beijing and Tianjin. The following year it demonstrated five-photon entanglement and open-destination teleportation, and in 2007 it built a quantum router for a four-port quantum cryptography network (USTC, n.d.). The key laboratory established a government quantum cryptography network in Wuhu city in 2009 and began providing services to eight departments of the Chinese Government – a first of its kind in the world at that time (X. Chen, 2009).

The transmission of quantum states through air – known as "free-space quantum teleportation" – has potential applications in cryptographic key exchange and long-distance communication is feasible with the help of quantum satellites. Such a global quantum communications network is one of the prime areas of research at the key laboratory given its geopolitical significance. Scientists at the key laboratory were able to increase quantum teleportation in free space from 16 km in 2010 to over 100 km in 2012 (C. Z. Peng et al., 2005; Yin et al., 2012). The key laboratory undertook the research project Quantum Experiments at Space Scale (QUESS) to develop a proof of concept for conducting quantum optical experiments over long distances. And in August 2016, the key laboratory placed the first satellite in the QUESS fleet with a quantum optical payload (named "Micius") in the sun-synchronous orbit.

The satellite has been instrumental in conducting experiments with quantum-key distribution between ground stations. After experiments with satellite-enabled quantum-key distribution within China (CAS, 2017a, 2017c), researchers from the CAS and the Austrian Academy of Sciences in 2018 succeeded in quantum-key distribution between "Micius" and the ground stations separated by 7,600 km – one at Xinglong near Beijing and the other at Graz near Vienna (Xinhua, 2018d). The strategic objective of the QUESS experiment is to build a hack-proof global quantum communications network, and China took a leap in that direction with the success of this experiment.

China has also advanced in the terrestrial segment of quantum communications network. This optical fibre network works in conjunction with the satellite-based quantum-key distribution network (eoPortal, n.d.). In 2017, China opened up a 2,000-km-long optical fibre backbone for quantum communication between Shanghai and Beijing – making it the world's first trunk line for quantum-key distribution (CAS, 2017d). The backbone basically connects quantum communication networks established in the cities of Beijing, Shanghai, Jinan, and Hefei. The integration of "Micius" with this network consolidates the terrestrial and space segments of China's quantum communications network (Z. Zhang, 2017). China anticipates expanding the quantum communications network into a global network by 2030. Such a network spread across land, space, and sea fulfils the need of the Government, CPC, and the PLA for ultra-secure communications. And that is one of the key reasons for this subject receiving the utmost Government attention and generous funding.

Quantum computers leverage the quantum mechanical phenomena of superposition and entanglement to perform operations on data which is stored in the form of quantum bits (qubits), unlike classical computers which store data as binary states of 0 or 1 (IBM, n.d.-b). They can overcome the computing limitations of classical computers. Quantum computing is another area of research where China has made advancements. Chinese scientists succeeded in building a quantum computer in 2017 (Xinhua, 2017d), and by 2018 they were able to achieve 18-qubit quantum entanglement (Y. Xu,

2018). The Center for Excellence in Quantum Information and Quantum Physics at USTC developed a 66-qubit processor in 2021 and in May 2023 upgraded it to support 176-qubits (Xinhua, 2023a).

China is also known to have made progress with experiments demonstrating Shor's algorithm, solving linear equations systems, entanglement-based machine learning, cloud quantum computing, and quantum metrology and sensors – some of these have practical applications in cryptanalysis. China began building the world's largest quantum research facility at Hefei in 2017, called as the National Laboratory for Quantum Information Sciences (S. Chen, 2017a; Superposition, 2017). Commercialisation of the research outcomes has also kept pace with the advancing research on quantum information sciences in China.

Along with security imperatives, commercial opportunities are also aplenty for quantum technology. Chinese private enterprises are deeply involved in research and technology development to harness business opportunities in services based on quantum technologies. Set up in collaboration with CAS, the Quantum Laboratory[4] at Alibaba DAMO Academy pursues research interests in quantum processors and computing systems, quantum algorithms, and simulations of quantum physics. The laboratory plans to build quantum computing prototypes of 50–100 qubits by 2030 (DAMO Academy, n.d.).

Baidu offers services to researchers for running quantum machine learning algorithms through its open-source machine learning toolkit called the Paddle Quantum platform (Swayne, 2020; Wiggers, 2020). The Quantum Computing Institute established in 2018 at Baidu Research has interests in the areas of *quantum artificial intelligence* (machine learning, information security), *quantum architecture* (hardware interface, quantum network and internet, quantum and post-quantum cryptography), and *quantum algorithm* (quantum simulation, quantum search, and quantum secure computation). The institute's long-term aim is to integrate quantum technologies into Baidu's core business (Baidu Research, n.d.-a).

Industry–academia integration in the case of quantum information sciences is now quite evident in China. QuantumCTek – a spin-out from the quantum physics research group at the Hefei National Laboratory for Physical Science and USTC – is a leader in quantum-based network security products and services for government organisations and the financial and energy industry (QuantumCTek, n.d.). HeFei Origin Quantum Computing Technology Company was founded by a team of scientists from the quantum information laboratory at CAS. This start-up is engaged in the development and application of quantum computers using scientific knowledge from the research at Key Laboratory of Quantum Information and CAS (Origin Quantum, n.d.).

Anhui Qasky Quantum Technology Company was formed out of a joint venture with USTC, and it builds commercial applications from quantum cryptography research at CAS. The company is a designated producer and licensed seller of commercial cipher products certified by the State Cryptography Administration and provides integrated solutions for quantum information security (Qasky, n.d.). Established by a team of academicians, QuantumDoor Technologies develops equipment for quantum key communication and optoelectronic components, and it provides quantum-based information security services to the government, defence, finance, and power sectors (QUDOOR, n.d.).

Publications in scientific journals of international repute and patents are one of the means to demonstrate leadership in a technology area. China's share in international research papers and patent applications in quantum information sciences has seen a sharp increase over the years. A contest among the great powers is unfolding at the frontiers of physics. In the disciplines of quantum computing and quantum information sciences, contributions from China to reputed scientific journals including *Science*, *Nature*, and *Physical Review Letters* have increased, which denotes the rising standards of research in these disciplines (CAS, 2017b). A McKinsey and Company report in 2015 had noted that China is among the top spenders in the world on non-classified quantum technology research, second to the US but ahead of Canada, Australia, Japan, and Russia (*The Economist*, n.d.). This report as well as some other studies found China to be leading in the number of patent applications for quantum cryptography and quantum-key distribution, but lagging behind in the case of quantum computing (Gibney, 2017).

A 2019 patent analysis of select quantum technologies concluded that after around ten years of constant patenting activity between 2003 and 2013, there has been a steep increase in patent filings after 2013 for quantum-key distribution attributed to applicants based in China (Travagnin, 2019). In the case of quantum computing, the study found that Chinese players have stepped up their patenting efforts since 2013, though the numbers remain limited. A 2022 academic study looking at the patent landscape of quantum technologies found China leading in quantum communications (Aboy et al., 2022). Another McKinsey and Company report in 2022 found that China holds more than half of the patents in quantum technologies and estimated the total of government funding in China for quantum technologies at USD 15.3 billion. This figure is almost double of what the European Union (USD 8.4 billion) has committed and more than triple of what the US ($3.7 billion) has announced as government funding for quantum technologies (Hart et al., 2023; Masiowski et al., 2022).

Standardisation of quantum technology is progressing mainly in three directions – quantum computing, quantum-key distribution, and quantum internet. For quantum computing, two study groups and an advisory group were established in 2018 and 2019, respectively, at ISO/IEC JTC 1 (ISO, n.d.). For quantum-key distribution, the network aspects of quantum information technologies are under study at ITU-T SG13 (Future Networks), while ITU-T SG 17 (Security) leads on the security dimensions (ITU-T SG 13, n.d.; ITU-T SG 17, n.d.; ITU News, 2019). In 2019, a focus group on quantum information technology for networks was established at ITU-T to support standardisation efforts underway at ITU-T study groups and other standard-setting organisations (ITU-T FG-QIT4N, n.d.). Standardisation of network engineering aspects such as routing, resource allocation, interoperability, and security of quantum internet is driven by IETF's quantum internet research group (IETF, n.d.).

With a globally recognised R&D programme in the discipline of quantum information sciences, China now anticipates playing a decisive role in the formulation of relevant standards. In 2015, the China Communications Standards Association initiated a study on quantum secure communication network security and established a special task force on quantum communication. China also initiated a study at ISO/IEC JTC 1 in 2017 on security requirements, tests, and evaluation methods for quantum key distribution (Q. Zhang et al., 2019). A coalition of the Beijing University of Posts and Telecommunications and eight Chinese companies (and one from the Republic of Korea) proposed setting up a focus group at ITU-T on quantum information technology for networks (ITU-T TSAG, 2019b). China is also working closely with the ITU for the standardisation of quantum-key distribution.

China is amongst the few countries in the world engaged in advanced research on this subject, and it has succeeded not just in experimental endeavours but also in the commercial development of scientific outcomes with an active involvement of the private sector. Over the course of the last two decades, China has built a strong research base, and integrated research with technology development and commercialisation which is evident from the cases of start-ups and joint ventures emerging from China's prominent quantum laboratories. From a negligible contribution to international scientific journals, China now leads in publications on quantum cryptography and quantum-key distribution. Put together, China could well be in a position to play a larger role in the formulation of standards for quantum computing, quantum cryptography, and other related technologies. Another emerging technology which has gained much limelight and global attention in recent times is artificial intelligence, and China's strides in artificial intelligence are again a matter of global discussion.

## Artificial intelligence

Artificial intelligence (AI) had a breakthrough moment in 1997 when IBM's computer *Deep Blue* defeated the world chess champion Gary Kasparov in a chess competition. The computer could explore up to 200 million possible chess positions per second (IBM, n.d.-a). Resurgence in the discipline of AI around 2010 and the progress thereafter is attributed to two factors – first is the availability of computing or processing power which can run AI algorithms, and second is the access to massive volumes of data, or large data sets, to train the algorithms (Council of Europe, n.d.). Substantive advancements in the associated fields of big data, cloud computing, the internet of things, and computing platforms (integrated circuits) propelled the rapid transition of deep neural networks from laboratories to real-world applications. AI is widely recognised as a game-changing technology, and it is being put into extensive use in the industry and governments to solve a wide spectrum of real-world problems. AI is also changing the way militaries train, deploy, and command their forces.

States anticipate AI to stimulate economic growth, but it is also expected to have a transformative or disruptive impact on economic competitiveness and the jobs market (Szczepański, 2019). Market intelligence company International Data Corporation forecasts worldwide revenues for the AI market (hardware, software, services) to surpass USD 300 billion by 2024 (IDC, 2020). A 2018 discussion paper by McKinsey and Company estimated that AI may deliver an additional global economic activity of around USD 13 trillion by 2030 (Bughin et al., 2018).

AI has been in the limelight of late as it is being closely associated with the strategic competition among states striving for supremacy in the realm of emerging technologies. President of the Russian Federation Vladimir Putin aptly put this state of competition in AI in his 2017 statement as, "whoever becomes the leader in this sphere will become the ruler of the world" (Gigova, 2017). Cognisant of the enormous potential of AI and its strategic implications, governments around the world are aggressively promoting research in the sub-fields of AI, developing capability, expediting its commercial development and adoption in the industry, and exploring its applications in the armed forces. The dormant race for supremacy in AI became apparent in 2017 when China announced its ambition to become the world leader in AI by 2030.

Two decades after IBM's *Deep Blue* defeated Gary Kasparov, in 2016 a computer programme developed by Google DeepMind called AlphaGo defeated South Korean professional "Go" player Lee Se-dol in a game (DeepMind, n.d.). Go is a classical board game which originated in China over 3,000 years ago and involves around 10 to the power of 170 ($10^{170}$) possible board configurations. Celebrated as a milestone in the field of AI, people from all over the world, 280 million in China alone, watched this match. It was dubbed "Sputnik moment" for the development of AI in China (K.-F. Lee, 2018: 3), though in 2016 AI was not new to China. A decade ago, the MLP had laid the foundations of R&D in AI prioritising the development of intelligent sensors and robotics as one of the frontier technologies (State Council, 2006). The research on intelligent sensors included image and natural language processing and biometric identification, while the focus areas for intelligent robots were manufacturing and control systems. Intelligent technologies were also meant to aid public security.

The *Made in China 2025* plan in 2015 prioritised the wide-scale use of intelligent systems in manufacturing, rail transportation, energy, power, and agriculture, and paved the way for research and development and industrialisation of intelligent industrial control systems, sensors, meters, reducers, vehicles, machinery, robots, and appliances (State Council, 2015a). The 2015 *Internet Plus Action Plan* also underscored the importance of nurturing the AI industry and investing in research and development of technologies such as computer vision, voice processing, biometric recognition, and natural language processing (State Council, 2015d). The NDRC in the following year rolled out *Internet plus Artificial Intelligence Three-year Action Plan* to boost the growth of AI sector in China and bring it at par with the global AI technology and industry (CAS, 2016; Y. Wang, 2017). The 13th Five-Year Plan also sought to foster AI as one of the strategic emerging industries (State Council, 2016). In continuation, the 14th Five-Year Plan identified AI as one of the key industries of the digital economy and committed carrying forward R&D in AI through establishment of national laboratories and formulation and implementation of strategic scientific plans.

China's AI ambitions received a major thrust when the State Council unveiled the *New Generation Artificial Intelligence Development Plan* ("AI Development Plan") in July 2017, setting the vision to develop China as a hub for global AI innovation and a leader in AI technology and applications by 2030 (Notice of the State Council on Issuing the Development Plan for the New Generation of Artificial Intelligence, 2017; Xinhua, 2017g). It officially marked the development of the AI sector as a national priority, and a few months later AI Development Plan also found a mention in Xi Jinping's report at the 19th National Congress of the CPC among other technology areas to be integrated with the real economy (Xi, 2017b). Noting that AI is now a focus of international competition and states are pursuing AI strategies to enhance national competitiveness and protect national security, the plan aspires to give China a first-mover advantage. And it seeks to build an influential position for China in AI research, thereby empowering it to seize the "commanding heights" of AI technology and enhance its scientific and technological power.

AI Development Plan has three milestones – placing China's AI industry at an equal footing with the global echelons of AI technology by 2020, making AI the main driving force behind China's industrial modernisation and economic transformation by 2025, and establishing China as a world leader in AI technology and applications and an innovation hub by 2030. Table 5.1 lists key tasks under the AI Development Plan and the corresponding focus areas. The plan has a strong international outlook too as it extends support to domestic enterprises to collaborate with leading international universities, research institutions, and groupings engaged in AI research and development, and it encourages domestic enterprises to "go global" through mergers and acquisitions, equity investments, and overseas R&D centres. The plan aspires to establish international organisations for AI, formulate international standards, and promote joint research centres and AI applications, especially in countries part of the Belt and Road Initiative. AI Development Plan further invigorated the existing research endeavours in China in the discipline of AI.

**TABLE 5.1** Key tasks under the New Generation Artificial Intelligence Development Plan

| Task | Focus areas |
| --- | --- |
| Building an open and collaborative AI technology innovation system | • Breakthroughs in applications and basic theoretical[5] research<br>• Multidisciplinary[6] exploratory research<br>• General technology systems[7]<br>• Development of AI academic discipline and skilled human resources |
| Fostering a high-end and efficient smart economy | • Development of emerging industries[8] in AI<br>• Modernisation of the industries such as manufacturing, finance, logistics, and agriculture using AI<br>• Establishment of innovation clusters |
| Building a safe and convenient intelligent society | • Provisioning of intelligent services such as in education and medical care[9]<br>• Intelligent governance in the areas of administration, courts, smart cities, and transportation<br>• Use of AI in monitoring and early warning and control systems to enhance public safety |
| Strengthening military–civilian integration in the field of AI | • Enhance communication and coordination among scientific research institutions, universities, enterprises, and military industry units to reap the benefits of dual-use nature of AI technologies |
| Building a ubiquitous, safe, and efficient intelligent infrastructure | • Improve network (5G, IoT, and industrial internet), big data, and high-performance computing infrastructure in order to meet the abovementioned needs |
| Making a blueprint for AI technology projects | • Integrate the new generation AI technology projects with the existing R&D projects being executed as part of national planning such as the National Key Research and Development Plan |

*Source*: Compiled by the author with inputs from the *New Generation Artificial Intelligence Development Plan.*

There are several parameters to gauge national capabilities in a technology field, and they could be a combination of scientific paper publications in reputed journals, patent filings and holdings, capital investments, technology infrastructure, availability of highly skilled human resources, and so on. Information from patent application documents could reveal the broader trends in research and innovation activity. Together with the analysis of scientific publications, this may provide better insights as a majority of the research output is not patented but published for knowledge dissemination in journals and conference proceedings. Moreover, lead in numbers or high volume alone does not necessarily translate into a better position in the high-technology competition, and it is important to factor in the quality of publications and patent holdings as well.

A 2018 study by the China Institute for Science and Technology Policy at Tsinghua University found that China has secured a position in the top echelons of AI technology development (Tsinghua University, 2018). The study assessed the development of AI in China on four parameters – S&T output and human resources, industry development and market applications, development strategy and policy environment, and public perception and general impact. The study found China to be leading the world in parameters that looked at AI research papers and highly cited AI papers publications, AI patents, and attracting AI venture capital investment. It ranked China second to the US in the number of AI-based enterprises and top-end human expertise pool. China's share in worldwide AI paper publications increased from 4.26 per cent in 1997 to 27.68 per cent by 2017, according to the study. A considerable number of these were an outcome of collaboration with scientists and researchers from the US, UK, and Australia, signifying China's growing engagement with these countries in advanced AI research. Different assessments find China leading in international journal publications in AI.

An analysis by the Allen Institute for Artificial Intelligence in 2018 of the most-cited AI research papers indexed on the scholarly search engine Microsoft Academic found that China had increased its share in the top 10 per cent of the most-cited papers from zero in 1982 to 26.5 per cent and it was just a little behind the US (O'Meara, 2019). As per the information on Artificial Intelligence publications from 1996 to 2022 in the SCImago Journal and Country Rank database, which uses the Scopus abstract and citation database to develop journals and country scientific indicators, China ranks number one in publications volume, ahead of the US, India, and Japan (Scimago Journal & Country Rank, 2022). The 2022 *AI Index Report* from the Stanford Institute for Human-Centered AI noted the increasing share of China in the number of citations of AI journal publications, though its share in the number of AI conference citations remained lower than the US despite leading in AI conference publications (D. Zhang et al., 2022). The 2023 *AI Index Report* found this gap narrowing and observed China leading in

AI journals, conferences, and repository publications (Maslej et al., 2023). China surpassed the US in 2008, and from 2014 onwards, China has succeeded in bridging the gap with the US in AI paper citations, which is an indicator of the improving quality of publications.

The 2019 World Intellectual Property Organization (WIPO) report on technology trends in AI – analysing data from nearly 340,000 AI-related inventions or patent families from 1960 until early 2018 – found 17 Chinese institutions among the top 20 academic players (universities and public research organisations) in AI patenting, and CAS to be the leading research organisation applicant (WIPO, 2019). The report observed that the patent filings by Chinese organisations grew more than 20 per cent per year on average between 2013 and 2016, outperforming organisations from other countries. China has been leading the world in patent filings since 2014 and Chinese institutions account for one-fifth of the top 500 patent applicants according to the report. According to the 2022 *AI Index Report*, China was filing over half of the world's AI patents then, but its share in patents granted stood at just about 6 per cent (D. Zhang et al., 2022).

Also in the private sector, Chinese technology giants Alibaba, Baidu, and Tencent have built substantial research capacity and made advances in all the key areas of AI (Alibaba AI Labs, n.d.; Baidu Research, n.d.-b; Tencent AI Lab, n.d.). Alibaba DAMO Academy's AI Lab pursues research in voice assistants, industrial manufacturing, robotics, and its cloud-based machine learning platform provides end-to-end data processing, feature engineering, model training, model prediction, and model evaluation (Alibaba AI Labs, n.d.; Alibaba Cloud, n.d.). Baidu Research – co-located in Silicon Valley, Seattle, and Beijing – has interests in natural language and speech processing, robotics and autonomous driving, computer vision, machine learning, and deep learning. Baidu hosts an open-source deep learning platform PaddlePaddle which helps developers and enterprises build applications for a wide range of industries. Tencent's AI Lab focuses on fundamental research in machine learning, computer vision, speech recognition, natural language processing, and their applications.

With the aim of leveraging the expertise and capacity of private sector enterprises, the MoST in 2017 began identifying the leading ones in specific sectors as "AI National Champions," basically to partner with and steer the AI Development Plan. The initiative began with Baidu (autonomous driving), Alibaba (smart cities), Tencent (medical diagnosis), and iFlyTek (speech recognition) and later included Huawei (infrastructure and software), Hikvision (video perception), Xiaomi (smart home), JD.com (supply chain), Qihoo 360 (cybersecurity), and Megvii and Yitu (facial recognition) (S. Dai, 2019). Advancing research at both public institutions and private sector enterprises underpins China's aspirations to play a key role in the AI standard-setting process, and global efforts towards this goal have already taken off.

Under the ISO/IEC JTC 1, the international standardisation committee SC-42 seeks to provide a framework and common vocabulary, address issues such as resiliency, reliability, accuracy, safety, security, and privacy, and foster collaboration with other committees spanning the entire AI ecosystem (ISO/IEC JTC1, n.d.). Focus group on artificial intelligence for health (FG-AI4H) established under the ITU-T Study Group 16 standardises the assessment framework for the evaluation of AI algorithms used in healthcare applications (ITU-T FG-AI4H, n.d.). Given the attention autonomous vehicles have received as an application of AI, the focus group on AI for autonomous and assisted driving (FG-AI4AD) under the ITU-T Study Group 16 supports the standardisation activities for services and applications enabled by AI systems in autonomous and assisted driving (ITU-T FG-AI4AD, n.d.).

China's AI Development Plan drew attention to the development of AI standards framework, and industry standards and norms based on the principles of security, availability, interoperability, and traceability. In 2018, the Standardization Administration of China established the National AI Standardization General Working Group and the National AI Standardization Expert Advisory Group charged with the responsibility of executing and coordinating national and international AI standardisation work.

The China Electronics Standardization Institute, a think-tank under the MIIT, published *Artificial Intelligence Standardization White Paper* in 2018, which was a joint effort of 30 organisations from academia and industry (CESI, 2018). Dividing the AI industry ecosystem into three layers of core business,[10] associated business,[11] and derived business,[12] the white paper underscored the key technology areas within the AI umbrella where China can step up its efforts to propose standards. It drew attention to foundational standards,[13] platform standards,[14] key technical standards,[15] products and services standards,[16] and application standards.[17]

Prioritising standards in the areas of ethics, security, and privacy in the development of AI, the Standardization Administration of China, the Office of the Central Cyberspace Affairs Commission, NDRC, MOST, and MIIT jointly issued the *Guidelines for the Construction of a National New Generation Artificial Intelligence Standards System* in July 2020. A year later, in July 2021, the second edition of *Artificial Intelligence Standardization White Paper* from China Electronics Standardization Institute presented the status of China's AI standardisation efforts[18] and shed some light on the problems and challenges thereof (CESI, 2021). The white paper made a few recommendations as well, such as improving coordination among domestic standardisation bodies, carrying out pilots, and increasing representation of China's standardisation institutions and enterprises in the formulation and revision of international AI standards. In spite of China's giant leap in AI research and innovation, there are formidable challenges in its path to the "commanding heights" of AI technology.

Most striking of these challenges pertains to the quality of research and patents, foundational technology of AI, and human resources. The 2019 *AI Index Report* had observed the field-weighted citation impact[19] of publications from the US to be 50 per cent higher than those from China (Perrault et al., 2019), which means that Chinese authors of research papers received fewer citations as compared to their counterparts from the US. The recent reports however find China closing in on the US. The 2018 study of the China Institute for Science and Technology Policy had made an explicit note of China's weakness in the core technologies of AI such as hardware and algorithm development. The study also found the domestic technology giants Baidu, Alibaba, and Tencent lagging behind their American counterparts like IBM, Microsoft, and Google in terms of research paper publications, patents, and attracting the best of the human resources in AI (Tsinghua University, 2018). The slack performance of Chinese private sector enterprises in research and patenting activity was also reflected in the 2019 WIPO report on technology trends in AI as only two companies from China made it to the top 20 list of companies filing AI-related patents (WIPO, 2019). China's private investment in AI (USD 13.4 billion) was less than a third of the US (USD 47.4 billion) in 2022, according to the 2023 *AI Index Report* (Maslej et al., 2023).

A 2019 report of the Center for Data Innovation analysing the six categories of talent (human resources), research, development, hardware, adoption, and data had found the US leading in the former four and China in the latter two categories (Castro, 2019). The report attributed this to the US's advantage in integrated circuits technology, AI open-source software, quality of the research papers, high-quality AI talent, and the vibrant start-up ecosystem, and observed access to data – a determining factor in AI – as China's primary advantage. A 2021 report on global AI talent distribution found that around 60 per cent of the top-tier AI researchers were working in the US, while only 11 per cent of them were engaged in research in China. Interestingly, in terms of the country of origin of top-tier AI researchers, China took the lead with a share of 29 per cent (MacroPolo, 2020; UNCTAD, 2021). This is because of Chinese researchers taking up higher studies or finding work in the US in large numbers.

China's private sector companies lag behind their US counterparts also in open-source machine learning and deep learning platforms such as Google's TensorFlow, Facebook's PyTorch, Microsoft's DMTK, and IBM's SystemML. In contrast, Baidu's open-source deep learning platform PaddlePaddle does not have much traction globally. In a bid to expand the global reach and adoption of China's open-source deep learning platforms, Tsinghua University rolled out an open-source deep learning framework named Jittor, Alibaba Cloud made its machine learning platform open-source in 2019, and Huawei too made its AI computing framework MindSpore open-source in

March 2020 (Huawei, 2020; Tsinghua University, n.d.). Also, the Institute of Computing Technology of the CAS developed Seetaface for facial recognition and Fudan University developed FudanNLP for natural language processing as open-source platforms. The 14th Five-Year Plan committed support to the development of open-source communities and urged enterprises to provide open-source code, hardware design, and application services.

Computing power is an essential building block of an advanced AI ecosystem and integrated circuits optimised for AI applications – also known as AI chips – provide that computing power. Traditional computing architectures are being optimised for specific AI application scenarios such as artificial neural networks, machine vision, and machine learning (ICFC, 2018). Integrated circuits or semiconductor technology in general is a major impediment for China in the development of a self-reliant AI industry, especially amidst the increasing technology export restrictions the US has imposed on China for the purchase and manufacturing of high-end semiconductor chips (BIS, 2022; Ernst, 2020). China acknowledges that it lags in materials, equipment, and manufacturing in the semiconductor industry (*People's Daily*, 2022).

China realises that its position in the upper echelons of AI technology depends a lot on how it inculcates an ecosystem integrated with the global R&D and talent hubs. The unified effort on the part of the Government, academic institutions, technology giants, and start-ups tends to rapidly bridge the gaps in basic research, AI technology ecosystem, foundational technologies and platforms of AI, AI open-source resources, top-rated AI experts, and AI standards and specifications.

Realising the economic and strategic imperatives, China's political leadership sees AI as a technology of the future. State-led policy measures have laid the foundations of research and directed the efforts of research institutions and industry towards the integration of AI with the prime sectors of China's economy such as manufacturing, healthcare, agriculture, transportation, and security. The CPC Central Committee Political Bureau undertook a study session on AI in 2018. Presiding the session, Xi Jinping in his speech urged to achieve "transformative and disruptive breakthroughs" in the direction, theory, methods, tools, and systems of AI and ensure a leading position of China in theoretical research and other critical and core technologies of AI (X. Zhou & Choi, 2018). A month before that, Xi Jinping had stressed on utilising AI for the benefit of mankind in a letter to the inaugural of the 2018 World Artificial Intelligence Conference held in Shanghai (CGTN, 2018).

Once integrated with the key sectors of Chinese economy, and the *Made in China 2025* plan and the *Internet Plus Action Plan* in particular, AI has the potential to usher China into a new generation of high economic growth. A globally leading position is understood to reinforce China's ambition to be among the leading technological superpowers, whether it is in basic research, applied research, technology empowering AI, or its applications. There was a sudden outburst of interest in AI among the political leaders from across the globe after China unveiled its AI Development Plan in 2017. In a way, this signifies the place China has eventually occupied in emerging technologies as its actions in the technology space now have global implications, even compelling other states to respond. Given its strategic relevance and boundless applications in both the civilian and military realms, and reiterating Vladimir Putin's words, "whoever becomes the leader in this sphere will become the ruler of the world," AI is being termed as the next battleground for great power competition.

## Discussion

China's technological and political leaders have for long related high technology with economic development and national power. Indigenous innovation in high technology is seen as the means to progressively reduce dependence on foreign technology or intellectual property and propel the much-needed economic growth. Long-term planning has therefore tried to address the gaps in China's S&T system keeping a close eye on the strategic needs – right from nuclear weapons and space to next-generation networks and quantum information sciences in the present era. The advances China has made in the emerging digital technology areas discussed in the chapter could be safely attributed to its persistent focus on R&D and ICT industrial development. Research paper publications in journals of international repute and intellectual property development, or patents, have become an instrument of China's claim on technology leadership in emerging technologies. To this end, activism in the international standards-setting processes is largely seen as an important indicator to gauge the maturity of China's technology ecosystem and a key lever to seize "commanding heights" of the competition in emerging technologies.

Technology leadership, or the so-called "commanding heights," in the eyes of the political leadership elevates China's standing in the international system and bestows China what they believed to be its "rightful place." China was left out of the previous generations of technology development, and as a result it had little or no role to play in the associated standards and rule-making processes. A lead position in the development of emerging technologies gives China the latitude to set or influence international standards and rules of the road for technology governance in conformity with its national interests and values. As geopolitical competition continues to permeate technology standardisation processes, China seeks a position commensurate with its rising global status and pursues a dominant position in international standard-setting organisations as a national priority. Development of standards for the next-generation of technologies and industrial revolution featured prominently in the *Made in China 2025* plan, and China is drawing up a national plan to do so for the leading technology sectors in the form of *China Standards 2035*.

The discussion on next-generation networks in the chapter revealed China's expectations from CNGI to be an enabler of its economic goals and an opportunity to have a greater say in the design, development, and technological improvements to the next generation of the internet. It facilitates China's early transition to the IPv6 standard and lays down the foundation for the wide-scale integration of traditional industries with the internet, resolving the IP address space and some of the security concerns. The ascend of China in the field of mobile communication networks holds immense economic value and simultaneously marks its entry to the select group of countries at the forefront of mobile broadband networks. Mobile communication networks (5G or 6G) are slated to be a key component of China's Digital Silk Road as more and more countries part of the Belt and Road Initiative are now planning to roll out 5G services given its applications in mobile broadband and a host of other industries, ranging from healthcare to smart manufacturing.

As part of China's larger focus on next-generation networks, the New IP proposal made at the ITU is an audacious attempt to replace the existing TCP/IP stack with a new one. Built on the grounds of technical limitations of the present architecture and schematics of the internet and the existing TCP/IP stack in the face of futuristic applications and security requirements, the proposal is a testament to China's aspirations to replace the very architecture of the internet and the approach to its technology evolution with the one that aligns with China's security interests. The idea of Network 2030 or New IP proposal is again a befitting example of China's inclination towards creating alternatives if the existing mechanisms, approaches, or architectures do not align with its economic and security needs. The previous chapter had also observed this with the cases of China's push for a multilateral approach to cyber governance and the Open-Ended Working Group at the UN, and its roll-out of the Global Initiative on Data Security and digital RMB.

The other two technology areas discussed in the chapter highlight how China is now reaping the benefits of the initiatives in R&D whose seeds were sown two decades back. Quantum computing and communication have been one of the focus areas for fundamental scientific research since the Tenth Five-Year Plan and the research on the subject began in China at the turn of the 21st century. China's share in international research paper publications and patent applications in quantum information sciences has witnessed a sharp increase. Quantum information sciences has also seen a close industry–academia collaboration, which is substantiated by the fact that academic research outputs have been converted into successful commercial applications by both big technology players and start-ups. With China's emergence as a leading hub or destination for R&D and technology development in quantum, it is certain to play a larger role in the standard-setting process of quantum computing, quantum cryptography, and other related technologies.

As far as AI is concerned, China has been the focus of several studies assessing its performance on various parameters related to R&D output, access to skilled human resources or talent, industrial development, and policy environment. The origins of China's R&D initiatives in AI could be traced back to the MLP, which eventually laid the foundation for research activities in image and natural language processing, biometric identification, robotics, and other intelligent system in manufacturing, transportation, and energy. The *Made in China 2025* plan and the *Internet Plus Action Plan* further fortified this endeavour, while the AI Development Plan gave it a strategic context, aiming to establish China as a world leader in AI technology and applications and an innovation hub by 2030.

The analysis of research papers published in the discipline of AI clearly indicates that China is now leading in terms of publication volume, and it has gradually improved the quality of publications as China's share in the most-cited research papers has increased. Chinese academic institutions dominate the list of top academic players in AI patenting, and China has been leading the world in AI-related patent filings since 2014. In order to convert these advancements into national and international standards, China has constituted an expert advisory group to spearhead the task. However, there remain to be some challenges in the form of quality of research and patents, access to human resources and talent, slack performance of private sector enterprises in research and patenting, and limitations in integrated circuits technology and open-source platforms.

With reference to the model for cyber power, the discussion on three technology areas in this chapter throws light on some of the *Capacities* listed as part of *Emerging Digital Technologies*. China's investments in the research and development of emerging digital technologies have grown significantly as these remain to be a priority both for the Government and the private sector. Building advanced laboratories for quantum technologies or AI in academia and private sector, or the facilities developed by Huawei and ZTE in other parts of the world indicate an influx in investments for R&D activities and research infrastructure. The ability of Chinese enterprises to commercialise research – as seen with Huawei and ZTE in the telecommunications sector, Alibaba and Baidu in the case of AI and quantum technologies, or the start-ups emerging from state laboratories – indicates that a technology industrial base is gradually developing in China. China's limitations in access to highly skilled workforce and attracting global talent are widely acknowledged and it plans to remedy this lacuna.

In terms of *Capabilities*, it is evident from the discussion in this chapter that China has made significant progress. The standards of research output from China at the cutting-edge of emerging digital technologies have shown considerable improvement. The increase in the contribution of researchers from China to reputed international scientific journals and also in the number of most-cited publications denotes rising standards of research. Another area which has seen remarkable change is the ability to forge collaboration between academia and the industry. As evident from the case studies in the chapter, there is a deeper integration of the efforts on the part of the Government, academic institutions, and technology giants and start-ups. The concept of New IP, for instance, was jointly proposed by a group of Chinese companies and the MIIT.

The growing number of laboratories in the private sector set up in collaboration with academia such as Quantum Laboratory at Alibaba DAMO Academy, and the increasing number of technology companies set up as spin-outs from the laboratories in academia indicate effective academia–industry collaboration as well as improvement in the maturity of the innovation ecosystem in China. China also continues to improve its ranking in the Global Innovation Index of WIPO, and stood at the 11th position in 2022 (NDRC, 2022; State Council, 2022; WIPO, 2021, 2022). As far as patents in these technologies are concerned, different patent analysis reports conclude that there has been a sharp increase in the number of patent filings from applicants based in China and the patent granted thereof. In these technology areas, China had a negligible presence a few decades ago.

Augmenting indigenous innovation in core technology areas is a key pillar of the objective of building China into a cyber superpower, and it is quite evident that China has made its presence felt in the global technology competition, especially with the rise of emerging digital technologies. China is amongst the few countries in the world engaged in advanced research in these disciplines. As part of this endeavour, China has succeeded in strengthening its research base, improving the quality of research, and integrating research with technology development and commercialisation. China's share in both international scientific publications and the most-cited papers has gradually increased. From a negligible presence in international scientific journals and patents a few decades ago, China now leads in some of the sub-domains of emerging digital technologies. As noted in the case of 5G, and some specific applications of quantum technologies and AI, Chinese entities are leading patent applicants or holders of SEPs.

China's leading private sector entities have built substantial research capacity and set up R&D facilities at global research hubs to tap the talent, while some of the laboratories have evolved into leading research hubs not just in China but globally. China has worked towards commercial development of scientific outcomes with an active involvement of the private sector, as evident from the increasing number of spin-outs from prominent laboratories. This also indicates a deeper interaction between academic and research institutions and the industry, who have also joined hands for the development of technology standards. The continuous improvement in China's rankings on global innovation metrics over the last decade or so is a testament to its advancing innovation ecosystem.

The chapter also noted certain gaps in the quality of research and patents, access to skilled workforce and global talent, industrial R&D, foundational technologies such as integrated circuits, and collaboration on open-source platforms that remain to be bridged. China's endeavour to secure the so-called "commanding heights" in technology competition has its own weaknesses. Despite all the efforts, the number of active IPv6 users in China trails significantly behind other countries. China's proposal for New IP at the ITU faced resistance, especially from the IETF and RIPE NCC on the grounds of a change in the traditional "bottom-up" approach to decision-making and taking away the process from IETF to ITU. Even with 5G, Chinese telecommunication equipment manufacturers face restrictions in many countries on security grounds or on account of trust deficit, which potentially dampens their prospects in the international market.

Though the quality of research in China has shown improvement, certain challenges persist. For example, in the case of AI, China is yet to catch up with the US in terms of the impact of research publications. China's own think-tanks have highlighted weaknesses in the core technologies of AI such as hardware and algorithm development, and found the domestic technology giants lagging their American counterparts in research papers publications, patents, and attracting talent. China's weakness in semiconductors is also a major impediment to the development of indigenous technology. Many assessment reports have flagged the shortage of talent China faces in some of these advanced technology areas such as AI as detrimental to its aim to be a global technology leader.

Augmenting indigenous innovation in core technology areas translates into technology leadership and dominance, which is largely seen by the political leadership in the context of China's rising status in the international system. Besides making economic gains, China aspires to leverage its advancements in emerging digital technologies to shape the rules, standards, and architectures for the future of technology or to pursue alternative approaches, and this is possible only when it has a dominant position in the respective technology areas. Another key driver of this quest for dominance in technology space is the competition in the military domain. With the US establishing a cyber command in 2010, which created reverberations in China as well, militaries became an integral part of how the cyber power of a state is constituted and projected. The next chapter examines PLA's perspective on cyber power and its efforts concentrated on building cyber military capabilities as part of the preparedness for conflicts of the future.

## Notes

1 Its full name is Zhongxin Technology Corporation, and it was founded as Zhongxing Semiconductor Co. Ltd in 1985 by the Ministry of Aerospace Industry as a state-owned enterprise. Later, in 1993, it was registered under the current name Zhongxin Technology Corporation (ZTE) as a "state-owned and private-run" enterprise.

2 TD-SCDMA is derived from SCDMA, an indigenous wireless access technology developed by Beijing Xinwei Telecom Technology Inc (a joint venture of China Academy of Telecom Technology and Cwill) in the mid-1990s.

3 The use cases include holographic type communications; tactile internet for remote operations; intelligent operation network; network and computing convergence; digital twin; space–terrestrial integrated network; industrial IoT; huge scientific data applications; application-aware data burst forwarding; emergency and disaster rescue; socialised IoT; and connectivity and sharing of pervasively distributed AI data, models, and knowledge.

4 Media reports from Novemver 2023 suggest that Alibaba's quantum laboratory has closed down.

5 Big data intelligence, autonomous coordination and control, optimised decision-making, advanced machine learning, quantum intelligent computing, etc.

6 Such as neurology, cognitive science, psychology, mathematics, economics, sociology, etc.

7 Knowledge-computing engines, autonomous systems, intelligent computing chips and systems, natural language processing technology, etc.

8 Software and hardware, robotics, self-driving vehicles, virtual and augmented reality, IoT devices, etc.

9 Surgical robots, diagnosis and treatment assistants, and physiological monitoring systems.

10 Core business includes *infrastructure* (smart chips, smart sensors, distributed computing frameworks), *information and data* (data acquisition, dataset analysis, data analysis processing), *technical services* (technology platforms, algorithmic models, integrated solutions), and *products* (intelligent speech processing, computer vision, intelligent voice, biometric feature recognition).

11 Associated business includes software product development, information technology consulting, electronic information materials, information system integration, internet information services, integrated circuit design, electronic computers, and electronic components.

12 Derived business forms include smart manufacturing, smart home, smart finance, smart education, smart transportation, smart security, smart medicine, and smart logistics.

13 Terminology, reference architecture, data, testing, and assessment.

14 Big data, cloud computing, edge computing, smart chips.

15 Machine learning, natural language processing, computer vision, biometric feature recognition.

16 Intelligent robots, intelligent delivery systems, smart terminals, and intelligent services.

17 Smart manufacturing, smart cities, smart transportation, smart health care, smart logistics, smart home, and smart finance fields.

18 Led by the National Information Technology Standardization Technical Committee (through AI and other technical subcommittees), the China National Technical Committee for Automation Systems and Integration Standardization, the National Audio, Video and Multimedia Standardization Technical Committee, the National Information Security Standardization Technical Committee, and the National Technical Committee on Intelligent Transport Systems.

19 The ratio of the total citations actually received by the denominator's output and the total citations that would be expected based on the average of the subject field.

# 6

# CHINA'S CYBER FORCE

## Preparing the PLA for "informatized war"

In recent years, China has embarked on ambitious reforms across nearly every function of the armed forces and the defence industry to build the People's Liberation Army (PLA) into a "world-class military" by "mid-century." The vision is to build a force capable of winning "informatized" wars, or in other words, a formidable force in the face of future conflicts. Since the early 1990s, China has demonstrated ample interest in the idea of information warfare, triggered by the American demonstration of its true extent during the Persian Gulf War. The chapter traces the origins and the subsequent evolution of information and cyber war in the Chinese military thinking, doctrine, and strategy.

Against the backdrop of reforms that seek to consolidate PLA's cyber force and build combat capabilities in the information and cyber domains, the chapter discusses different aspects of the Strategic Support Force and the relevant combat capabilities that generate asymmetric advantages. Synergising the strengths and resources of the civilian and the military sectors is all the more important in the case of cyber and emerging digital technologies. The chapter looks at China's strategy for military–civil fusion and its relevance to China's cyber force in terms of augmenting its capabilities or meeting its requirements of technical education and specialised training.

### Information and cyber warfare in the Chinese military thinking, doctrine, and strategy

The term "cyber" as such did not find much mention in the authoritative writings and doctrinal documents of the PLA until about 2010. The terms "informationization" or "informatization" rather found a widespread usage.

DOI: 10.4324/9781003473510-6

Much of the discourse on this subject within the PLA has been shaped under the aegis of "information warfare," which evolved out of the longstanding tradition in China's military thinking to closely follow the warfare practices of the US. As Feigenbaum noted, after the Korean Armistice Agreement in 1953, PLA began imparting lessons on modern, mechanised, and technologically oriented warfare gained from its encounter with the American technology in Korea (Feigenbaum, 2003: 18). Military thinkers and PLA officers examined publications and doctrine on information warfare of the US military for over a decade, but information warfare drew considerable attention in the PLA once the US demonstrated the true extent of information operations during the first Persian Gulf War in 1991.

The War actually triggered serious discussions in the PLA on the emerging nature of warfare, and it was assessed that the Persian Gulf War had altered the conduct of warfare. Consequently, in 1993 – two years after the first Persian Gulf War – the military strategic guidelines of the Central Military Commission (CMC) of the CPC directed the PLA to place the basis of preparations for military struggle on "winning local wars under modern especially high-technology conditions" (Burke et al., 2020; State Council, 2015b). As the highest level of national guidance and direction by the CMC to PLA, the military strategic guidelines serve as the basis for China's national military strategy and entail the general operational principles for the PLA essentially outlining China's plan to fight future wars. A change in the military strategic guidelines indicates a significant shift in China's threat perception or security environment, the strategic direction, or the characteristics of wars that the PLA will need to fight in the future. Between 1949 and 1993, there were four instances of change in the military strategic guidelines (Finkelstein, 2007).

Triggered by the impact of information warfare as demonstrated by the US military, the doctrinal change in 1993 sought to alter PLA's long-term preparedness, resource utilisation, and the development of its capabilities to fight and win wars. The change in military strategic guidelines was an outcome of the assessment that the PLA would need to fight its next war in China's geographical proximity or periphery with modern military hardware such as precision-guided weapons, and command, control, communications, computers, intelligence, surveillance, and reconnaissance (C⁴ISR) systems for enhanced situational awareness in all the physical domains of warfare. Building the PLA into an agile, technology-oriented modern armed force commensurate with China's rising international standing also required modernisation of the military science and technology infrastructure and defence manufacturing industry.

Following the change in military strategic guidelines, literature from the PLA began stressing on the critical role of information warfare in winning future wars. Though the first Persian Gulf War is largely known to have aggregated China's military thinking on information warfare, but deliberations on the concept and theory of information warfare in PLA writings actually predate this war. Shen Weiguang began researching and publishing on the strategic dimension of information warfare in 1985, and published a monograph titled *Information Warfare* in 1990. The monograph discussed the genesis of information warfare and the changes it could bring in the domains of military, politics, economics, science and technology, and international relations (W. Shen, 1995). Information warfare was described as command-and-control warfare or decision-control warfare where information is used as a weapon to target and disrupt the cognitive and information systems of the adversary, with the wider objective of changing the determination of policymakers. Such warfare encompasses psychological warfare, deterrence warfare, and political propaganda warfare, and it affects structural change for the armed forces from "material" to "information" and the development of "military soft science" (*PLA Daily*, 1996; W. Shen, 1995).

The contribution of Wang Pufeng, former Director of the Strategy Department of the Academy of Military Science, to the thinking on information warfare in PLA is highly regarded. Asserting that information warfare will control the form and future of war, Wang Pufeng beheld it as a force driving the modernisation of PLA and the catalyst of transition of PLA's weapons and equipment from the industrial age towards information technology, information weapons, and information networks (P. Wang, 1995). He considered information warfare a product of the information age which utilises information technology and information weapons on the battlefield spread over the tangible space on the ground, on the sea, in the air, and also in the intangible space of electromagnetic spectrum (J. C. Mulvenon and Yang, 1999). With control of information being the key to victory in information warfare, Wang believed the information weapons PLA should draw attention to are precision-guided weapons, air defence, electronic warfare weapons, and C$^4$I systems, which form the nervous system of the armed forces (P. Wang, 1995).

As the concept of information warfare gained traction, many articles from the PLA began discussing its characteristics, future trends, and the measures PLA needs to take. Some of the articles drew contrasts with the US's approach to information warfare, calling its conception of battlefield information warfare involving information protection and information attack a narrow sense of information warfare, and arguing that once warfare is dominated by information then only it could be termed as information warfare (B. Wang & Li, 1995). Future wars were seen to be a "contention for" and "confrontation of" information as information was perceived not just as a weapon of combat but also the object sought after by the belligerents (J. Wei, 1996). Some writings broadened the concept and characterised the aspects of psychological war, strategy war, culture war, and cyber war as part of information warfare (M. Chang, 1995; E. Su, 1996).

To ensure victory, PLA writings underscored the importance of "informationized military" or "information units" which embody combat theory, systems, qualified personnel, and weaponry congruent with the needs of information warfare (L. Liu, 1995; B. Wang & Li, 1995). Some articles distinguished key information systems or strategic information hubs of the adversary as the primary targets of offensive action, anticipating a widespread use of information technology to computerise weaponry, automate command and control, and digitise combat forces and battlefield (Niu et al., 1995; F. Peng, 1996). The ability of a state with weak information technology capability to cripple the information systems of technologically superior state and reduce its war-fighting capabilities was seen as a deterrent which could even limit the outbreak of a war (M. Chang, 1995). In terms of PLA's preparedness in the face of unfolding changes, some of the writers argued for augmenting research looking at the theory of information warfare and its applications and the ways and means to paralyse computer systems of the adversary in the event of a future regional war, at the same time drawing attention towards computer and information security of own systems to prevent security breaches and information leaks (Han, 1995; Zhai, 1995; D. Zhou, 1996).

Lieutenant General Huai Guomo, the then Vice Minister of the Commission for Science, Technology and Industry for National Defense, contended that thorough integration of the three factors – advanced weapon systems, pioneering military theory, and the corresponding force establishment – is fundamental to military revolution, indicating that policymakers and military specialists would need to conscientiously explore and study a new combat theory (Huai, 1996). This observation was against the backdrop of the changes brought in by military technology to the military theory and force establishment, pointing towards information warfare.

Towards the end of the decade of the 1990s, the general understanding of information warfare in China's military thinking encompassed battle in the political, economic, cultural, scientific, social, and technological spheres. A culmination of this thought process was the book *Unrestricted Warfare*, published in 1999. Authored by two senior colonels from PLA Air Force, it remains one of the most cited books from China on information and cyber warfare. As is the case with most of the PLA assessments of information warfare, the book also used the Persian Gulf War as the background. It described information technology-enabled real-time coordination between numerous weapons dispersed over vast geographical areas as unprecedented. The book took a special note of the integrated air campaign which blended all the combat operations during the war, be it reconnaissance, early-warning, bombings, communications, or command and control, and also the contest to dominate outer space and cyberspace (L. Qiao & Wang, 1999: 68).

The authors described "unrestricted warfare" as the warfare transcending all boundaries and limits, the war that keeps all the means in a state of readiness, makes the battlefield omnipresent, and dissolves all the boundaries between war and non-war and military and non-military. Unrestricted warfare goes beyond limits, and the practitioners of such warfare must break out of the confines of domains (L. Qiao & Wang, 1999: 12). The authors argued that the opening up of new domains of information warfare, financial warfare, trade warfare, and others breaks warfare from the confines of military sphere and the outcomes are largely governed by political, economic, diplomatic, cultural, technological, and other non-military factors (L. Qiao & Wang, 1999: 182–190). Unrestricted warfare essentially indicates towards the continuous expansion of the battlefield – from the traditional domains of land, sea, and air to cyberspace, cognitive space, and all the key functions of the state.

China's premier defence institute, the Academy of Military Science published the second edition of *Science of Military Strategy* in 2001 (the first was in 1987) which carried a dedicated section discussing the rise of high-tech local war, its features, characteristics of such a war that China may face, and strategic guidance for the PLA on it (G. Peng & Yao, 2005). An authoritative publication coming out of the PLA, *Science of Military Strategy*, details the strategic approach of PLA to address the threats and challenges in the coming years and its preparation for future conflicts.

Analysing the local wars fought after the end of the Cold War, *Science of Military Strategy* found them spread over a limited geographical area (a country or a region) and their size and intensity to be low, and it also noted the profound impact of high and new technology on military operations and the transformation from mechanised warfare towards information warfare (G. Peng & Yao, 2005: 400–401). Echoing the observation Qiao and Wang had made in *Unrestricted Warfare* on the extent of information warfare, *Science of Military Strategy* also found the space of such a war to be endlessly expanded with no clear division or distinction between the front and the rear and military and non-military targets as it brought in all the aspects of statecraft within the range of strike, even predicting a "new pattern of comprehensive cyberized war" (G. Peng & Yao, 2005: 406).

The *Science of Military Strategy* also adapted active defence – the mainstay of China's military strategy and PLA's strategic guidance – to the conditions of the high-tech local war as an operational necessity to engage with a technologically superior armed force. Active defence entails dominating the enemy by striking first once the adversary has jeopardised China's national interest. The *Science of Military Strategy* described the *modus operandi* to fight wars in modern high-tech conditions to attack and destroy the nodes of the information network or the critical points supporting the operational system of the adversary. This is the same argument Wang Baocun, Li Fei, and Shen Weiguang had made. It also mentioned exerting political, public opinion, and psychological pressure on the enemy so as to break its will to fight. On the aspect of strategy and the art of war, the *Science of Military Strategy* asserted that technology and new weapons alone do not necessarily decide the outcome of war.

At the turn of the 21st century, two common elements emerged – the PLA recognised the multidimensional nature of information warfare, and owing to PLA's inferiority in terms of technology it resorted to people's war as one of the guiding principles. Given the strategic relevance of information historically and its all-pervasive nature, the PLA viewed warfare in this domain to encompass the aspects of politics, public opinion, psychology, economy, diplomacy, culture, and technology spread over military as well as civilian realms. Under the conditions of war, the prime objective identified for PLA was to ensure disruption, or destruction, of the C⁴ISR systems or the hubs of decision-making to render the adversary blind or prevent the forces and the commanders from communicating.

Major General Dai Qingmin, who headed the former Fourth Department of the PLA General Staff Department, made a major contribution to China's military thinking on information warfare and the development of corresponding doctrine of the PLA. In a series of articles between 2000 and 2003, he emphasised on formulating an effective information warfare combat capability to gain strategic advantage, developing "informationized" arms and equipment, and integrating the use of both military and civilian forces in the information domain for future operations (J. Mulvenon, 2009; Thomas, 2004). Analysing the effectiveness of US operations during the Kosovo War in 1999 to force Yugoslavia to surrender, Dai Qingmin argued that the success or failure in the case of informationised war was "not to be determined by the ratio of casualties or in terms of territorial gains, but rather in forcing the adversary to submit to one's will" (Dai, 2004, cited in Thomas, 2007). In his view, information operations entail targeting the information infrastructure of the enemy with the purpose of destruction and control, and launching network-electronic attacks on select enemy targets (Wortzel, 2014).

The concept of "integrated network and electronic warfare," introduced by Dai Qingmin in 2000 and later elaborated in 2002, refers to the integrated use of electronic and network warfare measures as part of information operations to disrupt enemy's battlefield information systems while defending own systems. Derived from the increasing use of information technology in weapons systems and the proliferation of information systems, the concept advocates the coordinated use of electronic and network warfare as forms of information warfare rather than being seen as mutually independent (Thomas, 2005, 2007). The 2002 Defense White Paper of the State Council reflected on this concept and informed that the PLA departments are exploring the features and aspects of integrated network and electronic warfare. Taking note of the widespread utilisation of information technology and its extensive applications in the military domain, the white paper articulated that this phenomenon has "stretched the battlefield into multidimensional space which includes the land, sea, air, outer space, and electron" and the form of war is now increasingly becoming information-oriented (State Council, 2002).

In 2004, a year after the Iraq War, the military strategic guidelines of the CMC to PLA further substantiated the basis of preparations for military struggle from "winning local wars that might occur under modern especially high-technology conditions" to "winning local wars under conditions of informationization" (State Council, 2015b). This doctrinal change was not a radical shift from the previous iteration of 1993, but rather sought to adapt to the demands of increasing informationisation in armed forces and respond to the threats from a technologically superior adversary. The 2004 Defense White Paper had an unprecedented focus on informationisation, mainly in light of this change. The white paper recognised informationisation as a key factor in enhancing the warfighting capability of China's armed forces and pressed on the urgent need for PLA to undertake this transition as part of its modernisation process (State Council, 2004).

The first time "cyber" found a mention in China's defence white papers was in 2010. The 2010 Defense White Paper noted that some of the states have worked out warfare strategies for outer space, cyberspace, and the polar regions, and simultaneously developed the technical means to execute global strikes, deployed missile defence systems, and enhanced their capabilities to carry out cyber operations in a bid to occupy "commanding heights" in the respective domains (State Council, 2011). The white paper essentially extended the scope of China's national defence to the domains of space and cyberspace. Following this, the 2013 edition of the *Science of Military Strategy* of the Academy of Military Science emphasised heavily on the emergence of space and cyberspace as the domains of warfare. Cognisant of the possibilities of threat of war in space and cyberspace, it underscored the importance of achieving superiority in these domains to dominate the adversary and secure victory (Academy of Military Science, 2013).[1]

The book further propounded the integration of weapons, equipment and combat methods, and operations across all the domains of warfare attaching great importance to space and cyberspace. It also recognised local war under "informationization" conditions as a "system of systems vs. system of systems" warfare where the prime target of information operations is the vital networked warfighting system of the adversary. The book notes that network systems serve as the nerve centres of modern armed forces and their functions across different domains, and integrate their operational strengths, and this characteristic basically transforms the present state of war into "informationized" war. It pressed on the need for the PLA to practice "active defense" in the information domain, enhance its defence capabilities, and accelerate the raising of units that specialise in executing information warfare missions. The *Science of Military Strategy* also noticed the raising of professional cyber forces in other parts of the world, as the US Department of Defense by then had established a cyber command.

Thereafter, the 2015 Defense White Paper unveiled China's military strategy. With the aim of implementing the long-standing strategic guideline of "active defense" in the new situation, the CMC marked further adjustment in the basic point for preparations for the military struggle of the PLA from "winning local wars under conditions of informationization" to "winning informationized local wars" (State Council, 2015b). This doctrinal change enshrines the centrality of information in the conduct of warfighting and winning, rather than merely being a condition to strive for. It was again not a major change from the previous iterations of 1993 and 2004, but laid emphasis on information dominance, precision strikes, and joint operations to prevail in "system-vs-system" operations.

The military strategy discussed how cyberspace has emerged as a key pillar of economic and social development, and simultaneously as a new domain of national security. It noted the intense international strategic competition in cyberspace as states have started developing cyber military forces. With regard to the growing importance of cyberspace generally in military security calculus, the strategy informed objectives such as developing a cyber force and corresponding cyber capabilities for situational awareness in cyberspace, building cyber defence, and supporting national endeavours so as to be prepared for any cyber contingencies or crises and maintain national security and social stability (State Council, 2015b).

With the goal of developing strategic capabilities in this new domain of warfare, the PLA Strategic Support Force (PLASSF) came into being in the 2015 end. General Gao Jin, the then dean of the Academy of Military Science – who later became the inaugural commander of the PLASSF – had been quite articulate about the need for integrated joint operations of land, sea, air, space, cyber, and electromagnetic domains, noting the qualitative change in the form of warfare from mechanisation to informatisation (*PLA Daily*, 2015). He maintained that the control of information has now become important to the control of battlefield, and the mechanism of winning wars has profoundly changed (J. Gao, 2015).

Such a strong emphasis laid on cyberspace in the military realm around that time should also be seen in the context of the changes that China's cyber affairs had witnessed in the civilian domain. By early 2014, Xi Jinping had taken over the lead of the national cybersecurity initiatives under the former Central Leading Group for Cybersecurity and Informatization, representing a greater centralisation of authority over cyber affairs, and at the launch of the Leading Group, he had called upon for collective efforts to build China into a cyber superpower. From about 2010 till the release of the military strategy in 2015, events such as the Stuxnet malware, then the Arab Spring followed by the Snowden revelations have had a profound impact on Chinese thinking on the threats emanating from cyberspace.

A series of policy measures implemented in the civilian domain recognised the growing role of armed forces in cyberspace. The revised outline of the *State Informatization Development Strategy* in 2016 mentioned the development of military informatisation theories, the integrated use of information systems, adapting to the evolving nature of warfare, and the transformation of military training based on the information-enabled battlefield. China's *National Cyberspace Security Strategy* criticised cyber deterrence for aggravating an arms race in cyberspace and posing challenges to global peace, but it endorsed the use of military measures, along with others, in the defence of sovereignty in cyberspace. China's *International Strategy of Cooperation on Cyberspace* also deemed deterrence in cyberspace to be detrimental to international security, but simultaneously proclaimed that armed forces have a key role to play in protecting China's sovereignty and other interests in cyberspace. The strategy mentioned enhanced defence capability in cyberspace as an important segment of China's defence modernisation exercise, in line with the strategic guideline of "active defense," and it also spoke of building a cyber force to meet those objectives. The key policy or strategy documents in the civilian space have explicitly supported the use of military for securing China's interests in cyberspace.

The 2019 Defense White Paper identified safeguarding China's security interests in outer space, electromagnetic space, and cyberspace as one of the fundamental goals of China's national defence in the new era. The White Paper perceived cybersecurity as a severe threat to China's national security, and to thwart cyber threats it promulgated accelerating enhancement of cyber capabilities of the armed forces, development of cybersecurity, building of cyber defence capabilities consistent with China's international standing and status as a major cyber power, and maintaining China's cyber sovereignty (State Council, 2019).

The National Defense University released a revised version of the *Science of Military Strategy* in 2020 (earlier published in 1999 and 2015, the revised versions of the 2015 edition were later released in 2017 and 2020) discussing in detail military conflict in cyberspace, cyber warfare, and the requirements of cyber capability and cyber force development for building cyber power (National Defense University, 2020).[2] The book recognises cyber power as a key element of military power and the shift in the role of cyber forces from auxiliary to key warfare forces, and it lays down reconnaissance, cyber-attack, and cyber defence as the requirements of cyber combat capability. For the development of cyber power, the book presses on the need for building an integrated command and mobilisation system for cyber combat capability, comprehensive combat training regime and exercises for cyber force, and raising a professional cyber force composed of military commanders and personnel and civilians specialising in cyber warfare and network security.

Keeping an eye on the emergence of new domains of warfare and the unfolding military competition, China has correspondingly developed new doctrinal principles and modified the basis of preparations for military struggle from time to time, redefining the general operational principles for the PLA and reorienting the force formation to fight future wars. China's emphasis now is on building a technology-intensive, lean, and agile armed force capable of operating as a unified force across all the domains of warfare, with space and cyberspace being the new additions. To that end, the reforms in the force structure and administration initiated in the 2015 end envision PLA as a technology-oriented agile armed force capable of conducting full-spectrum operations, cutting-across different services and arms, and dominating all the domains of warfare. The reforms also sought to consolidate PLA's cyber force and build combat capabilities to engage a superior adversary in the information and cyber domains.

## The PLA Strategic Support Force

The structural changes Xi Jinping initiated in cyber affairs and informatisation in the civilian domain after assuming the office as the President of the People's Republic of China were discussed at length in the third chapter. With Xi Jinping as Chairman of the CMC, similar eagerness was visible in the military realm to leverage the new domains in PLA's preparation for future military conflicts. In 2014, he had called on the PLA to create a new strategy for "information warfare," which would require establishing "a new military doctrine, institutions, equipment systems, strategies and tactics and management modes" (*China Daily*, 2014b). China's military strategy had also made the intent to develop a cyber force quite explicit, and informed that integrated combat forces will be employed to "prevail in system-vs-system operations" which feature information dominance, precision strikes, and joint operations (State Council, 2015b).

In spite of several modernisation efforts, the basic structure of the PLA had remained intact since the times of Mao Zedong and Deng Xiaoping, and it was felt that this structure is falling short in the face of modern warfare which is turning "informationized" and warrants joint combat capability extending to the new domains of space and cyberspace. Beginning 31 December 2015, Xi Jinping unveiled a series of wide-ranging military and national defence reforms, designed to transform the PLA from a regional defence-oriented force to a modern combat force capable of conducting a full spectrum of operations – dismantling the long-established system of general departments, military area commands, and the dominance of the army (Ministry of National Defense, 2016).

The reforms established five joint theatre commands, a new Joint Staff Department, and reorganised the four General Departments of the PLA – General Staff Department, General Political Department, General Logistics Department, and General Armaments Department – into 15 organs under the centralised leadership of the CMC. The reforms redefined the relationships between and among the arms of the PLA and the CMC. The seven military area commands (Shenyang, Beijing, Lanzhou, Jinan, Nanjing, Guangzhou, and Chengdu) were reorganised into five joint theatre commands – Eastern Theater Command, Southern Theater Command, Western Theater Command, Northern Theater Command, and Central Theater Command. The structural reforms created a separate PLA Army headquarters, elevated the PLA Second Artillery Force to a full-service PLA Rocket Force, and established the PLA Joint Logistic Support Force and the PLA Strategic Support Force (PLASSF), which combined strategic support forces across the services and CMC organs (State Council, 2019).

One of the main tasks of the reforms was to put in place an integrated joint operations command system with the overarching objective of improving the ability of the PLA to conduct joint operations across multiple domains (Xinhua, 2016a). To that end, the raising of PLASSF as a special force for space and cyber operations was meant to integrate the capacities to protect China's interests spread across the domains of space, cyberspace, and electromagnetic spectrum, and take full advantage of cross-domain synergy among these frontiers. The PLASSF essentially consolidated China's space, electronic, cyber, and information warfare capabilities under a single bureaucratic umbrella or a centralised command, which were earlier dispersed across the former four General Departments (Ni & Gill, 2019).

Under the new structure, the Space Systems Department is responsible for the space operations of the PLASSF, while the Network Systems Department unifies signals intelligence, cyber espionage, electromagnetic warfare, and psychological operations. The PLASSF inherited much of the PLA's electronic and information warfare capabilities, such as the Third Department (3PLA) and Fourth Department (4PLA) of the General Staff Department. It is mainly built around the Third Department, which was responsible for signals intelligence collection and analysis, technical reconnaissance, network operations, espionage (through 12 operational bureaus), and three research institutes,[3] and specialised in cryptography and code-breaking (D. Cheng, 2016).

The Fourth Department had the responsibility for military electronic intelligence and electronic warfare, and it managed the major research institutes involved in the R&D of new electronic countermeasure systems. Some of the technical reconnaissance bureaus from PLA's service and former military regions also came under the aegis of the PLASSF and the psychological operations earlier executed under the General Political Department were also brought into the fold of the PLASSF (Costello & Mcreynolds, 2018). Such a comprehensive consolidation of the full spectrum of war-fighting capacities and capabilities in the domains of space, cyberspace, and electromagnetic spectrum earlier spread all over the PLA departments and services signifies the shift in China's approach to regard them as full-fledged war-fighting domains in their own right, and not merely as the functions supporting warfighting in other domains. Since its establishment, the political and military leadership and PLA analysts have commended PLASSF as one of its kind in the world – a PLA officer even hailed it as the "most decisive and forward-looking high-end force" among the modern militaries (*PLA Daily*, 2016b).

Soon after unveiling the reforms, Xi Jinping had called PLASSF "a new type of combat force to maintain national security" (Ministry of National Defense, 2016). General Gao Jin, the inaugural commander of the PLASSF, stated that one of the prime tasks of the PLASSF would be to seize the commanding heights of future military competition and secure the new frontiers of national security (*People's Daily*, 2016). Major General Hao Yeli, former deputy director of the Fourth Department, called PLASSF "a sword of deterrence and a shield of national defense," noting that it is necessary to integrate PLA's cyber combat power with the national security strategy (Y. Hao, 2016).

The PLASSF is supposed to provide the much desired "information umbrella" to PLA's joint forces as it is integrated with the operations of the army, navy, air force, and rocket force. The role of PLASSF extends throughout the lifecycle of a military operation – right from reconnaissance, target detection and early warning to the transmission, processing, and dissemination of information, and then later to battle damage assessment or even second strike if required (CCTV, 2016). The 2019 Defense White Paper characterised PLASSF as a "new type of combat force tasked with the safeguarding of China's national security and a key driver of the development of new combat capabilities of PLA" (State Council, 2019). The PLASSF is projected as a key enabler of the objective of building PLA into a "world-class military" by the mid-century.

The placing of Space Systems Department and Network Systems Department under PLASSF reflects the recognition of the synergy among the capabilities under these two domains which are regarded as new "commanding heights" in strategic competition, and it is supposed to help the PLA achieve information dominance in its future combat operations. More specifically, the concentration of cyber, electronic, and psychological warfighting capabilities under the new organisational settings to generate the desired effects is evidence of PLA's integrated approach to information operations. This is in line with the concept of integrated network and electronic warfare from the early 2000s which advocated combining network and electronic attacks in future information operations rather than considering them as standalone efforts.

The *Science of Military Strategy* also calls for the use of space, cyber, and electronic warfare means in cohesion as strategic weapons. Strategic cyber operations of PLASSF are therefore supposed to target the politics, economy, science and technology, culture, and foreign affairs of the adversary (J. Chen et al., 2021). The new structure for the execution of PLA's information operations aims to fully operationalise the strategic concepts for information warfare which the authoritative publications from the PLA have for long contemplated on, but could not be achieved due to the separation of capabilities between the former Third Department and the Fourth Department.

The key functions of PLASSF, as described in the 2019 Defense White Paper, include supporting the forces on the battlefield, providing information, communications, and information security, and testing of new technology (State Council, 2019). The primary missions of PLASSF could be categorised as – strategic information support to other PLA services in the form of communications, positioning and navigation, and intelligence, surveillance, and reconnaissance; protection of PLA's own information infrastructure; and to engage in information operations leveraging synergies across space, cyber, electromagnetic, and psychological domains. The PLASSF is slated to be the key enabler to realise the principles of PLA's doctrinal approach to information operations, the instrument for PLA's engagement in "informationized" wars, and the cornerstone of China's power projection in the space and cyber domains.

One of the main features that finds frequent mention in the context of organisational reforms and the description of PLASSF is to improve PLA's ability to conduct joint operations. This is one of the key differentiators of modern armed forces as they are desired to execute joint operations cutting across the areas of responsibility of traditional services of the army, navy, and air force, spread over a wide geographical area and that too beyond the political boundaries if required.

### PLASSF and joint exercises

Modern warfare warrants not just the services and branches of the armed forces to operate together, but also the platforms and weapons deployed across different domains to work in conjunction with each other to generate the desired effects. The need for the PLA to possess the capability to execute joint operations has long been part of the modernisation drive. Joint operations have been discussed in PLA publications as early as the mid-1990s, deliberating on the need for the combat units to break their traditional service arm operating limits, adoption of tri-service structures, and execution of missions beyond the capabilities of single-service arms (Huai, 1996; B. Wang & Li, 1995; J. Wu, 1995). The 2001 edition of *Science of Military Strategy* had noted that single-service dominated operations are disappearing and the traditional division of roles and responsibilities among the army, navy, and air force is gradually blurring (G. Peng & Yao, 2005).

The PLASSF aims to fulfil a critical role in PLA, whose need and relevance have long been a subject under consideration, and after its creation, this specific aspect of joint operations has been underscored time and again. For instance, at the first inspection of PLASSF, Xi Jinping called it "an important aspect of PLA's joint operations system" (Xinhua, 2016d). Joint operations of the armed forces also featured in Xi Jinping's address at the 19th and 20th National Congress of the CPC as he mentioned developing strong and efficient joint operations command institutions for theatre commands and improving combat capabilities for joint operations.

Reports suggest that PLASSF units have trained with the other PLA services in joint exercises. The 2019 Defense White Paper informed that the PLASSF has made efforts to integrate into the joint operations system, and also carried out combat exercises (State Council, 2019). Engagement in joint exercises and trainings could serve as an indicator of the growing combat capabilities of the PLASSF; however, it must be noted that open sources do not contain much information about the composition or the design of these exercises, or even the role of PLASSF in these exercises. The PLA has had a long history of conducting exercises having information warfare overtones, which even predate the raising of PLASSF.

One of the early instances of "integrated high-technology" exercises dates to 1997–1998, and the numerous information or cyber warfare exercises reported since then denote the transition in PLA from theoretical understanding to the practice of information or cyber warfare. One of the first information warfare exercises was held in 1997 in the former Shenyang military region, followed by another one in 1998 which simulated an integrated high-technology battlefield environment and involved multiple military regions (Thomas, 2004). In 1999 and 2000, military exercises embodying the use of high technologies such as computer networks and reconnaissance, sensing, and simulation to train under the new operational concepts were reported from the former Beijing, Chengdu, and Guangzhou military regions (State Council, 2002). One of them held by the PLA General Staff Department in October 2000 even had Jiang Zemin in attendance.

As early as 2004, the PLA had established a "Blue Force" at the Zhurihe training base to train "Red Forces" in information warfare. Opposite to the usual practice, in the case of PLA the "Blue Force" acts as the adversary or the opposing force, and the "Red Force" represents PLA units (Krekel, 2009). The prominent information warfare exercises of the PLA are Leap

Forward 2009, Mission Action 2010, and Joint-2011. Leap Forward 2009 (*Kuayue – 2009*) was held in Guangzhou with division-size units participating from three different military regions. Mission Action 2010 (*Shiming Xingdong – 2010*) involved division-size units and 30,000 soldiers from the former Beijing, Chengdu, and Lanzhou military regions. Joint-2011 (*Lianhe – 2011*) focused on joint information operations such as joint strikes, joint campaign planning, and joint reconnaissance and early warning (Krekel et al., 2012; Thomas, 2004).

These exercises reportedly featured attacks on command and control systems using computer networks and included information confrontation as part of the missions, and even tested combat capability in high-tech warfare, or under the so-called "complex information environment" (*China Daily*, 2010). They also involved long-distance mobilisation and participation of different arms from aviation, communications, reconnaissance, artillery, and armoured using the integrated command information system (Raman, 2011).

The overall training apparatus of the PLA received an overhaul under Xi Jinping. The Zhurihe training base has evolved as a key joint arms training centre for the PLA. The dedicated "Blue Force" (195th mechanised infantry brigade of the former Beijing military region) established at the Zhurihe training base in 2014 became the cornerstone of the famous "Stride" exercise series, which brought significant changes in PLA's existing approach to exercises and even went on to expose shortcomings of the combat units in command, collaboration, and utilisation of new equipment in the battlefield (G. Li, 2015; Sina, 2016). Since its inception, the "Blue Force" at the Zhurihe training base has had a very high winning rate in the exercises, and it also works closely with military academies for research, joint education, and training (Sina, 2016; S. Wang, 2021; Yan & Yao, 2019). Primarily aimed at improving the combat capability of the PLA, joint exercises have raised the level of trainings in the PLA, and the theatre commands and individual services are now reported to be establishing "Blue Forces" based on the same model.

The PLASSF began participating in joint training exercises soon after its raising. One of the first ones was held in February 2016 with the PLA Rocket Force for joint combat readiness training, and the exercise simulated a communication network attack on a PLA Rocket Force unit and a counterattack (*PLA Daily*, 2016a). The PLASSF thereafter participated in the 2016 Stride exercise at the Zhurihe training base, which had participating units from all the five newly established theatre commands. The exercise simulated the anti-Taiwan independence military mission (Sina Military, 2016; Xinhua, 2016b). The PLASSF again contributed to the 2017 Stride exercise at Zhurihe, training jointly with other services to improve reconnaissance and situational awareness capabilities in an "informatized battlefield environment" (Xinhua, 2017h).

In February 2018 PLASSF exercised with the PLA Rocket Force (Y. Yang & Tian, 2018). In July, 50 units involving around 2,100 officers from the five theatre commands joined an exercise held simultaneously at the Zhurihe training base and four military institutes, testing their skills in reconnaissance, electronic communication, cybersecurity, air strikes, and other battlefield tactics (M. Chan, 2018). A PLASSF base trained with an army brigade from the Central Theater Command in October 2018 and also delivered lectures on reconnaissance and counter-reconnaissance tactics, deception, electronic countermeasures, and network attack and defence (R. Hu & Xia, 2018).

In February 2019, PLASSF was part of an offshore joint naval exercise held by Southern Theater Command in the Pacific Ocean, along with PLA Air Force and PLA Rocket Force units (Q. Zhou et al., 2019). As part of its "ingenious soldiers" military skills competition held in 2018 and 2019, the PLA conducted a cyber-simulation exercise at Heifei, called "ingenious cyber-electromagnetic soldier," which saw participation from 200 soldiers (China Military Online, 2018, 2019; US DoD, 2020). The PLASSF continued to be part of the joint exercises through 2020 and 2021, integrating the concepts of information dominance with exercise planning to prepare for future "information-based" operations (CCTV, 2021; NetEase, 2021; Pang et al., 2020; Sina, 2021).

Joint exercises, and especially the annual Stride exercise, have emerged as the preferable mechanism to build and test new combat capabilities and also to verify the outcomes of PLA reforms (NetEase, 2022). Around 200 commanders from the five theatre commands observed the 2021 edition of Stride exercise (S. Wang, 2021), indicating the traction this exercise now has within the PLA. Joint exercises also seek to overcome the capability gap of PLA commanders who generally have long experience in single-service operations but now need to be adept at commanding a diverse set of combat forces.

The military leadership for long has emphasised on more practical trainings and exercises to be better prepared for future conflicts. High-quality trainings and exercises are also regarded as the primary means to hone the combat capabilities of the PLA given its lack of combat experience (*People's Daily*, 2021). The PLA in 2018 had published an outline for establishing mechanisms to make exercises combat-oriented and inclusive of joint operations (Xinhua, 2018c). Following Xi Jinping's call for the PLA to train under "real combat conditions," in early 2021 the CMC made a decision to bring in a new system for military training so as to ensure that PLA's exercises imbibe combat-oriented training and get close to "real war" conditions (*People's Daily*, 2021; Xinhua, 2020b).

The PLA's exercises earlier were often criticised for their overly scripted and insufficiently realistic design and execution, and the failure to fully exploit their potential to improve the combat readiness of the forces (Campbell, 2021; Logan, 2017). The changes in training and exercise regimen aim to make them professional and draw learning lessons to improve the operational capabilities of the PLA to fight modern conflicts. While the specifics of these exercises are sparse and the after-action reports remain absent, the regular participation of PLASSF in these joint exercises indicates its increasing integration with other services and growing importance in PLA's preparedness for future "information-based" operations.

## Cyber and asymmetric warfare capabilities

China's growing cyber capabilities have drawn focus of the countries who perceive China as a threat. Being the prime target of the rising cyber threat from China, the US has devoted serious attention to this matter. The 2002 annual US Department of Defense (US DoD) report to the US Congress on *Military Power of China* took note of China's capability to penetrate poorly protected computer systems in the civilian and military infrastructures, and it warned of the risks to operational centres such as $C^4I$ systems, airbases, and aircraft carrier battle groups located around the periphery of China (US DoD, 2002). The subsequent annual reports of the US DoD to the US Congress underscored the rising complexity of information warfare components in PLA's military exercises, and the likelihood of pre-emptive use of information operations capabilities by the PLA to blind or disrupt the information and $C^4I$ systems of the adversary (US DoD, 2003, 2004, 2006). But the reports assessed this capability to be limited given that PLA's systems were older and China lacked domestic production of such systems.

By 2010, as China's cyber activities picked to pace the annual US DoD reports to the US Congress began emphasising the risks from China's cyber warfare capabilities, which were mostly cyber intrusions targeting the US Government institutions having strategic or military utility. The reports could not ascertain whether the known instances of cyber-attacks on the US were conducted by the PLA or any other government-related entity, but they found the capabilities consistent with the authoritative writings from the PLA (US DoD, 2010). The reports observed cyber warfare capabilities to be helping China in information collection for intelligence purposes through cyber intrusions and a useful tool to constrain an adversary by disrupting its networked operations (such as logistics and communications), and also to serve as a force multiplier coupled with kinetic attacks (US DoD, 2011, 2013, 2015, 2018).

The 2019 annual report of the US DoD to the US Congress noted PLA's improving proficiency to act as a joint combat force capable of conducting the full-range of land, air, maritime, space, electronic warfare, and cyber operations in near and distant battlefields (US DoD, 2019). The subsequent reports in 2020, 2021, and 2022 assessed that China's cyber capabilities pose significant and persistent cyber espionage and attack threat to the US military and critical infrastructure as China could seek to generate disruptive and destructive effects leveraging its amassed cyber capabilities to aid data collection for intelligence, target civilian and defence critical infrastructure, and use them as force-multiplier during an armed conflict (US DoD, 2020, 2021, 2022). It is interesting to note that China's cyber capabilities assessed as "rudimentary" in the 2000 report were denoted as a significant threat to the US after two decades.

Taiwan has long been a prime target of China's cyber operations, deployed along with military, economic, and diplomatic measures in support of CPC's principal objective of Taiwan's reunification with mainland China. In fact, some of the PLA's exercises simulate a cross-strait war. Taiwan now perceives China's growing cyber military capabilities as a threat to its national security. The quadrennial defence reviews of the Taiwanese Ministry of National Defense over the years have noted that the PLA is likely to employ cyber and information operations to disrupt Taiwan's critical political, economic, military infrastructures and information systems, and interfere with the surveillance, reconnaissance, and command and control systems, or cripple the counter strike capabilities of the armed forces (MND, 2009, 2017b, 2021b). As early as the mid-2000s, Taiwan's National Defense Reports began airing concerns over PLA's likely use of "hackers, computer viruses, and information time bombs" to paralyse tactical and strategic command and control and surveillance systems of Taiwanese armed forces in a conflict situation (MND, 2006, 2008).

The National Defense Reports from the mid-2010s highlighted the increasing use of social engineering and malware to intrude into the networks of Taiwanese Government and private enterprises, and assessed that China's cyber forces now possess the capabilities to target command and control and surveillance systems of Taiwanese armed forces (MND, 2013, 2015, 2017a). The impact of China's disinformation campaigns and interference in Taiwan's electoral processes on the Taiwanese society featured in the 2019 National Defense Report (MND, 2019). Various other reports confirm China's interference in Taiwan's elections, earlier in 2018 local elections and then the 2020 Presidential elections (Kurlantzick, 2019; McKenzie et al., 2019; O'Connor et al., 2020; V-Dem Institute, 2019). The 2021 National Defense Report, in addition to China's peacetime and wartime cyber activities, threw light on its use of cognitive warfare, military intimidation, and psychological tactics in support of China's geopolitical objectives (MND, 2021a). The use of media and social media to mould public opinion in conjunction with political and military measures stands in line with China's long-standing interpretation of information operations.

China's use of information or cyber campaigns against the activists and supporters of Tibetan and Uyghur separatist movements and the Southeast Asian countries having overlapping maritime territorial claims in the South China Sea are also well reported. The issues such as the longstanding demand for Taiwan's independence, the aggravating Uyghur and Tibetan separatist movements, and the maritime territorial disputes in the East and South China Seas have repeatedly been highlighted as serious threats to China's sovereignty and territorial integrity in the Defense White Papers, along with the military presence of the US and its involvement in the security affairs of Asia-Pacific, especially the arms support to Taiwan (State Council, 1998, 2004, 2009, 2013).

The Tibetan Government-in-Exile and Tibetan and Uyghur dissidents in exile or those living in other countries have been subject to China's incessant cyber espionage and disruption operations since the early 2000s (Horenbeeck, 2008; Nairne, 2002). There is a long history and strong evidence in the form of technical analysis of malware being delivered through spear-phishing and watering hole attacks targeting Windows, Mac, iOS, and Android platforms to steal files on the devices and gather information related to the contacts and communications of the targeted individuals (Beer, 2019; Blasco, 2012; Falcone and Miller-Osborn, 2016; Lookout, 2020; Marczak et al., 2019; Raiu, 2012).

Additionally, the instances of sophisticated cyber operations attributed to China, and the PLA in specific, targeting prominent government agencies, military, private sector entities, and critical infrastructure across different countries could serve as an indicator of its growing cyber capabilities. Some of these cyber operations date back to the early 2010s and are attributed to the units within PLA (Council on Foreign Relations, 2010). The PLA also came into the limelight following the 2013 Mandiant report on an advanced threat actor group engaged in cyber espionage attributed to 3PLA (Mandiant, 2013). Different reports have attributed other advanced threat actor groups to the PLA (Leonard, 2022; Mandiant, 2014; MITRE, n.d.), not to mention China's increasing use of cyber coercive measures against countries embroiled in territorial disputes with it – targeting their critical infrastructure such as telecommunications and electricity grids as well as a host of key government and private sector entities (Insikt Group, 2021a, 2021b, 2022; Tomoyuki, 2021).

Cyber or information domain gives a militarily weaker actor an asymmetric advantage (Lindsay, 2013). Weaker actors resort to surprise in order to overwhelm a stronger adversary, and cyber warfare, to that end, could be a good proposition given that modern armed forces are highly dependent on information systems for almost every function, from logistics to command and control (Goldman & Arquilla, 2014). Under the conditions of conventional asymmetry among the actors, the weaker one is more likely to use cyber means rather than conventional means to erode opponent's ability or willingness to resist, and it is mainly attributed to the perceived ease or cost-effectiveness of conducting cyber operations (Borghard & Lonergan, 2017: 472). In the case of China, asymmetrical warfare has largely been analysed with reference to the US, mainly based on the premise that it provides advantages to the weaker actor. The concept has long been deliberated upon in PLA's authoritative writings.

Way back in 1995, Wang Pufeng had argued that China "must use all types, forms, and methods of force, and especially nonlinear warfare (asymmetric warfare) and information warfare" to target the weaknesses of the adversary to secure victory given China's inferiority in information technology (P. Wang, 1995). The book *Unrestricted Warfare* also discussed the concept in greater detail and suggested considering asymmetrical factors and using the principle as an important fulcrum to accomplish objectives. The book cited historical antecedents where weaker countries and non-state actors have used asymmetrical combat methods such as guerrilla war, terrorism, protracted war, and network war against powerful adversaries (L. Qiao & Wang, 1999: 211–212).

Deliberating on the conditions of high-tech war, the 2001 edition of the *Science of Military Strategy* noted that since the strong actor will leverage all its advantages in combat forces, technology, and operational methods, the weaker one tends to make the most of its own advantages using asymmetric means and operational methods. Since high-tech weaponry and equipment and the stronger actor have their own vulnerabilities, the book argued that the weaker actor therefore must rely on its advantages against the weaknesses of the adversary as superiority does not necessarily mean an advantageous position across the entire spectrum of operations all the time.

Recognising that China needs to focus on those niche areas where it enjoys an advantage or its ability is at par with the competitors, the 2013 edition of the *Science of Military Strategy* identified space and cyberspace as an integral part of the command and control system of the modern armed forces and suggested using these domains to create asymmetry against an enemy (Academy of Military Science, 2013: 128–129). It advocated the development of space weapons to gain superiority so as to target and destroy the critical assets in the adversary's space systems and proposed to exploit land, sea, air, space, cyberspace, and electromagnetic spectrum to disrupt the terrestrial–space communication system and deny the adversary access to its own space systems. Assuming that offence has an advantage over defence in cyberspace, the book emphasised the use of cyber-attacks to disrupt the adversary's information systems (both hardware and software) in war time, and in a general sense, characterised it as asymmetrical (Academy of Military Science, 2013: 130–131, 193).

In the other PLA writings too, cyberspace is deemed as a strategic means to obtain asymmetrical advantages (W. An, 2016), and cyber warfare as a covert tool to destroy, paralyse, or control the military network systems of the adversary (W. Chen, 2019). Some of the writings advocated the use of offensive cyber operations, noting the dependency of the so-called "cyber hegemons" – indicating towards the US – on information networks which renders them vulnerable to cyber-attacks and the ensuing disruption (Ye & Zhao, 2014). The development of cyber forces and the extensive use of cyber options (malware, cyber-attacks, or cyber weapons) by the US and the advantage it enjoys in the cyber domain find a frequent mention in PLA's writings, expressing apprehensions over China's comparative disadvantage (W. An, 2016; H. Chen, 2017; China Military Network, 2019; Dossi, 2019).

Elaborating the impressions of the so-called "assassin's mace" weapons in the Chinese statecraft, Fisher argues that such weapons are developed in utmost secrecy, they are employed with an element of surprise to target the weaknesses of the enemy, and their development in the present times is part and parcel of asymmetrical warfare strategy and capabilities (D. Fisher, 2010: 81). Such weapons enable a weaker actor to confront a stronger adversary. Western think-tanks and scholars, both civilian and military, have analysed Chinese views on asymmetrical warfare and the development of corresponding capabilities in China mainly from the vantage point of US–China geopolitical rivalry, stressing on the gulf between their conventional military capabilities and also the respective defence budgets (Anderson and Engstrom, 2009; Cordesman, 2016; Horta, 2013; Roberts et al., 2020; Twomey, 2005). A key takeaway from these analyses is that China intends to invest in technologies which radically improve its strategic capabilities with respect to the US, without the need to match the US in conventional weaponry.

Looking at the history of the use of cyber weapons by strong powers against the weak and noting that strong powers continue to expand their asymmetrical advantages in cyberspace, a PLA article argued that strong powers have the technological wherewithal to attack, retaliate, and even build asymmetrical defence capabilities which makes it difficult for the weak to fight against the strong powers and their asymmetrical advantage also withers away (S. Wei, 2021). This view indicates that the most credible and potent threats to China in cyberspace will originate from countries that are technologically advanced, mainly the US. Asymmetrical weapons allow China to develop a credible deterrent as well as an effective wartime advantage, without the need to engage in direct competition with the US (Blasko, 2011), and in the cyber realm such weapons are likely to exploit the dependence of the US military, economy, and society on information networks. China's weakness in conventional capabilities *vis-à-vis* the US has forced China to focus on its asymmetrical strategies, and use cyber capabilities as asymmetric means to confront the superior military power of the US (Miller & Kuehl, 2009: 2).

Cyber or information warfare, however, is one amongst the asymmetric capabilities China is known to have developed in the other domains of warfare. For instance, recognising the heavy dependence of the US military on its space assets, China's asymmetric capabilities in space are primarily devised to deny or even destroy space assets as demonstrated by the 2007 anti-satellite test using a kinetic kill vehicle. China's anti-ship ballistic missile – DF-21D – is yet another asymmetric weapon to deter a potential American or any other external intervention during a crisis in the Taiwan Strait (Cropsey, 2010; Der Spiegel, 2008). It also affords China the ability to maintain an assertive posture with respect to its maritime territorial claims in the South and East China Seas.

In the pursuit of geopolitical aims, China is inclined to utilise advancements in emerging technologies as well to augment its asymmetric warfare capabilities. The 2019 Defense White Paper took a note of the growing adoption of cutting-edge technologies such as AI, quantum information systems, big data, and cloud computing in the military and the thrust on long-range precision, intelligent, stealthy, and unmanned weaponry and equipment – denoting it as "intelligentized" warfare (State Council, 2019). Intending to enhance military capabilities using AI, the *New Generation Artificial Intelligence Development Plan* aspires to leverage AI to support command and battlefield situational awareness and decision-making systems, training, simulation, and war-gaming, and to improve defence equipment such as airborne, ground, and maritime unmanned systems in both combat and reconnaissance roles (S. Chen, 2018; Government of Canada, n.d.; F. E. Morgan et al., 2020; Xinhua, 2019d). The applications of AI in PLA are also being extended to the next-generation cruise missiles (Zhao, 2016a).

Since the publication of the 2019 Defense White Paper, commentaries have appeared in the official PLA media discussing concepts like "intelligentized" warfare, unmanned and autonomous weapon systems, and cognitive warfare. Military thinking on the transformative impact of AI on war planning and warfighting is advancing within the PLA in line with the global developments in this space, while some of writings have even been mindful of the ethical considerations of the military use of AI (*China Youth Daily*, 2019; F. Yang & Li, 2020; Yufu Zheng, 2019). Some of the writings advocate prioritising AI development on similar lines to nuclear and space projects executed in the 1950s and 1960s, better known as "Two Bombs and One Satellite" project (Qi, 2019).

The 2020 edition of *Science of Military Strategy* of the National Defense University also lays emphasis on the impact of AI in military operations and warfare against the backdrop of the increased focus on AI in the military domain. In the PLA writings, AI is also discussed within the context of information warfare and its increasingly important role in modern cognitive warfare where advantages in AI become decisive, and superior technology and algorithms provide a unilateral asymmetric advantage as information superiority shifts to intelligence superiority in the battlefield (D. Chen, 2021; Fu et al., 2020; C. Xu et al., 2020). Some of the writings have even termed cognitive space as "the strategic commanding height of future wars" (Y. Li, 2020).

The general understanding of AI in the military context within PLA is that it has an impact on weapon platforms, command systems, combat terminals, and battlefield environment, and the relationship between human and machine intelligence is symbiotic with the human in a decisive role (Fu et al., 2020; C. Xu et al., 2020). Military operations under such conditions will see close cooperation between information networks, soldiers, and intelligent unmanned equipment (Linjuan et al., 2019), and the side with better algorithms can quickly and accurately predict the battlefield situation to help devise effective combat methods and thus secure victory (Xinhua, 2019a). Reports suggest that China is integrating AI with its military modernisation efforts, and the focus of PLA's AI technology procurement is primarily on intelligence analysis, predictive maintenance, information warfare, target recognition for autonomous vehicles, and training and simulation (Fedasiuk et al., 2021; X. Liu, 2021).

Another technology that has garnered deep interest of the PLA is quantum, whose military applications range from secure communications to accurate navigation and positioning. Given its wide-ranging applications, quantum technology is seen as a disruptive technology in future warfare (Qiu, 2019). With quantum information technology and quantum computing, the interests of PLA span communications security, code-breaking, operations optimisation, stealth submarine metrology, coastal surveillance, and anti-submarine warfare (Sharma, 2018). Quantum communication technology was one of the 11 new research directions identified by the PLA University of Science and Technology in 2011 (Z. Yang et al., 2011). The PLA envisions quantum communications to foster its stealth capabilities and fortify precision combat platforms (Wang, 2014), and hails quantum communications to be a game changer (W. An, 2017).

State owned enterprises having close associations with the PLA, such as China Electronics Technology Group Corporation, China Aerospace Science and Industry Corporation, and China Aerospace Science and Technology Corporation are known to be exploring military applications of quantum technology (*Global Times*, 2016; Reuters, 2017; Zhao, 2016b). The upcoming National Laboratory for Quantum Information Sciences at Hefei is going to house research expertise and capacity for military applications of quantum information technology, eyeing the areas mentioned above (S. Chen, 2017b; *China Daily*, 2017).

Quantum-based positioning and navigation can improve the ability of the PLA to execute missions in satellite navigation-denied or degraded environments and extend the reach of submarine operations which may improve

PLA's visibility over maritime areas of interest. With quantum sensing and meteorology, improved detection capabilities of the PLA in air, maritime, and space domains can potentially erode the strategic advantage of the adversary. Moreover, the likely use of quantum computing to break encryption schemes will lead to the loss of cryptographic infrastructure and render existing encryption algorithms unsafe, which are used widely by governments and militaries all over the world for secure communications. On the other hand, advances in quantum cryptography are anticipated to lay the foundations of hack-proof communications for the PLA.

China's pursuit of the so-called "game-changing" strategic technologies in the digital space seeks to augment its cyber and information warfare capabilities and generate asymmetric advantages. A combat force of the composition and mandate as that of PLASSF has technology at its core. And in modern times, technology R&D is a much more collaborative exercise, breaking the confines of the military, government establishments, private sector, and academia. This is so because the expertise and facilities are no more found to be concentrated in any one of these sectors. The expanse and pace of technology development also warrant all the players in the technology sector to synergise their respective strengths and resources towards a common national goal.

To achieve that, building an ecosystem conducive for the civilian and military sectors to cooperate, collaborate, and corroborate on technology research and development becomes important. With the strategy for military–civil fusion, China is known to have prioritised deeper integration of capacities and capabilities of military and civilian sectors with the objective of enabling a swift transfer of pertinent breakthroughs among the universities, private sector enterprises, scientific research institutes, and military establishment. Cyber is one of the technology areas where military–civil fusion is quite relevant and the PLASSF plays an important role in this initiative.

### Cyber in the military–civil fusion strategy

The term "military–civil fusion" began to gain traction under Hu Jintao in the late 1990s when he was the Vice Chairman of the CMC, though combining the forces of military and civilian sectors had long been a priority dating back to the founding of the People's Republic of China (Bruyère & Picarsic, 2021). Hu Jintao's report at the 17th National Congress of the CPC in 2007 called for the reforms of defence-related science, technology, and industry system, and integration of military and civilian purposes and efforts for development – indicating holistic convergence of institutions spread over the civilian and military sectors (J. Hu, 2007). A similar emphasis on integrated development of military and civilian sectors was found in the subsequent report of Hu Jintao at the 18th National Congress of the CPC (J. Hu, 2012a). At the 19th National Congress of the CPC, Xi Jinping shared his vision of an ecosystem which enhances and complements capacities and capabilities of the civilian-scientific and military-scientific spheres, and spoke about coordinating strategies and sharing resources between the military and civilian sectors at the 20th National Congress of the CPC.

Military–civil fusion has appeared consecutively in the Five-Year Plans since the 10th Five-Year Plan. The 13th Five-Year Plan sought to strengthen coordination between the military and civilian sectors in the sharing of advanced technologies, industries, and infrastructure, and to implement joint development projects in the areas of ocean, space, and cyberspace. The 14th Five-Year Plan further added new energy, AI, and quantum science and technology to this list. The Defense White Papers too have carried a section on military–civil integration ever since the first edition in 1998, reporting on the contribution of the armed forces to scientific research projects and the transfer of scientific and technological findings to the civilian sector (State Council, 1998, 2004, 2013). Against the backdrop of the blurring boundaries between peacetime and wartime and military and civilian activities in cyberspace, the 2013 edition of the *Science of Military Strategy* spoke of joining hands and espoused combining civil and military capacities and forces during war times (Academy of Military Science, 2013: 130–131).

In March 2015, military–civil fusion was elevated to a national strategy, also featuring in the military reforms initiated at the end of 2015 (China National Radio, 2015; Xinhua, 2016a). Two years later, in 2017, the Central Commission for Integrated Military and Civilian Development – the highest decision-making body for issues related to military–civil fusion – was established with the objective of accelerating implementation of the strategy, to be headed by Xi Jinping (Xinhua, 2017a). Military–civil fusion or "deepening integrated military and civilian development" envisions harnessing the expertise and capacity residing in the civilian science and technology entities for the technological modernisation of China's armed forces (Stone & Wood, 2020; Xinhua, 2017f). It aims to combine research capabilities of the military and civilian sectors and making defence S&T part of the civilian sector by encouraging defence-related research institutes to work on civilian research topics and opening up defence-related R&D activities to civilian research institutes and industries. Military–civil fusion synergises production, education, and research activities of the military and civilian sectors and enables sharing of resource (laboratories, facilities, and expertise) and collaboration between them (State Council, 2017b; Xinhua, 2016c).

Xi Jinping, while speaking at the National Cybersecurity and Informatization Work Conference in 2018, pointed out that cybersecurity and informatisation are the frontiers of military–civilian fusion and they hold vast potential (Qiushi, 2018). Implementation of the military–civil fusion strategy in the information and cyber domains is deemed essential to the advancement of China's national defence, winning future information wars, and the goal of building China into a cyber superpower (He et al., 2018; Jin, 2018; M. Li, 2018; Z. Zhang, 2018a). Under Xi Jinping, military–civil fusion has gained renewed interest and attention, especially given the strategic importance of emerging technologies for the PLA, whose development is largely led by commercial enterprises. The establishment of the Central Commission for Integrated Military and Civilian Development further reflects the sense of urgency and importance of this task. With the authority vested in the Commission, it intends to overcome the institutional barriers and ensure the flow of resources, talent, and innovation across the government, military, and industry.

Military–civil fusion, in general, is relevant for dual-use infrastructure, national defence-related science and technology industry, weapons and equipment, and training, and under China's strategy for military–civil fusion, areas such as outer space, cyberspace, biology, new energy, and maritime domain have received utmost attention (Jin, 2018; G. Zhang, 2017). Amongst others, quantum computing, big data, semiconductors, 5G, advanced nuclear technology, aerospace technology, and AI are the prioritised technology areas (Xinhua, 2017b). There were reports of an official policy document *Opinion on Promoting In-depth Military-Civil Fusion in Cyberspace Security and Informatization* to guide the development of military–civil fusion for cyberspace, though it is not available in the public domain (Stone & Wood, 2020).

As China's civilian sector has made a substantial contribution to the national informatisation effort, growth of China's digital economy, and research and technology development, it could augment the cyber capabilities of the PLA, and the PLA's leadership also believes that military–civil fusion is the only way to build China's cyber force (Y. Hao, 2016). As the boundaries between military and civilian sectors and peace and war continue to blur and information warfare no longer being a direct contest between the military systems, military–civil fusion is argued to be the only way for the PLA to proceed on the path of informatisation and meet the requirements of weapons for the new combat forces as well as to elevate combat effectiveness (L. Jiang, 2017; Xinhua, 2018b).

In cyberspace, military–civil fusion has vast applicability ranging from reducing the costs of weapons research and development and improving PLA's ability to maintain network security to the real-time monitoring of security incidents and joint exercises (X. Cheng, 2018; M. Li, 2018). In security operations, the areas that may gain significantly are intrusion detection, encryption, next-generation firewalls, network security monitoring, early warning and emergency response, and exchange of cyber threat intelligence

(Jin, 2018; H. Zhou & Zhang, 2018a, 2018b). Integration of such systems across the civilian and military sectors may also require alignment of technology standards (He et al., 2018; H. Zhou & Zhang, 2018a). Cyber exercises, hackathons, and building cyber-ranges are also expected to gain from this increased interaction among the entities from military and civilian sectors (Z. Zhang, 2018b).

China has made some progress in this segment of military–civil fusion strategy. For instance, the Cybersecurity Military–Civil Fusion Innovation Center was established in 2017. Led by 360 Enterprise Security Group, the centre provides cyber defence systems, enables threat intelligence sharing, and offers cyber emergency response services and threat analysis and monitoring services to the PLA and other Government bodies (*People's Daily*, 2017b). In 2017, China began building the National Cybersecurity Talent and Innovation Base at Wuhan – commonly known as National Cybersecurity Center. The sprawling campus spreads over 40 km² and includes seven centres for research, talent development, and entrepreneurship; two laboratories; and a cybersecurity academy (Cary, 2021; Eastmoney Securities, 2017; Xinhua, 2019c).

Denoted as a carrier of China's cyber power, the centre aspires to meet the strategic requirements of China's cybersecurity across the three areas of training and talent development, technological innovation, and industrial development (*Changjiang Daily*, 2022; HUST, 2019). The centre has received ardent policy support since establishment. In fact, a ten-point policy measure for the next three years came into force in June 2022 encompassing support for talent, think-tanks and new R&D institutions, scientific and technological innovation, development of enterprises, financial incentive, and industrial development fund (Wuhan Municipal People's Government, 2022). In addition to the National Cyber Security College of Wuhan University and the Cyberspace Security College of Huazhong University of Science and Technology relocating to the National Cybersecurity Center, around 200 cybersecurity companies in China – including all the top 50 companies – have also settled there (*Changjiang Daily*, 2022; Sina, 2022; WHU, 2021). In 2021, the first batch of students from undergraduate, masters, and doctoral programmes in cybersecurity graduated from the Center (Wuhan Municipal Cyberspace Administration, 2021).

Aligning with the military–civil fusion strategy, the National Cybersecurity Center could play an important role in addressing the requirements of the PLASSF, in terms of both training and the development of technology solutions to support its cyber operations. For instance, the Sixth Bureau of Networks Systems Department of the PLASSF is headquartered in Wuhan, which is likely to have a training mission (Cary, 2021; Stokes et al., 2011). Moreover, both Wuhan University and the Huazhong University of Science and Technology are known to have close ties with the

PLA. Wuhan University conducts defence-related research in the areas of navigation, computer simulation, aerospace remote sensing, materials science, and cybersecurity, and it functions under a joint-supervision agreement between the Ministry of Education and the State Administration for Science, Technology, and Industry for National Defense, which is an agency under MIIT that supports research for the requirements of the PLA (ASPI, 2019c). The Cyber Attack and Defense Center of Wuhan University reportedly runs in collaboration with PLA's Hubei Military District (Sina, 2009). The focus areas of defence-related research at the Huazhong University of Science and Technology include artificial intelligence, image processing, navigation, electronics, and materials, and it also works with the PLA (ASPI, 2019b; SICAS, n.d.).

Military–civil fusion in China is still at a nascent stage, requiring structural and behavioural changes going forward to break the silos in which the research institutions and defence technology industry are traditionally used to be working (Ruili Municipal People's Government, 2019). The lack of competition, institutional barriers, and structural issues are broadly seen as impediments in achieving true integration of the capacities of military and civilian domains in defence technological research and development (G. Zhang, 2017; H. Zhou & Zhang, 2018b). The strategy for military–civil fusion also puts obligations on civilian entities to meet PLA's requirements of compliance, licensing, standards, and confidentiality of information while executing research projects. Moreover, the international academic partnerships of some of the Chinese universities and commercial engagements of some of the companies are already under scrutiny owing to their relations with the PLA and as a result their contribution to enhancing China's defence capabilities. Closer engagement with the PLA as part of the military–civil fusion strategy might lead to restrictions on these Chinese universities and companies in their international partnerships and associations.

The shortage of cybersecurity talent in China is often highlighted as a pressing issue, and it is estimated to be close to 1.4 million (*Beijing News*, 2020; M. Li, 2018). The strategy for military–civil fusion actively seeks to bridge this gap, not just in numbers but also in terms of requisite skill sets, training, and operational experience. The PLASSF in particular needs a well-trained workforce for various roles in cybersecurity analysis, emergency response, research and development for hardware and software security, etc., not to mention the requirements for conducting offensive cyber operations (H. Zhou & Zhang, 2018b). Military–civil fusion will allow the PLA to leverage the capacities residing in the civilian sector for imparting education and training and developing the desired skills.

## Cyber in military education and training

Human resources are vital to building cyber capabilities, and the PLA is no exception. Military education and training system is the lynchpin to develop the skills required for cyber and information operations, and the premier educational and research institutions of the PLA have stepped up their efforts to meet the requirements of "informationized" warfare. The PLA Academy of Military Science, for instance, has been central to the advancement of strategic thought on information warfare within the PLA, as observed earlier in the chapter on how the subject has received attention in its publications. The appointment of General Gao Jin from the Academy of Military Science as the inaugural commander of PLASSF in 2016 indicates the close interaction between PLASSF and the Academy of Military Science from the very beginning.

As part of the restructuring initiated in 2017, the Academy of Military Science was tasked with combining its strengths in military theoretical research with military scientific and technological research with the aim of integrating the development of doctrine and strategy with technology innovation (D. Chen, 2018; Xinhua, 2017f). Six research institutes subordinate to the former general departments of the PLA – including the Institute of War Studies, System Engineering Institute, and National Defense Science and Technology Innovation Institute – were merged into the Academy of Military Science (The Paper, 2017; Wuthnow, 2019).[4] These three institutions conduct research in the disciplines of software engineering, information and communication engineering, computer science, network engineering, cybersecurity, and intelligent systems. And they began recruiting civilians in 2018 for various research positions to meet their demand for scientific researchers (China University of Petroleum, 2019; Huatu Education, 2019; Ministry of Education, 2021; Tay, 2020).

Two technology schools – the National University of Defense Technology (NUDT) and Information Engineering University (IEU) – largely fulfil the training and educational requirements of the PLA for cyber and related disciplines. The NUDT offers information security and cybersecurity courses under the School of Computer Science and School of Electronic Science, and it is responsible for the technical education and training of senior scientists and engineers, serving officers, newly commissioned officers, noncommissioned officers, and academics of the PLA (NUDT, n.d.-d). It ranks among China's top universities in the disciplines of computer science, optical engineering, and communications engineering (ASPI, 2019a; AT0086, n.d.). NUDT is acclaimed for its research on high-performance computing (NUDT, 2012), and Tianhe-1A and Tianhe-2A developed by NUDT were the world's fastest supercomputers from October 2010 to June 2011 and June 2013 to November 2015 respectively (TOP500, n.d.-a, n.d.-b).

The School of Computer Science trains personnel in combat roles and offers majors in the disciplines of computer science, network engineering, software engineering, the internet of things, integrated circuit design, and cybersecurity. The school began offering doctoral degrees in cybersecurity in 2016 (NUDT, n.d.-b). The School of Electronic Science has doctoral programmes in information and communication engineering, electronic science and technology, military command, and cybersecurity (NUDT, n.d.-a). The School of Intelligent Science is an epicentre for training and research in artificial intelligence and biological intelligence focusing on the requirements of unmanned operations (NUDT, n.d.-c).

The School of Computer Science and the School of Electronic Science have consistently offered admissions in their cybersecurity post-graduate and doctoral programmes to both serving military personnel and civilians, while the School of Electronic Countermeasures has intermittently offered such admissions (NUDT, 2019a, 2019b, 2020, 2021a, 2021b, 2022a, 2022b). The academic programmes offered by NUDT across these schools at various levels are pertinent to meet the PLA's requirement of skilled human resources in both defensive and offensive aspects of cyber capabilities. With its academic and research orientation towards the military applications of emerging technologies such as artificial intelligence, NUDT is also playing a key role in developing the relevant capacity within the PLA to meet the needs of future conflicts.

The former PLA Institute of Information Engineering, the PLA Institute of Surveying and Mapping, and the PLA Institute of Electronic Technology were merged in 1999 to form the Information Engineering University (IEU) (China Kaoyan, n.d.; GKZY, 2014). As part of the restructuring, the PLA Foreign Languages University was merged with IEU in 2017 and brought under the ambit of Network Systems Department of the PLASSF. The IEU for long had been providing technical education and training to the personnel of 3PLA in the disciplines of electrical engineering, communications engineering, computer science, and network security, while the linguists received their language training at the PLA Foreign Languages University (Stokes et al., 2011). IEU has served as the academy for electronic and cyber warfare arms of the PLA with a focus on research and training in cryptography, signals, information security, information engineering, and network exploitation (ASPI, 2021). As the primary educational institute of Network Systems Department, IEU is now central to the development of human resources and meeting the technology requirements of PLASSF for offensive cyber operations (McReynolds & Luce, 2021).

For its doctoral programme, the IEU recruits recent master's graduates, in-service personnel with a master's degree, and personnel who have a bachelor's degree and worked for more than six years in a discipline closely related to their proposed doctoral area of study or have published academic papers. Civilian candidates with publications in reputed journals are also recruited for the IEU's doctoral programme (IEU, 2018, 2019). The development and deployment of exploits as part of information and cyber operations also need linguistics support, and the IEU fulfils this requirement as well for the PLASSF.

Along with the expansion of educational, training, and research capacity on its own, civilian universities and private sector companies are deeply involved in augmenting the cyber capabilities of the PLASSF. It has signed strategic cooperation agreements with nine civilian academic institutions, which include the University of Science and Technology, Shanghai Jiaotong University, Xi'an Jiaotong University, the Beijing Institute of Technology, Nanjing University, the Harbin Institute of Technology, China Aerospace Science and Technology Corporation, China Aerospace Science and Industry Corporation, and the China Electronic Technology Group Corporation. The agreements encompass training and education, scientific and technological research, and building cyber ranges among others (*People's Daily*, 2017a).

The strategy for military–civil fusion is largely shaping how the PLASSF accesses the vast pool of human capital in the civilian domain. One of the prime goals of this strategy is to integrate skilled human resources at multiple levels in the military. Research and training segments are likely to benefit PLASSF the most from this collaboration with the industry and universities in the civilian domain. In parallel, PLASSF also seeks to directly recruit civilian talent in research positions (Military Talent Net, 2022). To attract top talent in the areas of cybersecurity, network security, and emerging technologies such as artificial intelligence and quantum information sciences, PLASSF has to directly compete not just with the Government ministries and agencies but also with China's private sector. The private sector however could be more lucrative in terms of compensation, benefits, and the work culture.

## Discussion

The changes brought in by the information age to the conduct of war have been influencing strategic thinking in China's military establishment. The realisation that information would play a decisive role in modern conflicts, rather than being merely an enabler, has engendered changes in doctrine and strategy for the military use of capabilities in this domain to prepare the PLA for future conflicts. Shifts in the basis of preparations for the military struggle to calibrate general operational principles have sought to ascertain PLA's long-term preparedness and development of right capabilities in the face of future wars. The thinking on information and cyber warfare, operational concepts, and the corresponding force structuring of the PLA have evolved over the last two decades.

The PLA perceives cyber as an elemental feature of "informationized" wars, in which information is both the domain where such war occurs and a weapon of combat. From this understanding stems the conviction that cyber capabilities are pivotal to winning modern conflicts, and cyber forces are now central to warfighting and no longer an auxiliary force. Cyber combat capability in this context refers to an integrated use of reconnaissance, cyber-attacks, and cyber defence. A key element of PLA's view of modern warfare is the continuous expansion of the battlefield – from the physical domains to cyberspace and cognitive space, and encompassing key functions of the state – with no distinction between military and non-military targets. This essentially brings political and military decision-makers, public opinion, military information systems, and information systems of critical infrastructure under the ambit of information operations.

Cyber means also align well with China's longstanding inclination towards asymmetrical tools to overcome the military capabilities of a superiority adversary, as seen in the space and maritime domains. Cyber means allow China to apply its capabilities against the vulnerabilities or weaknesses of a superior adversary dependent on cyberspace and information systems for military operations. In, and through, the cyber domain, China seeks to build a credible deterrent and an effective wartime advantage in order to meet its geopolitical objectives, without the need to engage in a direct military confrontation with superior powers it deems as an impediment to meeting those objectives. In the pursuit of a leading position in emerging digital technologies, China also seeks to generate asymmetric advantages by leveraging technologies such as artificial intelligence and quantum in the military domain for long-range precision, intelligent, stealthy, and unmanned weaponry and equipment, secure communications, military code-breaking, stealth submarine metrology, and anti-submarine warfare.

The raising of PLASSF integrated the capacities of PLA's information operations units which were earlier grouped according to mission type such as espionage, attack, defence, and psychological operations, and dispersed across the former four General Departments. Cyberspace now plays a central role in military planning, force structuring, and warfighting practices of the PLA. The appointment of General Ju Qiansheng as commander of the PLASSF in July 2021 further signals that CMC is prioritising professional leadership of the force as he has the experience of commanding the Network Systems Department of PLASSF (T.-H. Wu & Hung, 2021). The previous commanders of PLASSF, General Gao Jin and General Li Fengbiao, had spent much of their service career in the former PLA Second Artillery Force and the PLA Air Force, respectively.

Combining the forces of China's military and civilian sectors for technological advancement had for long been a priority, which under Xi Jinping has received ample attention and push with a sense of urgency in the form of military–civil fusion strategy. The strategy prioritises deeper integration of universities, private sector enterprises, scientific research institutes, and military R&D and industrial establishments for swift transfer of scientific and technological breakthroughs among them. Cyber and the associated technology areas are likely to gain substantially from this increased interaction between military and civilian entities. The National Cybersecurity Center is conceived to meet the long-term requirements of training and talent development, technological innovation, and industrial development in cybersecurity. The PLASSF is slated to leverage the National Cybersecurity Center for its advancing requirements for training as well as technology solutions.

With reference to the model for cyber power, this chapter throws light on China's development of *Capacities* listed as part of *Military Cyber Policy*. The existence of cyber force in China is very much evident with the raising of PLASSF and its further integration with the operations of other services of the PLA is also well reported. Moreover, with the mandate of providing strategic information support and conducting information operations, PLASSF does not merely serve an auxiliary function and it is projected as a combat force central to PLA's warfighting doctrine, strategy, and tactics for future conflicts. It is integral to PLA's joint operations, and to China's power projection in the space and cyber domains. Since its raising, the PLASSF has regularly been part of PLA's flagship joint exercises, such as the annual Stride exercise, which are essential for combat and operational readiness. Information or cyber warfare component in PLA's exercises beginning the late 1990s, and the efforts to integrate PLASSF with other services exemplify PLA's transition from theoretical understanding to the practice of information or cyber warfare.

Given PLA's lack of combat experience, high-quality trainings and exercises are considered vital to building combat capabilities and improve operational readiness to be better prepared for future conflicts. The lack of publicly available information whether on the specifics or composition of PLA's exercises or their after-action reports makes it difficult to analyse the quality of the trainings for China's cyber force. The impact of CMC's decision of late to bring in a new system for military training with the aim of making PLA's trainings combat-oriented and close to "real war" conditions is yet to be seen. A major shortcoming is China's lack of participation whatsoever at the reputed international cyber defence exercises. Because of geopolitical reasons and its growing aggression along borders as well as in the maritime, space, and cyber domains, China is kept out of international cyber defence exercises which also restricts its access to technology, and knowledge and experience sharing.

Deliberations on the impact of information on warfare have long been part of PLA's writings and publications. Since cyber is seen as an elemental feature in China's overarching conceptualisation of information warfare, and looking at the focus cyber domain has received in China's military doctrine and strategy and the authoritative publications and other writings from the PLA over the past decade or so, it is safe to conclude that cyber now occupies a prominent position in China's military thinking and strategy. As far as cyber in military education and training is concerned, the premier PLA academic institutions – the Academy of Military Science, NUDT, and IEU – under different schools or institutes impart technical education and training and conduct research on a range of disciplines associated with cyber. The post-graduate and doctoral programmes for serving military personnel and civilians at these institutions seek to meet PLASSF's requirements of talent for both defensive and offensive aspects of cyber operations. Moreover, keeping an eye on the requirements of future battlefield, some of the technology schools even have academic and research orientation towards emerging digital technologies.

In terms of *Capabilities* identified as part of *Military Cyber Policy* in the cyber power model, the discussion in this chapter suggests that China has made steady progress in most of these aspects. China pursues military-civil fusion (civil–military integration) as a national strategy (since 2015) with the aim of synergising the expertise and resources of military and civilian sectors for increased interaction and collaboration, driven by a central commission established in 2017 and headed by Xi Jinping. With this strategy, China's civilian sector is slated to propel the technological modernisation of the armed forces, and with respect to cyberspace, the strategy will augment the capabilities of China's cyber force and meet its requirements of skilled manpower, technology, weapons, and exercises.

In this respect, the establishment of Cybersecurity Military–Civil Fusion Innovation Center and National Cybersecurity Center demonstrates that China has made some advancements. The former fulfils the requirements of cyber defence and cyber threat analysis, while the latter, denoted as a carrier of China's cyber power, is more focused on the strategic requirements of innovation, talent, and industrial development in cybersecurity. With the cybersecurity schools of Wuhan University and the Huazhong University of Science and Technology relocating to National Cybersecurity Center and the leading cybersecurity companies also settling in, the envisioned schema of the centre has started taking shape. Given the convergence of information security and cybersecurity skills in the military and civilian sectors, the military–civil fusion strategy will largely direct PLASSF's access to the talent pool in the civilian sector. This is manifesting not just in the form of collaboration with private sector entities and leading academic institutions, but also through direct recruitment of civilians for various research positions in cybersecurity and emerging digital technologies at PLA affiliated institutions.

As regards the experience of armed forces in conducting cyber operations, the growing offensive capabilities of the PLA are quite apparent from the increasing instances of cyber espionage and cyber-attacks attributed to it which have targeted defence and civilian critical infrastructure across different countries. The recent annual reports of the US DoD to the US Congress on military developments in China have also underscored PLA's improving ability to conduct full-range of land, air, maritime, counter-space, and cyber operations as a joint combat force. China for long has directed information and cyber operations against the Taiwanese Government, military, private sector, and society in support of CPC's principal objective of Taiwan's reunification. China's disinformation campaigns and electoral interference in Taiwan, and the increasing use of cyber coercive measures against countries with which it has ongoing boundary or maritime disputes also stand as a testament to the proficiency of PLA in conducting information and cyber operations.

There is ample evidence to conclude that China has by and large succeeded in integrating cyber with its military doctrines, strategies, and tactics. Information domain was central to the last two doctrinal changes made by the CMC, seeking to maintain PLA's combat readiness in the face of contemporary battlefield realities. The Defense White Papers since 2010 have stressed on the need to secure China's growing interests in the cyber domain and achieve superiority, especially against the backdrop of emerging strategic competition in cyberspace. China's military strategy recognises cyber as a domain of national security and clearly states the objectives of China's development of cyber force and corresponding capabilities. The raising of PLASSF and the thrust on enhancing its capabilities to maintain national security and social stability and defend sovereignty in cyberspace are further in line with the considerations of the military strategy, which indicates the integration of cyber with China's military strategy. The PLASSF essentially operationalises the principles of PLA's conception of "informationized" wars and it is purposed to be the mainstay of China's power projection in the cyber domain – which it regards as a full-fledged war-fighting domain in its own right.

Cyber military capabilities are a key enabler of the objective of building China into a cyber superpower, and the evidence from this chapter suggests that the military leadership has persistently sought to prepare the PLA for modern conflicts, where they expect information and cyber domains to play a decisive role. The decisions to adapt the military doctrine to the emerging realities of the battlefield, to focus on information and cyber domains in the military strategy, to raise PLASSF and integrate its combat capabilities with other services of the PLA, and to synergise the activities of military and civilian sectors reflect the deep desire and intent of China's military leadership to develop PLA as a force to be reckoned with.

## Notes

1 Translated into English by the China Aerospace Studies Institute.
2 Translated into English by the China Aerospace Studies Institute.
3 First Bureau (Unit 61786) was responsible for information security across PLA; the Second Bureau (Unit 61398) engaged in computer network espionage; the Third Bureau (Unit 61785) looked at communications intelligence over radio and wireless networks; the Fourth Bureau (Unit 61419) focused on Japan and Korea; the Fifth Bureau (Unit 61565) and Eleventh Bureau (Unit 61672) focused on Russia; Sixth Bureau (Unit 61726) focused on Southeast and South Asia; the Seventh Bureau (Unit 61580) was believed to be engaged in information technology development, the Eighth Bureau (Unit 61046) covered Europe, Africa, the Middle East, and South America; the Ninth Bureau (Unit 61221) was responsible for strategic intelligence analysis; the Tenth Bureau (Unit 61886) focused on missile tracking and telemetry; and the Twelfth Bureau (Unit 61486) was responsible for space-related activities (D. Cheng, 2016).
4 Other research institutes are – the Academy of Military Medicine, National Defense Engineering Research Institute, Military Political Work Research Institute, Chemical Defense Research Institute, and Military Legal Research Institute.

# 7

# CONCLUSION

The steadfast progress towards the goal of building China into a cyber superpower since Xi Jinping's clarion call could have varying interpretations and implications extending well beyond China's periphery. The book has examined resources and capabilities arranged in four dimensions – national cyber policy, cyber diplomacy, emerging digital technologies, and military – where China's initiatives are largely concentrated to understand its interpretation of cyber power and its device to accomplish the goal of building China into a cyber superpower. China's treading on the path to cyber superpower should be seen as a composite of the motives and actions across this broad spectrum of state functions.

The status of a cyber superpower in China's conceptualisation of cyber power and in the eyes of the political leadership essentially translates into self-sufficiency in information technology, greater say in internet and cyber governance, ability to define international cyber norms and technical standards and transform institutions that reflect its values and priorities, and unchallenged pursuit of interests in cyberspace pertaining to CPC's supremacy and political stability. It also affords China the ability to institute architectural changes and ingrain its values into the technology and governance model of cyberspace which presently has a deep influence of the West and libertarian values, and becomes a pathway to international acceptability of China's perceptions, principles, and practices of cyber governance. Cyber military capabilities and emerging digital technologies in this conceptualisation generate asymmetric advantages and they are considered pivotal to win modern conflicts.

The strategic utility of cyberspace for China reflects in the tenets the political leadership has repetitively laid stress upon while deliberating on

DOI: 10.4324/9781003473510-7

cyber power. The potential of cyber or digital economy as a prime driver of the much-needed economic growth for China is highly recognised and underpins Government's flagship initiatives to expand ICT infrastructure and integrate information technology and emerging digital technologies with the traditional sectors of the economy. Indigenous innovation, in this context, is not only seen as the modality to progressively reduce China's dependence on foreign technology and intellectual property, but also as the means to lay claim to global technology leadership. The former assuages cybersecurity and cyber espionage risks that come along with the technology and services of foreign origin, while the latter affords China the long-sought footing to play an influential role in the international processes for the development of standards and norms and the governance of emerging technologies having strategic relevance. Global technology leadership elevates China's standing in the international system, and the activism at international standards development organisations could serve as a key indicator of China's growing prowess in some of the emerging digital technologies which of late have taken the centre stage in the unfolding geopolitical competition.

As a cyber superpower, China envisions best of the defensive ability to secure its growing economic and developmental interests in cyberspace and protect its information systems and critical information infrastructure. Referring to cybersecurity as a precondition to development rests its management and policy formulation with the highest echelons of political leadership and makes cyber an elemental feature of state's instruments for maintaining political stability and curbing subversion and separatism. This also prepares the ground for sweeping censorship measures, controls on the free flow of information, suppression of internet freedom, and invasion of privacy. Though this is not a new phenomenon in China as some of these measures date back to the mid-1990s and late 1990s, but their intensity and technological sophistication have strengthened progressively as cyberspace gained prominence in China's economic and security policy.

The legal and regulatory measures, coupled with state-of-the-art technological means to monitor internet traffic and manage online content, work precisely towards strengthening the control of the CPC over information and protecting its supremacy. Instead of opening up to the internet and embracing openness and the principles of freedom of expression and freedom of information, the CPC regime has rather not only subsumed the internet under its vast censorship apparatus but also leveraged it extensively to mould public opinion. The CPC regime has managed to do so while reaping the enormous benefits of this technology for China's economy. Absolute authority of the CPC over the planning, development, and regulatory aspects of internet or cyberspace in China is regarded as essential to attain the objective of building China into a cyber superpower. At the same time, propagating the concept of cyber sovereignty seeks to legitimise these measures for the suppression of free flow of information and freedom of expression.

China's predisposition for stringent controls and censorship also tends to inform its preference for multilateral approach to internet and cyber governance and shape the directions of its cyber diplomatic engagement. The latter has actively sought to expand China's normative influence internationally and garner acceptability of China's vision for internet and cyber governance. Cyber sovereignty – the organising principle of cyber governance for China – forms the very premise of China's cyber diplomacy which desires to legitimise it in the international community. A key element of China's cyber diplomacy in recent times is the advancement of Digital Silk Road initiative. Leveraging China's progression up the technology value chain, Digital Silk Road is a device to project China as a digital technology provider or digital infrastructure builder for developing countries and transpose its own technology standards and principles for the governance of cyberspace and digital technologies. Data security could perhaps emerge as a new direction of China's cyber diplomatic efforts with discussions on issues pertaining to security and trust in cross-border data flows picking pace at many multilateral forums.

Cyberspace also informs China's military ambitions and drives the envisioned modernisation goals of the armed forces as the military leadership is mindful of the distinctive ability of cyberspace to influence events in the other domains beyond cyberspace. Considerate of the changes wrought in by information and cyber domains to the conflicts and wars in the modern era, the leadership has calibrated the general operational principles and the requisite force structuring of the PLA to ascertain its long-term preparedness and development of relevant cyber military capabilities. The PLASSF therefore operationalises the principles of PLA's conception of "informationized" wars and it is purposed to be the mainstay of China's power projection in the cyber domain – which is regarded as a full-fledged warfighting domain in its own right. The advancing thought within PLA on the impact of artificial intelligence on warfighting signals a shift towards the superiority of intelligent systems in the battlefield, the prominence of unmanned and autonomous weapon systems, and merging of cyber with the cognitive domain.

Cyber force, or in a way the ability to utilise cyber operations to generate effects and influence events in other operational environments, affords CPC a tool to achieve political objectives, which could be deployed against a superior adversary or for that matter even against a weaker adversary or non-state actors. The endeavour to build a cyber force is being supported in no small measure by the civilian sector as part of the strategy for military–civil fusion. Increased interaction and exchange between military and civilian entities is expected to meet PLA's long-term requirements of training and talent development, technological innovation, and industrial development in cybersecurity as well as emerging digital technologies.

Notwithstanding the aggressive pursuit of the objective of building China into a cyber superpower, there are some factors that could impede anticipated outcomes. China presently lacks thought leadership in global internet and cyber governance issues. It purports to speak on behalf of developing countries, but China's ideas in this sphere have failed to gain much traction internationally, except perhaps the SCO. China's attempts, moreover, to alter the existing multistakeholder approach to the internet and cyber governance and put in place a multilateral approach have largely failed to bring about any substantive changes. China's normative influence in this realm is rather limited, and it has not yet demonstrated the ability to establish new institutions or forge noteworthy international partnerships to drive the agenda of internet or cyber governance. The authoritarian practices of one-party state ruled by the CPC to suppress civil liberties fail to find consonance among countries with democratic values.

Regarding the technology innovation ecosystem, China faces the acute challenges of improving the quality of research and the impact of research publications, attracting talent of international repute, and overcoming weakness in the core aspects of emerging technologies such as artificial intelligence. Chinese technology giants are yet to be seen empowering global technology communities in their quests for innovation and collaboration. A major impediment to the global prospects of Chinese private sector entities is the growing security concerns and widening trust deficit over risks of espionage and their proximity to the PLA or the CPC, which has led to restrictions on their market access in different parts of the world. These apprehensions are further compounded by the provisions in China's domestic laws on cybersecurity, data security, and personal information protection that require Chinese enterprises to share data with state agencies on national security matters.

Impediments in the technology realm also have bearing on China's cyber force as the PLA looks up to the civilian sector to meet the growing requirements of PLASSF for technology, workforce, skill sets, and operational experience. The strategy for military–civil fusion is still at a nascent stage and certainly requires structural and behavioural changes to break the silos in which the research institutions and defence technology industry are traditionally used to be working. Repetitive calls by the leadership for military–civil fusion indicate lacunae in the integration of the capacities and capabilities of military and civilian domains in defence technological research and development. The same shortcomings are seen in military exercises as well, whose utility in overcoming PLA's lack of combat experience finds much emphasis and the past ones have attracted criticism for the failure to fully exploit their potential to improve combat readiness.

As an aspiring cyber superpower, China should have been driving premier international cyber offense and defence exercises, but on the contrary China is not part of the prominent ones. Owing to its unabating military and cyber aggression, Chinese universities and companies having close working relations with the PLA will continue to face restrictions in their international partnerships so that such associations do not eventually end-up contributing to China's defence capabilities. International scepticism and exclusion from engagements tend to diminish China's influence and cyber superpower prospects.

The ensemble of increased leadership involvement in cyber policy-making, deeper integration of cyber with different state functions including foreign policy, extensive investments in cybersecurity and emerging digital technologies, and results-driven structural reforms is going to make China more confident of its cyber capabilities in the long term. In pursuit of its cyber superpower ambitions, in all likelihood China will continue to challenge the existing internet or cyber governance processes or even the technology architecture until they align with China's interests and priorities.

Leveraging the advances in domestic information and telecommunications technology industry, China's attempts to extend the reach of its technology in these sectors to other parts of the world – especially to the countries part of the BRI – will become more resolute. More than bolstering China's soft power or international standing, modalities like Digital Silk Road will serve as the vehicle to push China's own technology standards to these geographies, which is getting more relevant with the intensifying global competition in emerging digital technologies. Moreover, the technologies of Chinese origin for governance services and security and surveillance, or the Chinese mass surveillance model at large, will remain an attractive proposition for regimes seeking technology know-how to implement such stringent measures in the digital space.

China as a cyber superpower will not hesitate to full-scale utilisation of cyber power or its overt use in support of myriad geopolitical objectives or to generate desired effects. In the meantime, it will not shy away from demonstrating the strength and depth of its contemporary offensive cyber capabilities at opportune time. China's readiness to take risks with offensive cyber means in political and military conflicts against a strong opponent is a double whammy for smaller powers lacking cyber defence capabilities and whose offensive cyber capabilities many not be a match to China's might. Such flexing of "cyber-muscles" will have consequences during conflicts or skirmishes arising out of China's more than a dozen boundary and maritime territorial disputes across East Asia, South Asia, and Southeast Asia. China's opponents should expect aggressive deployment of cyber-enabled information operations during escalating geopolitical tensions. The fallout of China's accumulating experience in offensive cyber campaigns coupled with its imprudent and risky experiments with cyber power will be well beyond its periphery.

China's leaders interpret cyberspace from the prisms of economic prosperity, social development, national security, and military power. The call for building China into a cyber superpower – a cyber power of global reckoning – translates into mobilisation of all national assets and resources residing in the government, industry, academia, and armed forces towards a common cause. The party-state apparatus has left no stone unturned in pursuit of this goal, whose imperatives and urgency have been emphasised time and again over the last decade or so. What remains to be seen is to what extent this endeavour empowers China to regain its "rightful place" in the international system.

# REFERENCES

Aboy, M., Minssen, T., & Kop, M. (2022). Mapping the patent landscape of quantum technologies: Patenting trends, innovation and policy implications. *IIC – International Review of Intellectual Property and Competition Law, 53*(6), 853–882. https://doi.org/10.1007/s40319-022-01209-3

Academy of Military Science. (2013). *The science of military strategy.* Military Academic Works, Academy of Military Science.

Ackerman, E. (2012, December 14). The U. N. fought the Internet – And the Internet won; WCIT summit in Dubai ends. *Forbes.* https://www.forbes.com/sites/eliseackerman/2012/12/14/the-u-n-fought-the-internet-and-the-internet-won-wcit-summit-in-dubai-ends/?sh=2854f12637cc

Alibaba AI Labs. (n.d.). *Research focus.* https://damo.alibaba.com/labs/ai

Alibaba Cloud. (n.d.). *Machine learning platform for AI: Data mining & analysis.* Retrieved December 13, 2020, from https://www.alibabacloud.com/product/machine-learning

An, J. (2016, February 25). Internet sovereignty is a necessary choice of global cyber governance. *People's Daily.* http://theory.people.com.cn/n1/2016/0225/c143844-28150601.html

An, W. (2016, January 13). Deputy commander: China should develop its killer power to achieve future advantages. *People's Daily.* http://military.people.com.cn/n1/2016/0113/c1011-28046287.html

An, W. (2017, September 27). Quantum communication triggers military field reform to reshape war system. *PLA Daily.* http://jz.chinamil.com.cn/n2014/tp/content_7278464.htm

Anderson, E. C., & Engstrom, J. G. (2009). *Capabilities of the Chinese People's Liberation Army to carry out military action in the event of a regional military conflict.* https://www.uscc.gov/sites/default/files/Research/CapabilitiesoftheChinesePeople'sLiberationArmytoCarryOutMilitaryActionintheEventofaRegionalConflict.pdf

APNIC. (2023a). *IPv6 capable rate by country (%)*. Asia Pacific Network Information Centre. https://stats.labs.apnic.net/ipv6/

APNIC. (2023b). *Use of IPv6 for China (CN)*. Asia Pacific Network Information Centre. https://stats.labs.apnic.net/ipv6/CN

ASPI. (2019a, November). *National university of defense technology – Chinese defence universities tracker*. Australian Strategic Policy Institute. https://unitracker.aspi.org.au/universities/national-university-of-defense-technology/

ASPI. (2019b, November 18). *Huazhong university of science and technology – Chinese defence universities tracker*. Australian Strategic Policy Institute. https://unitracker.aspi.org.au/universities/huazhong-university-of-science-and-technology/

ASPI. (2019c, November 18). *Wuhan university – Chinese defence universities tracker*. Australian Strategic Policy Institute. https://unitracker.aspi.org.au/universities/wuhan-university/

ASPI. (2021, May). *Information engineering university – Chinese defence universities tracker*. Australian Strategic Policy Institute. https://unitracker.aspi.org.au/universities/information-engineering-university-2/

AT0086. (n.d.). *National university of defense technology*. Retrieved August 22, 2022, from http://www.at0086.com/nudt/whyus.aspx

Austin, G. (2016). *Mapping and evaluating China's cyber power*. http://ww1.prweb.com/prfiles/2016/09/19/13694501/Policy-Papers-Issue-2-Greg-Austin-Chinas-Cyber-Power.pdf

Austin, G., Tay, K. L., & Sharma, M. (2022). *Great-power offensive cyber campaigns: Experiments in strategy*. https://www.iiss.org/blogs/research-paper/2022/02/great-power-offensive-cyber-campaigns

Baidu Research. (n.d.-a). *Research areas*. http://research.baidu.com/Research_Areas/index-view?id=75

Baidu Research. (n.d.-b). *Research areas*. http://research.baidu.com/Research_Areas?id=55

Barnett, M., & Duvall, R. (2005). Power in international politics. *International Organization, 59*(1), 39–75.

BBC. (n.d.). *The thoughts of Chairman Xi*. Retrieved December 12, 2020, from https://www.bbc.co.uk/news/resources/idt-sh/Thoughts_Chairman_Xi

BBC. (2005, June 14). *Microsoft censors Chinese blogs*. http://news.bbc.co.uk/2/hi/technology/4088702.stm

BBC. (2010, June 29). *Timeline: China's net censorship*. https://www.bbc.com/news/10449139

Beam, C. (2009, April 3). *China and Russia want a new global reserve currency*. Slate. https://slate.com/news-and-politics/2009/04/china-and-russia-want-a-new-global-reserve-currency-what-would-it-look-like.html

Bebber, R. J. (2017). Cyber power and cyber effectiveness: An analytic framework. *Comparative Strategy, 36*(5), 426–436. https://doi.org/10.1080/01495933.2017.1379833

Beer, I. (2019, August 29). *Project zero: A very deep dive into iOS exploit chains found in the wild*. Google Project Zero. https://googleprojectzero.blogspot.com/2019/08/a-very-deep-dive-into-ios-exploit.html

Beijing News. (2020, September 18). Dialogue with the director of the national cyber security base office: Cybersecurity talents should be cultivated on the "battlefield." *Beijing News.* https://www.bjnews.com.cn/detail/160040212515806.html

Belt & Road News. (2019, June 26). China Unicom to build 5G networks on Belt & Road. *Belt & Road News.* https://www.beltandroad.news/2019/06/26/china-unicom-to-build-5g-networks-on-belt-road/

Belt and Road Portal. (2016, September 20). *Promote the "Belt and Road" construction special plan for technological innovation cooperation.* Belt and Road Portal. https://www.yidaiyilu.gov.cn/zchj/jggg/326.htm

Betz, D. J., & Stevens, T. (2011). *Cyberspace and the state: Towards a strategy for cyber-power.* Routledge.

Bi, J. (2001). The Internet revolution in China: The significance for traditional forms of communist control. *International Journal, 56*(3), 441. https://doi.org/10.2307/40203576

Bi, J., Xu, K., Li, X., Williams, M. I., Wu, J., & Ren, G. (2008). *A source address validation architecture (SAVA) testbed and deployment experience – RFC, 5210.*

Biddle, B., Curci, F. X., Haslach, T. F., Marchant, G. E., Askland, A., & Gaudet, L. (2012). The expanding role and importance of standards in the information and communications technology industry. *Jurimetrics, 52*(2), 177–208.

Bin, Z., & Taylor, R. (2005). Modeling IT for growth: How China's informatization index system informs its development policy. Presented at *PTC05 broadband and content: From wires to wireless conference.* Honolulu.

Bird&Bird. (n.d.). *Who is leading 5G development.* Retrieved December 13, 2020, from https://www.twobirds.com/~/media/pdfs/who-is-leading-5g-development.pdf?la=en&hash=AB57AC4B01AD1F8BE

BIS. (2022, October 7). *Commerce implements new export controls on advanced computing and semiconductor manufacturing items to the People's Republic of China (PRC).* https://www.bis.doc.gov/index.php/documents/about-bis/newsroom/press-releases/3158-2022-10-07-bis-press-release-advanced-computing-and-semiconductor-manufacturing-controls-final/file

Björk, M. (2019, April 26). Towards a European response to the emerging "geopolitics of standards": The role of China. *Geopolitics of Standards.* https://www.ui.se/globalassets/ui.se-eng/research/europe/proceedings-geopolitics-of-standards.pdf

Blasco, J. (2012, June 29). *New MaControl variant targeting Uyghur users, the Windows version using Gh0st RAT | AT&T Alien Labs.* AT&T. https://cybersecurity.att.com/blogs/labs-research/new-macontrol-variant-targeting-uyghur-users-the-windows-version-using-gh0s

Blasko, D. J. (2011). "Technology determines tactics": The relationship between technology and doctrine in Chinese military thinking. *Journal of Strategic Studies, 34*(3), 355–381. https://doi.org/10.1080/01402390.2011.574979

BOFIT. (2023). China's central bank ongoing digital yuan pilot project enters its fourth year. *The Bank of Finland Institute for Emerging Economies Weekly Review, 28.* https://www.bofit.fi/en/monitoring/weekly/2023/vw202328_1/

Booz Allen Hamilton. (2012, January 12). New index ranks ability of G20 nations to withstand cyber attacks, harness digital environment. *Business Wire.* https://www.businesswire.com/news/home/20120112005941/en/New-Index-Ranks-Ability-of-G20-Nations-to-Withstand-Cyber-Attacks-Harness-Digital-Environment

Borghard, E. D., & Lonergan, S. W. (2017). The logic of coercion in cyberspace. *Security Studies*, 26(3), 452–481. https://doi.org/10.1080/09636412.2017 .1306396

Bowman, J. (2000). *Columbia chronologies of Asian history and culture*. Columbia University Press.

Breznitz, D., & Murphree, M. (2013). *The rise of China in technology standards: New norms in old institutions*. https://www.uscc.gov/sites/default/files/Research /RiseofChinainTechnologyStandards.pdf

Brooks, R. A. (2007). The impact of culture, society, institutions, and international forces on military effectiveness. In R. A. Brooks & E. A. Stanley (Eds.), *Creating military power: The sources of military effectiveness*, pp. 1–26. Stanford University Press.

Bruyère, E. de la, & Picarsic, N. (2020). *China standards 2035: Beijing's platform geopolitics and "standardization work in 2020."* https://www.horizonadvisory .org/chinastandards

Bruyère, E. de la, & Picarsic, N. (2021). *Defusing military-civil fusion: The need to identify and respond to Chinese military companies*. https://www.fdd.org/ analysis/2021/05/26/defusing-military-civil-fusion/

Bughin, J., Seong, J., Manyika, J., Chui, M., & Joshi, R. (2018). *Notes from the AI frontier: Modeling the impact of AI on the world economy*. https://www .mckinsey.com/featured-insights/artificial-intelligence/notes-from-the-ai-frontier -modeling-the-impact-of-ai-on-the-world-economy#

Burke, E. J., Gunness, K., Cooper III, C. A., & Cozad, M. (2020). *People's liberation army operational concepts*. https://www.rand.org/content/dam/rand/pubs/ research_reports/RRA300/RRA394-1/RAND_RRA394-1.pdf

Buzan, B., Woever, O., & De Wilde, J. (1998). *Security: A new framework for analysis*. Lynne Rienner.

CAC. (2016). *National cyberspace security strategy*. http://www.cac.gov.cn/2016 -12/27/c_1120195926.htm

CAC. (2017a, January 23). *Defend cyberspace sovereignty and consolidate the cornerstone of cyber power*. Cyberspace Administration of China. http://www .cac.gov.cn/2017-01/23/c_1120366736.htm

CAC. (2017b, September 15). Thoroughly implement General Secretary Xi Jinping's strategic thinking of strengthening the country through the Internet, and solidly promote network security and informatization work. *Qiushi*. http://www .qstheory.cn/dukan/qs/2017-09/15/c_1121647633.htm

CAC. (2019, December 15). *Regulations on the ecological governance of network information content*. Cyberspace Administration of China. http://www.cac.gov .cn/2019-12/20/c_1578375159509309.htm

Cadell, C. (2017, July 29). Apple says it is removing VPN services from China App Store. *Reuters*. https://www.reuters.com/article/us-china-apple-vpn -idUSKBN1AE0BQ

Cai, C. (2015). Cybersecurity in the Chinese context: Changing concepts, vital interests, and prospects for cooperation. *China Quarterly of International Strategic Studies*, 1(3), 471–496. https://doi.org/10.1142/S2377740015500189

Cai, C. (2018). Global cyber governance: China's contribution and approach. *China Quarterly of International Strategic Studies*, 4(1), 55–76. https://doi.org/10.1142 /S2377740018500069

Cai, P. (2017, March 22). *Understanding China's Belt and Road Initiative.* Lowy Institute. https://www.lowyinstitute.org/publications/understanding-belt-and -road-initiative

CAICT. (2020). *Digital economy development in China (2020).* China Academy of Information and Communications Technology.

CAICT. (2021). *China digital economy white paper.* http://www.caict.ac.cn/english /research/whitepapers/202104/P020210429540525737660.pdf

CAICT. (2022). *China digital economy development report (2022).* http://www.caict .ac.cn/english/research/whitepapers/202208/P020220819505049573088.pdf

Cambridge English Dictionary. (n.d.). *POWER | Meaning in the Cambridge English Dictionary.* Retrieved December 10, 2020, from https://dictionary.cambridge .org/dictionary/english/power

Campbell, C. (2021). *China's military: The People's Liberation Army (PLA).* https:// crsreports.congress.gov

Cary, D. (2021). *China's national cybersecurity center: A base for military-civil fusion in the cyber domain.* https://cset.georgetown.edu/wp-content/uploads/ CSET-Chinas-National-Cybersecurity-Center.pdf

CAS. (2016, May 24). China Rolls out three-year program for AI growth. *Chinese Academy of Sciences.* http://english.cas.cn/newsroom/archive/china_archive/ cn2016/201605/t20160524_163411.shtml

CAS. (2017a, June 19). Chinese scientists successfully beam "entangled" Photons from space in landmark experiment. *Chinese Academy of Sciences.* http://english .cas.cn/newsroom/archive/research_archive/rp2017/201706/t20170619_178278 .shtml

CAS. (2017b, July 10). A life of quantum entanglement. *Chinese Academy of Sciences.* http://english.cas.cn/newsroom/archive/news_archive/nu2017/201707/ t20170711_179511.shtml

CAS. (2017c, August 10). China's satellite sends unbreakable cipher from space. *Chinese Academy of Sciences.* http://english.cas.cn/head/201708/t20170810 _181862.shtml

CAS. (2017d, October 9). China opens 2,000-km quantum communication line. *Chinese Academy of Sciences.* http://english.cas.cn/newsroom/archive/news _archive/nu2017/201710/t20171009_183701.shtml

Castro, D. (2019). *Who is winning the AI race: China, the EU or the United States?* https://datainnovation.org/2019/08/who-is-winning-the-ai-race-china-the-eu-or -the-united-states/

Cavelty, M. D. (2018). Europe's cyber-power. *European Politics and Society, 19*(3), 304–320. https://doi.org/10.1080/23745118.2018.1430718

CCDCOE. (2015). *An updated draft of the code of conduct distributed in the United Nations – What's new?* https://ccdcoe.org/incyder-articles/an-updated -draft-of-the-code-of-conduct-distributed-in-the-united-nations-whats-new/

CCTV. (2016, August 30). What kind of force is the strategic support force inspected by Xi Jinping? *CCTV.* http://news.cctv.com/2016/08/30/ARTI2Xi1zgynCfj6TYs ecOcb160830.shtml

CCTV. (2021, December 17). A certain department of the strategic support force: Carry out emergency drills to improve awareness of combat readiness. *CCTV.* http://military.cctv.com/2021/12/17/ARTIHe7uRGvLpFkBicaxqZg7211217 .shtml

CECC. (n.d.). *Agencies responsible for censorship in China.* Congressional-Executive Commission on China. Retrieved December 12, 2020, from https://www.cecc.gov/agencies-responsible-for-censorship-in-china

Cerf, V. G. (2012, May 25). Keep the Internet open. *The New York Times.* https://www.nytimes.com/2012/05/25/opinion/keep-the-internet-open.html

CESI. (2018). *Artificial intelligence standardization white paper (2018) – Translation by center for security and emerging technology.* https://cset.georgetown.edu/wp-content/uploads/t0120_AI_standardization_white_paper_EN.pdf

CESI. (2021). *Artificial intelligence standardization white paper – Translation by center for security and emerging technology.* China Electronics Standardization Institute.

CGTN. (2018, September 17). Xi says China willing to cooperate with other countries in AI industry. *CGTN.* https://news.cgtn.com/news/3d3d514e32556a4d7a457a6333566d54/share_p.html

Chan, J. H. (2019, April 30). China's digital silk road: A game changer for Asian economies. *The Diplomat.* https://thediplomat.com/2019/04/chinas-digital-silk-road-a-game-changer-for-asian-economies/

Chan, J. H., & Rawat, D. (2019). *China's digital silk road: The integration of Myanmar.* www.rsis.edu.sg

Chan, M. (2018, July 11). Welcome to the modern military: China's new combat units prepare for electronic warfare. *South China Morning Post.* https://www.scmp.com/news/china/diplomacy-defence/article/2154550/welcome-modern-military-chinas-new-combat-units-prepare

Chang, A. (2014). *Warring state: China's cybersecurity strategy.* https://www.cnas.org/publications/reports/warring-state-chinas-cybersecurity-strategy

Chang, M. (1995, March 5). Information intensified-A mark of 21st century weapons and military units. *International Aviation [FBIS-CHI-95-114].*

Changjiang Daily. (2022, March 31). Half of the top 50 domestic cybersecurity companies have settled in the Dongxihu District National Cybersecurity Base. *Changjiang Daily.* http://news.cjn.cn/whpd/yw_19947/202203/t4004452.htm

Chapelle, B. de la. (2007). The Internet governance forum: How a United Nations summit produced a new governance paradigm for the Internet age. In C. Möller & A. Amouroux (Eds.), *Governing the Internet: Freedom and regulation in the OSCE region.* Organization for Security and Co-operation in Europe. www.osce.org/fom

Chase, M. S., & Mulvenon, J. C. (2002). *You've got dissent!: Chinese dissident use of the Internet and Beijing's counter-strategies.* RAND Corporation. https://www.rand.org/pubs/monograph_reports/MR1543.html

Chen, D. (2018, March 31). Adhere to the path of modernization of military theory with the characteristics of our army. *Qiushi.* http://www.qstheory.cn/dukan/qs/2018-03/31/c_1122594901.htm

Chen, D. (2021, November 4). Artificial intelligence: The winning blade of cognitive warfare. *PLA Daily.* http://www.81.cn/jfjbmap/content/2021-11/04/content_302370.htm

Chen, H. (2017, March 14). What is the main purpose of U.S. cyber warfare? *China Military Network.* http://www.81.cn/jskj/2017-03/14/content_7366108.htm

Chen, J., McReynolds, J., & Green, K. (2021). The PLA strategic support force: A "joint" force for information operations. In J. Wuthnow, A. S. Ding, P. C. Saunders, A. Scobell, & A. N. D. Yang (Eds.), *The PLA beyond borders*, pp. 151–179. National Defense University Press.

Chen, S. (2017a, September 11). China building world's biggest quantum research facility. *South China Morning Post*.

Chen, S. (2017b, September 11). China building world's biggest quantum research facility. *South China Morning Post*. https://www.scmp.com/news/china/society/article/2110563/china-building-worlds-biggest-quantum-research-facility

Chen, S. (2018, February 4). China's plan to use artificial intelligence to boost the thinking skills of nuclear submarine commanders. *South China Morning Post*. https://www.scmp.com/news/china/society/article/2131127/chinas-plan-use-artificial-intelligence-boost-thinking-skills

Chen, S., Zhao, J., & Peng, Y. (2014). The development of TD-SCDMA 3G to TD-LTE-advanced 4G from 1998 to 2013. *IEEE Wireless Communications*, 21(6), 167–176. https://doi.org/10.1109/MWC.2014.7000985

Chen, W. (2019, March 1). Cyber war. *PLA Daily*. http://www.81.cn/jfjbmap/content/2019-03/21/content_229747.htm

Chen, X. (2009, May 21). China builds world's first quantum encrypted gov't network. *China.Org.Cn*. http://www.china.org.cn/government/local_governments/2009-05/21/content_17813415.htm

Cheng, D. (2016). *Cyber dragon: Inside China's information warfare and cyber operations*. Praeger. https://www.cengage.com/search/productOverview.do;jsessionid=D4AADE6EDBD9AC7CB732E9EC1778A8CA?N=28+197&Ntk=P_EPI&Ntt=1852580308297716025159608370220452407938&Ntx=mode%2Bmatchallpartial

Cheng, X. (2018, April 3). Military-civilian integration to build a national cyberspace defense system. *PLA Daily*. http://www.81.cn/jfjbmap/content/2018-04/03/content_203077.htm

China Briefing. (2021, August 24). *The PRC personal information protection law (final): A full translation*. https://www.china-briefing.com/news/the-prc-personal-information-protection-law-final-a-full-translation/

China Copyright and Media. (1996, April 16). *State council general office notice concerning establishing the state council leading group for informatization work*. https://chinacopyrightandmedia.wordpress.com/1996/04/16/state-council-general-office-notice-concerning-establishing-the-state-council-leading-group-for-informatization-work/

China Copyright and Media. (1999, December 23). *State council general office notice concerning establishing a leading group for national informatization work*. https://chinacopyrightandmedia.wordpress.com/1999/12/23/state-council-general-office-notice-concerning-establishing-a-leading-group-for-national-informatization-work/

China Copyright and Media. (2006, March 19). *2006–2020 national informatization development strategy*. https://chinacopyrightandmedia.wordpress.com/2006/03/19/2006-2020-national-informatization-development-strategy/

China Copyright and Media. (2016a). *Outline of the national informatization development strategy*. https://chinacopyrightandmedia.wordpress.com/2016/07/27/outline-of-the-national-informatization-development-strategy/

China Copyright and Media. (2016b, April 26). *Speech at the work conference for cybersecurity and informatization.* https://chinacopyrightandmedia.wordpress.com/2016/04/19/speech-at-the-work-conference-for-cybersecurity-and-informatization/

China Copyright and Media. (2018, April 22). *Xi Jinping's speech at the national cybersecurity and informatization work conference.* https://chinacopyrightandmedia.wordpress.com/2018/04/22/xi-jinpings-speech-at-the-national-cybersecurity-and-informatization-work-conference/

China Daily. (2002, March 26). *Public pledge of self-regulation and professional ethics for China Internet industry.* http://govt.chinadaily.com.cn/s/201812/26/WS5c23261f498eb4f01ff253d2/public-pledge-of-self-regulation-and-professional-ethics-for-china-internet-industry.html

China Daily. (2010, November 25). Mission action 2010 transregional joint exercise. *China Daily.* https://www.chinadaily.com.cn/china/2010-11/25/content_11607284.htm

China Daily. (2014a, February 27). Xi Jinping leads Internet security group. *China Daily.* http://www.chinadaily.com.cn/china/2014-02/27/content_17311358.htm

China Daily. (2014b, September 1). Army needs "information warfare" plan, declares Xi. *China Daily.* http://www.chinadaily.com.cn/china/2014-09/01/content_18520930.htm

China Daily. (2015, December 16). Top official says ITU can help in Digital Silk Road. *China Daily.* https://www.chinadaily.com.cn/china/2015-12/16/content_22727868.htm

China Daily. (2016). *Evolution of the Internet in China.* http://www.chinadaily.com.cn/china/2016even/index.html

China Daily. (2017, September 13). World's biggest quantum facility in E China to equip stealth submarines. *China Daily.* https://www.chinadaily.com.cn/china/2017-09/13/content_31932221.htm

China Economic Net. (2012, July 31). Solidly promote the innovation-driven development strategy. *Economic Daily Multimedia Digital Newspaper.* http://paper.ce.cn/jjrb/html/2012-07/31/content_125344.htm

China Internet Information Center. (2019, November 5). Press conference on the fourth plenary session of the 19th CPC Central Committee. *China.Org.* http://www.china.org.cn/china/2019-11/05/content_75376452_3.htm

China Kaoyan. (n.d.). *Introduction to PLA university of information engineering.* Retrieved August 23, 2022, from http://www.chinakaoyan.com/graduate/intro/schoolID/568.shtml

2016 Cybersecurity Law. (2016). https://www.chinalawtranslate.com/2016-cybersecurity-law/

China Law Translate. (2022, January 3). *Cybersecurity review measures* (2022 ed.). https://www.chinalawtranslate.com/en/17598-2/

China Market Regulation News. (2020, January 19). *Comprehensively deepen the reform of standardization and give full play to the basic, strategic and leading role of standardization.* China Market Regulation News. http://www.cicn.com.cn/zggsb/2020-01/19/cms123351article.shtml

China Military Network. (2019, June 14). Stepping up preparations for war, the United States wants to drag the world into the history of cyber warfare. *China Military Network.* http://www.81.cn/theory/2019-06/14/content_9530549.htm

China Military Online. (2018, July 9). PLA army holds "ingenious soldiers" military skills competition. *China Military Online.* http://english.chinamil.com.cn/view /2018-07/09/content_8084257.htm

China Military Online. (2019, May 17). PLA ground force holds "ingenious engineering soldier-2019" competition. *China Military Online.* http://eng .chinamil.com.cn/view/2019-05/17/content_9506269.htm

China National Radio. (2015, March 13). Xi Jinping: Upgrading the development of military-civilian integration to a national strategy. *China National Radio.* http://m.cnr.cn/news/20150313/t20150313_517988703.html

China Telecom. (n.d.). *IPv6 deployment best practice by China Telecom.* Retrieved December 13, 2020, from https://www.ipv6forum.com/dl/presentations/v6CT.pdf

China University of Petroleum. (2019, December 17). *Chinese people's liberation army academy of military sciences.* Career Centre of China University of Petroleum. https://career.cup.edu.cn/news/view/aid/86666/tag/lecture

China Youth Daily. (2019, October 17). *The artificial intelligence arms race is quietly emerging.* https://m.chinanews.com/wap/detail/zw/gn/2019/10-17 /8981224.shtml

Choi, C. (2016, August 19). Beijing clamps down on news portals, ordering round the clock monitoring. *South China Morning Post.* https://www.scmp.com/news /china/policies-politics/article/2005820/beijing-clamps-down-news-portals -ordering-round-clock

Christchurch Call. (n.d.). *About Christchurch call.* Retrieved December 12, 2020, from https://www.christchurchcall.com/call.html

CISA. (2022). *China cyber threat overview and advisories.* Cybersecurity and Infrastructure Security Agency. https://www.cisa.gov/uscert/china

CNCERT. (n.d.). *About us.* Retrieved February 1, 2019, from http://www.cert.org .cn/publish/english/index.html

CNET. (1997, June 27). *Golden projects.* https://www.cnet.com/news/golden -projects/

CNGI. (2010, December 20). *CNGI background.* China Next Generation Internet Expert Committee. http://www.cngi.cn/class/view?id=10222

CNNIC. (2012a, June 28). *The Internet timeline of China 1986–2003.* https://cnnic .com.cn/IDR/hlwfzdsj/201306/t20130628_40563.htm

CNNIC. (2012b, August). *Introduction.* https://cnnic.com.cn/AU/Introduction/ Introduction/201208/t20120815_33295.htm

Cooper, A. (2020, March 30). *Liaison statement: Response to "LS on new IP, shaping future network."* Internet Engineering Task Force. https://datatracker .ietf.org/liaison/1677/

Cordesman, A. H. (2016). *Chinese military spending estimates of Chinese military spending.* http://csis-website-prod.s3.amazonaws.com/s3fs-public/publication /160928_AHC_Estimates_Chinese_Military_Spending.pdf

Costello, J., & Mcreynolds, J. (2018). *China's strategic support force: A force for a New Era.* National Defense University Press. https://ndupress.ndu.edu/Portals /68/Documents/stratperspective/china/china-perspectives_13.pdf

Council of Europe. (n.d.). *History of artificial intelligence.* Retrieved December 13, 2020, from https://www.coe.int/en/web/artificial-intelligence/history-of-ai

Council on Foreign Relations. (2010). *Operation Aurora.* Council on Foreign Relations. https://www.cfr.org/cyber-operations/operation-aurora

Creemers, R., Costigan, J., & Webster, G. (2022, January 28). *Translation: Xi Jinping's speech to the politburo study session on the digital economy – October 2021*. DigiChina. https://digichina.stanford.edu/work/translation-xi-jinpings -speech-to-the-politburo-study-session-on-the-digital-economy-oct-2021/

Creemers, R., Dorwart, H., Neville, K., Schaefer, K., Costigan, J., & Webster, G. (2022, January 24). *Translation: 14th five-year plan for national informatization – December 2021*. DigiChina. https://digichina.stanford.edu/work/translation -14th-five-year-plan-for-national-informatization-dec-2021/

Creemers, R., Triolo, P., Sacks, S., Lu, X., & Webster, G. (2018, March 26). *China's cyberspace authorities set to gain clout in reorganization*. https://www .newamerica.org/cybersecurity-initiative/digichina/blog/chinas-cyberspace -authorities-set-gain-clout-reorganization/

Creemers, R., Triolo, P., & Webster, G. (2017). *Translation: Cybersecurity law of the People's Republic of China*. https://www.newamerica.org/cybersecurity -initiative/digichina/blog/translation-cybersecurity-law-peoples-republic-china/

Creemers, R., Webster, G., Triolo, P., Tai, K., Coplin, A., & Laskai, L. (2018, May 31). *Lexicon: 网络强国 Wǎngluò Qiángguó*. DigiChina. https://digichina .stanford.edu/work/lexicon-网络强国-wangluo-qiangguo/

Cropsey, S. (2010). The US navy in distress. *Strategic Analysis, 34*(1), 35–45. https:// www.hudson.org/content/researchattachments/attachment/766/cropsey_us _navy_in_distress.pdf

Fisher, R. D. (2010). *China's military modernization: Building for regional and global reach*. Stanford University Press.

Dai, Q. (2004). Discourse on armed forces informationization building and information warfare building. In W. Shen (Ed.), *On the Chinese revolution in military affairs*, pp. 39–47. New China Press.

Dai, S. (2019, August 30). China adds Huawei, Hikvision to expanded 'national team' spearheading country's AI efforts. *South China Morning Post*. https:// www.scmp.com/tech/big-tech/article/3024966/china-adds-huawei-hikvision -expanded-national-team-spearheading

DAMO Academy. (n.d.). *Quantum Lab – DAMO Academy*. Retrieved December 13, 2020, from https://damo.alibaba.com/labs/quantum

Dann, G. E., & Haddow, N. (2008). Just doing business or doing just business: Google, Microsoft, Yahoo! and the business of censoring China's Internet. *Journal of Business Ethics, 79*(3), 219–234.

DeepMind. (n.d.). *AlphaGo*. Retrieved December 13, 2020, from https://deepmind .com/research/case-studies/alphago-the-story-so-far

Deering, S., & Hinden, R. (1998). *Internet protocol, version 6 (IPv6) specification*. https://www.rfc-editor.org/rfc/pdfrfc/rfc2460.txt.pdf

Deering, S., & Hinden, R. (2017). RFC 8200 – Internet protocol, version 6 (IPv6) specification. In *Internet engineering task force*. https://tools.ietf.org/html/rfc8200

Defense Science Board. (2019). *Defense applications of 5G network technology*. https://apps.dtic.mil/sti/pdfs/AD1078719.pdf

Dekker, B., Okano-Heijmans, M., & Zhang, E. S. (2020). *Unpacking China's Digital Silk Road*. www.clingendael.org

Deng, X. (1988, October 24). *China must take its place in the field of high technology*. https://cpcchina.chinadaily.com.cn/2010-10/26/content_13918471.htm

Der Spiegel. (2008, March 19). Spiegel interview with top Chinese military strategist: "We will defend our sovereignty with all means". *Der Spiegel*. https://

www.spiegel.de/international/world/spiegel-interview-with-top-chinese-military -strategist-we-will-defend-our-sovereignty-with-all-means-a-542506.html

Deutsche Bank. (2020). *Moving to digital wallets and the extinction of plastic cards part III. Digital currencies: The ultimate hard power tool.*

Devanesan, J. (2020, April 16). 5G patent wars – Asia surges ahead of Europe & US. *Techwire Asia.* https://techwireasia.com/2020/04/5g-patent-wars-asia-surges -ahead-of-europe-us/

Dossi, S. (2019). On the asymmetric advantages of cyberwarfare. Western literature and the Chinese journal Guofang Keji. *Journal of Strategic Studies, 43*(2), 281– 308. https://doi.org/10.1080/01402390.2019.1581613

Du, Z., & Yuxia, N. (2014). An analysis of the relationship between network sovereignty and state sovereignty. *Journal of Southwest Petroleum University, 16*(6), 79–84. http://www.xml-data.org/XNSYDXXBSKB/HTML/2014-6-79.htm

Eastmoney Securities. (2017, February 6). *Well-known central enterprise projects will be settled in Wuhan national cyber security base.* https://guba.eastmoney .com/news,601857,601889787.html

EDRi. (2012, December 19). *WCIT: What happened and what it means for the Internet.* European Digital Rights. https://edri.org/our-work/edrigramnumber10 -24wcit-what-happend/

Embassy of PRC in India. (n.d.). *Introduction to ZTE.* Retrieved December 13, 2020, from http://in.chineseembassy.org/eng/jjmy/zymywl/zzgs/t112583.htm

eoPortal. (n.d.). *QUESS (quantum experiments at space scale) / Micius.* Sharing Earth Observation Resources. Retrieved December 13, 2020, from https:// directory.eoportal.org/web/eoportal/satellite-missions/q/quess

Ericsson. (2020). *Ericsson mobility report.* https://www.ericsson.com/4adc87/ assets/local/mobility-report/documents/2020/november-2020-ericsson-mobility -report.pdf

Ermert, M. (2015, December 16). WSIS+10: Roles, responsibilities remain hot; cybersecurity treaty demanded by many states. *Intellectual Property Watch.* https://www.ip-watch.org/2015/12/16/wsis10-roles-responsibilities-remain-hot -cybersecurity-treaty-demanded-by-many-states/

Ernst, D. (2020). *Competing in artificial intelligence chips: China's challenge amid technology war.* https://www.cigionline.org/sites/default/files/documents/com petinginartificialintelligencechips-dieterernst_web.pdf

Eurasia Group. (2020). *The Digital Silk Road: Expanding China's digital footprint.* https://www.eurasiagroup.net/files/upload/Digital-Silk-Road-Expanding-China -Digital-Footprint-1.pdf

European Commission. (2020, September 10). *EU-China: Commission and China hold first high-level digital dialogue.* https://ec.europa.eu/commission/ presscorner/detail/en/ip_20_1600

Falcone, R., & Miller-Osborn, J. (2016, January 24). *Scarlet mimic: Years-long espionage campaign targets minority activists.* Unit 42 Palo Alto Networks. https://unit42.paloaltonetworks.com/scarlet-mimic-years-long-espionage -targets-minority-activists/

Fang, K. (2015, December 18). *Diplomacy is the point of China's world Internet conference.* The Initium. https://theinitium.com/article/20151218-opinion-world -internet-conference-foreign-policy-fangkecheng/

Fang, X., & Hu, H. (2014). *The great game of China-US in cyberspace.* Publishing House of Electronics Industry.

Farrell, J., Hayes, J., Shapiro, C., & Sullivan, T. (2007). Standard settings, patents, and hold-up. *Antitrust Law Journal, 74*(3), 603–670.

FAS. (2000). *Ministry of information industry.* https://fas.org/nuke/guide/china/agency/mii.htm

Fedasiuk, R., Melot, J., & Murphy, B. (2021). *Harnessed lightning: How the Chinese military is adopting artificial intelligence.* https://cset.georgetown.edu/wp-content/uploads/CSET-Harnessed-Lightning.pdf

Feigenbaum, E. A. (2003). *China's techno-warriors: National security and strategic competition from the nuclear to the information age.* Stanford University Press.

FG NET-2030. (n.d.). *Focus group on technologies for network 2030.* ITU-T Focus Group Technologies for Network 2030. Retrieved December 13, 2020, from https://www.itu.int/en/ITU-T/focusgroups/net2030/Pages/default.aspx

Financial Times. (2020, February 12). *Patents reveal extent of China's digital currency plans.* https://www.ft.com/content/f10e94cc-4d74-11ea-95a0-43d18ec715f5

Finkelstein, D. M. (2007). China's national military strategy. *Asia Policy, 4,* 67–72.

Finnemore, M., & Hollis, D. B. (2016). Constructing norms for global cybersecurity. *American Journal of International Law, 110*(3), 425–479. https://doi.org/10.5305/amerjintelaw.110.3.0425

FMPRC. (2020a, September 8). *Foreign ministry spokesperson Zhao Lijian's regular press conference.* Ministry of Foreign Affairs of the People's Republic of China. https://www.fmprc.gov.cn/ce/cesb/eng/fyrth_17/t1813183.htm

FMPRC. (2020b, September 8). *Global initiative on data security.* Ministry of Foreign Affairs of the People's Republic of China. https://www.fmprc.gov.cn/mfa_eng/wjdt_665385/2649_665393/202009/t20200908_679637.html

FMPRC. (2020c, September 8). *The Chinese side proposes a global initiative on data security.* Ministry of Foreign Affairs of the People's Republic of China. https://www.fmprc.gov.cn/ce/cgmb/eng/zgyw/t1813730.htm

Frankel, J. (2019, October 24). Trump's weaponisation of the dollar could threaten its dominance. *The Guardian.* https://www.theguardian.com/business/2019/oct/24/trumps-weaponisation-of-the-dollar-could-threaten-its-dominance

Fu, W., Yang, W., & Xu, C. (2020, January 14). Intelligent warfare, where is the constant. *PLA Daily.* http://www.81.cn/jfjbmap/content/2020-01/14/content_252163.htm

Future Networks. (2017). *Internet 2030: Towards a new Internet for the year 2030 and beyond.* https://www.itu.int/en/ITU-T/studygroups/2017-2020/13/Documents/Internet_2030.pdf

Gady, F.-S. (2015, February 7). The Wuzhen summit and Chinese Internet sovereignty. *HuffPost.* https://www.huffpost.com/entry/the-wuzhen-summit-and-chi_b_6287040

Gao, J. (2015, November 2). President of the academy of military sciences: Reforms must solve the institutional obstacles that fetter a strong army – Teller Report. *Chinanews.* https://www.chinanews.com.cn/mil/2015/11-02/7600724.shtml

Gao, P. (2008). WAPI: A Chinese attempt to establish wireless standards and the international coalition that resisted. *Communications of the Association for Information Systems, 23.* https://doi.org/10.17705/1cais.02308

Geng, Z. (2021, February 24). *Accurately promote the direction of building a strong cyber country.* Cyberspace Administration of China. http://www.cac.gov.cn/2021-02/24/c_1615744064919664.htm

Gibney, E. (2017, May). Europe's billion-euro quantum project takes shape. *Nature*. https://www.nature.com/news/europe-s-billion-euro-quantum-project-takes -shape-1.21925

Gigova, R. (2017, September 2). Who Putin thinks will rule the world. *CNN*. https:// edition.cnn.com/2017/09/01/world/putin-artificial-intelligence-will-rule-world/ index.html

Gill, B., & Ni, A. (2017, October 16). Expect a shakeup of China's military elite at the 19th Party Congress. *The Conversation*. https://theconversation.com/expect -a-shakeup-of-chinas-military-elite-at-the-19th-party-congress-84060

Giovannini, M. (2020, June 10). The Digital Silk Road's growing strategic role during the epidemic. *CGTN*. https://news.cgtn.com/news/2020-06-10/The-Digital-Silk -Road-s-growing-strategic-role-during-the-epidemic-RbN21gC6xW/index.html

GIP. (n.d.). *UN GGE and OEWG | GIP Digital Watch observatory for Internet governance and digital policy*. Retrieved December 10, 2020, from https://dig .watch/processes/un-gge

GKZY. (2014). *The people's liberation army information engineering university*. College Entrance Examination Volunteer Network. http://www.gkzy.com/ college/brief_127.html

Global Times. (2013a, June 14). China deserves explanation of PRISM. *Global Times*. https://www.globaltimes.cn/content/788734.shtml

Global Times. (2013b, June 16). *World reacts to Edward Snowden's leak*. https:// www.globaltimes.cn/content/789098.shtml

Global Times. (2014, October 9). *Beijing bids farewell to era of "undefended" Internet, moving to cyber power status*. https://www.globaltimes.cn/content/885408.shtml

Global Times. (2016, September 9). China successfully develops quantum radar system. *Global Times*. https://www.globaltimes.cn/content/1005525.shtml

Global Times. (2020, April 28). Chinese standards going global an unavoidable trend. *Global Times*. https://www.globaltimes.cn/content/1187060.shtml

Global Times. (2021, July 16). Seven of China's top regulators enter Didi to undergo cybersecurity review. *Global Times*. https://www.globaltimes.cn/page/202107 /1228838.shtml

Goldman, E. O., & Arquilla, J. (2014). *Cyber analogies*. https://core.ac.uk/download /pdf/36732393.pdf

Goldsmith, J., & Wu, T. (2006). *Who controls the Internet?: Illusions of a borderless world*. Oxford University Press.

Gong, S., & Li, B. (2019). The digital silk road and the sustainable development goals. *IDS Bulletin*, *50*(4). https://bulletin.ids.ac.uk/index.php/idsbo/article/view /3061/3037

Government of Canada. (n.d.). *Chinese military innovation in emerging technologies*. Retrieved December 15, 2020, from https://www.canada.ca/ en/security-intelligence-service/corporate/publications/china-and-the-age-of -strategic-rivalry/chinese-military-innovation-in-emerging-technologies.html

Gray, C. S. (2013). *Making strategic sense of cyber power: Why the sky is not falling*. Strategic Studies Institute and U.S. Army War College Press. http://www.strateg icstudiesinstitute.army.mil/

GSMA. (2019). *The mobile economy 2019*. https://data.gsmaintelligence.com/api-web/ v2/research-file-download?id=39256194&file=2712-250219-ME-Global.pdf

Gu, Z., & Liu, J. M. (2005, September 21). ZTE's solution to China next generation Internet (CNGI). *ZTE Communications*. https://www.zte.com.cn/global/about/magazine/zte-communications/2005/3/en_58/162362.html

Guan, C. (n.d.). *Huawei – Chinese telecommunications giant Huawei: Strategies to success.*

Guo, Y. (2017, December 4). Digital economy cooperation to empower Belt, Road. *China.Org.* http://www.china.org.cn/world/2017-12/04/content_50083923.htm

Guterres, A. (2017, May 14). Remarks at the opening of the Belt and Road Forum. *United Nations Secretary-General.* https://www.un.org/sg/en/content/sg/speeches/2017-05-14/secretary-general's-belt-and-road-forum-remarks

Haas, B. (2017, July 19). China blocks WhatsApp services as censors tighten grip on Internet. *The Guardian.* https://www.theguardian.com/technology/2017/jul/19/china-blocks-whatsapp-services-as-censors-tighten-grip-on-internet

Hachigian, N. (2001, March). China's cyber-strategy. *Foreign Affairs.* https://www.foreignaffairs.com/articles/asia/2001-03-01/chinas-cyber-strategy

Haldane, M., & Shen, X. (2022, October 6). China blocks Internet anticensorship tools ahead of 20th party congress as the Great Firewall grows in sophistication. *South China Morning Post.* https://www.scmp.com/tech/policy/article/3195045/china-blocks-internet-anticensorship-tools-ahead-20th-party-congress

Han, Y. (1995, June 27). The invisible battlefront. *PLA Daily [FBIS-CHI-95-193].*

Hansen, S. (2014). *China's cyberpower: International and domestic priorities.*

Hao, X., Zhang, K., & Yu, H. (1996). The Internet and information control: The case of China. *Electronic Journal of Communication*, 6(2). http://www.cios.org/EJCPUBLIC/006/2/00625.HTML

Hao, Y. (2016, February 2). Forward-looking thoughts on the construction of China's cyber army under the background of global co-government cyber security. *People's Daily.* http://theory.people.com.cn/n1/2016/0202/c386965-28104957.html

Harold, S. W., Libicki, M. C., & Cevallos, A. S. (2016). *Getting to yes with China in cyberspace.* https://www.rand.org/content/dam/rand/pubs/research_reports/RR1300/RR1335/RAND_RR1335.pdf

Harper, J. (2018, August 27). Germany urges SWIFT end to US payments dominance. *DW.* https://www.dw.com/en/germany-urges-swift-end-to-us-payments-dominance/a-45242528

Hart, B., Lin, B., Lu, S., Price, H., Liao, Y. (Grace), & Slade, M. (2023). *Is China a leader in quantum technologies?* China Power. https://chinapower.csis.org/china-quantum-technology/

Harwit, E. (1998). China's telecommunications industry: Development patterns and policies. *Pacific Affairs*, 71(2), 175–194. https://doi.org/10.2307/2760975

Harwit, E. (2007). Building China's telecommunications network: Industrial policy and the role of Chinese State-owned, foreign and private domestic enterprises. *China Quarterly*, 190, 311–322.

Hassan, M., & Kumar, A. (2020). *Who owns 5G patents? – A detailed analysis of 5G SEPs – GreyB.* https://www.greyb.com/5g-patents/

Hathaway, M., Demchak, C., Kerben, J., Mcardle, J., & Spidalieri, F. (2015). *Cyber readiness INDEX 2.0.* www.potomacinstitute.org

He, G., Meng, Q., & Zhang, J. (2018, April 23). Cyber security military-civilian integration is imperative. *People's Daily*. http://theory.people.com.cn/n1/2018/0423/c40531-29943961.html

Hogewoning, M. (2020). *Response to "new IP, shaping future network" proposal*. https://assets.documentcloud.org/documents/6876493/RIPE-NCC-TSAG-New-IP.pdf

Hong, S. (2016). China and global Internet governance: Toward an alternative analytical framework. *Chinese Journal of Communication* . https://doi.org/10.1080/17544750.2016.1206028

Hong, S. (2018). Building a digital silk road? Situating the Internet in China's Belt and road initiative. *International Journal of Communication, 12*, 2683–2701. http://ijoc.org

Horenbeeck, M. Van. (2008, March 21). *Cyber attacks against Tibetan communities*. InfoSec Handlers Diary Blog. https://isc.sans.edu/diary/Cyber+attacks+against+Tibetan+communities/4176

Horta, L. (2013, October 17). *The Dragon's spear: China's asymmetric strategy*. YaleGlobal Online. https://yaleglobal.yale.edu/content/dragons-spear-chinas-asymmetric-strategy

Hu, H. (2018, July 16). Use development finance to better serve the Belt and Road construction. *People's Daily*. http://opinion.people.com.cn/n1/2018/0716/c1003-30148128.html

Hu, J. (2007, October 24). *Full text of Hu Jintao's report at 17th Party Congress*. https://www.chinadaily.com.cn/china/2007-10/24/content_6204564.htm

Hu, J. (2012a, November 18). *Full text of Hu's report at 18th Party Congress*. https://www.chinadaily.com.cn/china/19thcpcnationalcongress/2012-11/18/content_29578562.htm

Hu, J. (2012b, November 27). *Full text of Hu Jintao's report at 18th Party Congress*. http://www.china-embassy.org/eng/zt/18th_CPC_National_Congress_Eng/t992917.htm

Hu, R., & Xia, H. (2018, October 14). *A brigade of the army in the central theater and a base of the strategic support force conduct a confrontation exercise*. Ministry of National Defense. http://www.mod.gov.cn/power/2018-10/14/content_4826663.htm

Hu, Y. (2016, October 15). The core meaning of the cyber power strategy. *Sohu*. https://www.sohu.com/a/116225177_119861

Huai, G. (1996). On meeting the challenge of the new military revolution. *China Military Science [FBIS-CHI-96-130]*, 1.

Huang, Y. (2019, April 24). Construction of digital Silk Road lights up BRI cooperation. *People's Daily*. http://en.people.cn/n3/2019/0424/c90000-9571418.html

Huatu Education. (2019). *Military civilian position list of the institute of systems engineering, academy of military science*. https://ah.huatu.com/zw/jdwz/bw2019/85.html

Huawei. (2015, May 14). Huawei launches new European Research Institute to gear up European digitization progress and achieve win-win outcomes. *Huawei Press Center*. https://www.huawei.com/en/news/2015/05/hw_427623

Huawei. (2020, March 30). *MindSpore goes open source, empowering global developers with an all-scenario AI computing framework.* https://www.huawei .com/en/news/2020/3/huawei-mindspore-open-source

HUST. (2019, August). *Basic overview of the national cybersecurity talent and innovation base.* School of Cyber Science and Engineering, Huazhong University of Science and Technology. http://cse.hust.edu.cn/xygk/jdjj.htm

IBM. (n.d.-a). *Deep blue.* Retrieved December 13, 2020, from https://www.ibm.com /ibm/history/ibm100/us/en/icons/deepblue/

IBM. (n.d.-b). *What is quantum computing?* Retrieved December 13, 2020, from https://www.ibm.com/quantum-computing/learn/what-is-quantum-computing/

IBM. (n.d.-c). *What is the Golden Shield Project and how does it affect access to the eluminate.js files on my website when its accessed within China?* Retrieved December 12, 2020, from https://www.ibm.com/support/pages/what-golden -shield-project-and-how-does-it-affect-access-eluminatejs-files-my-website-when -its-accessed-within-china

ICANN. (2000). *Contract between ICANN and the United States government for performance of the IANA function.* https://www.icann.org/resources/unthemed -pages/iana-contract-2000-02-09-en

ICFC. (2018). *White paper on AI chip technologies.* https://www.080910t.com/ downloads/AIChip2018EN.pdf

IDC. (2020, August 4). *IDC forecasts strong 12.3% growth for AI market in 2020 amidst challenging circumstances.* https://www.idc.com/getdoc.jsp?containerId =prUS46757920

IETF. (n.d.). *Quantum Internet research group.* Retrieved December 10, 2020, from https://datatracker.ietf.org/rg/qirg/about/

IETF. (2011). *Source address validation improvements (Savi) working group.* https://datatracker.ietf.org/wg/savi/about/

IEU. (2018, November 2). *2019 Ph.D. application instructions.* Information Engineering University. http://zhaosheng.plaieu.edu.cn/contents/252/1018.html

IEU. (2019, November 7). *2020 Ph.D. application instructions.* Information Engineering University. http://zhaosheng.plaieu.edu.cn/contents/252/1138.html

IGF. (2015a). *About the Internet governance forum.* https://www.intgovforum.org /multilingual/tags/about

IGF. (2015b). *The Internet governance forum.* https://www.intgovforum.org/cms /2015/IGF.24.06.2015.pdf

IISS. (2021). *Cyber capabilities and national power: A net assessment.* https://www .iiss.org/blogs/research-paper/2021/06/cyber-capabilities-national-power

IMF. (n.d.). *World currency composition of official foreign exchange reserves.* International Monetary Fund. https://data.imf.org/regular.aspx?key=41175

Inkster, N. (2015). *China's cyber power* (Vol. 55). International Institute for Strategic Studies.

Insikt Group. (2021a, February 28). *China-linked group RedEcho targets the Indian power sector amid heightened border tensions.* Recorded Future. https:// www.recordedfuture.com/redecho-targeting-indian-power-sector

Insikt Group. (2021b). *Threat activity group RedFoxtrot linked to China's PLA Unit 69010; targets bordering Asian countries.* https://go.recordedfuture.com/ hubfs/reports/cta-2021-0616.pdf

Insikt Group. (2022, April 6). *Continued targeting of Indian power grid assets by Chinese State-sponsored activity group.* Recorded Future. https://www.recordedfuture.com/continued-targeting-of-indian-power-grid-assets

Interim regulations on the management of international networking of computer information. (1997). http://www.asianlii.org/cn/legis/cen/laws/irotmoinoci880/

Internet Society. (n.d.-a). *IANA transition.* Retrieved December 10, 2020, from https://www.internetsociety.org/iana-transition/

Internet Society. (n.d.-b). *What is IPv6?* Retrieved December 13, 2020, from https://www.internetsociety.org/deploy360/ipv6/

Internet Society. (2012). *Internet Society submission for the ITU world conference on international telecommunication regulations (WCIT-12).* https://www.internetsociety.org/resources/doc/2012/internet-society-submission-for-the-itu-world-conference-on-international-telecommunication-regulations-wcit-12/

Ip, K., Robinson, M., Lau, N., & Gong, J. (2017). *China tightens control on Internet news and content – Lexology.* Herbert Smith Freehills LLP. https://www.lexology.com/library/detail.aspx?g=b2aa77aa-0270-40f8-9f18-ad65b6130259

ISO/IEC JTC1. (n.d.). *Artificial intelligence – JTC 1.* Retrieved December 13, 2020, from https://jtc1info.org/technology/subcommittees/artificial-intelligence/

ISO. (n.d.). *ISO – ISO/IEC JTC 1 — Information technology.* International Organization for Standardization. Retrieved December 13, 2020, from https://www.iso.org/isoiec-jtc-1.html

ITU-T FG-AI4AD. (n.d.). *Focus group on AI for autonomous and assisted driving (FG-AI4AD).* Retrieved December 13, 2020, from https://www.itu.int/en/ITU-T/focusgroups/ai4ad/Pages/default.aspx

ITU-T FG-AI4H. (n.d.). *Focus group on "artificial intelligence for health."* Retrieved December 13, 2020, from https://www.itu.int/en/ITU-T/focusgroups/ai4h/Pages/default.aspx

ITU-T FG-QIT4N. (n.d.). *ITU-T focus group on quantum information technology for networks (FG-QIT4N).* Retrieved December 13, 2020, from https://www.itu.int/en/ITU-T/focusgroups/qit4n/Pages/default.aspx

ITU-T SG 13. (n.d.). *SG13: Future networks, with focus on IMT-2020, cloud computing and trusted network infrastructures.* Retrieved December 13, 2020, from https://www.itu.int/en/ITU-T/studygroups/2017-2020/13/Pages/default.aspx

ITU-T SG 17. (n.d.). *SG17: Security.* Retrieved December 13, 2020, from https://www.itu.int/en/ITU-T/studygroups/2017-2020/17/Pages/default.aspx

ITU-T TSAG. (2019a, September 10). *[83] "New IP, shaping future network": Propose to initiate the discussion of strategy transformation for ITU-T.* https://www.itu.int/md/T17-TSAG-C-0083

ITU-T TSAG. (2019b, September 10). *[97] Proposal to set up a new ITU-T focus group on quantum information technology for networks (FG-QIT4N).* ITU-T TSAG (Study Period 2017) Contribution 97. https://www.itu.int/md/T17-TSAG-C-0097/en

ITU-T TSAG. (2019c, September 18). *[598] Tutorial on C83 – New IP: Shaping the future network.* https://www.itu.int/md/T17-TSAG-190923-TD-GEN-0598/en

ITU. (2005). *WSIS: Tunis agenda for the information society.* http://www.itu.int/net/wsis/docs2/tunis/off/6rev1.html

ITU. (2012). *WCIT-12 final acts of the world conference on international Telecommunication.*

ITU. (2017). *ICT development index 2017 – China*. International Telecommunication Union. https://www.itu.int/net4/ITU-D/idi/2017/index.html#idi2017economycard-tab&CHN

ITU. (2018). *Setting the scene for 5G: Opportunities & challenges*. International Telecommunications Union. https://www.itu.int/en/ITU-D/Documents/ITU_5G_REPORT-2018.pdf

ITU. (2020). *Global cybersecurity index*. International Telecommunication Union. https://www.itu.int/en/ITU-D/Cybersecurity/Pages/global-cybersecurity-index.aspx

ITU News. (2019, December 3). New ITU standard for networks to support quantum-safe encryption and authentication. *ITU News*. https://news.itu.int/new-itu-standard-networks-support-quantum-safe-encryption-authentication/

Jiang, C. (2010). Cyber: The invisible new battlefront. *Qiushi*, *13*, 53–55.

Jiang, L. (2017, February 3). Why did the development of military-civilian integration become a national strategy. *The Paper*. https://www.thepaper.cn/newsDetail_forward_1611165

Jiang, L., Zhang, X., & Xu, F. (2013). The international cybersecurity dilemma and a way out. *Contemporary International Relations*, *9*, 52–58.

Jiang, M. (2010). Authoritarian informationalism: China's approach to Internet sovereignty. *SAIS Review of International Affairs*, *30*(2), 71–89. https://muse.jhu.edu/article/403440/pdf

Jiang, Z. (2009). *On the development of China's information technology industry*. Academic Press. https://www.elsevier.com/books/on-the-development-of-chinas-information-technology-industry/zemin/978-0-12-381369-5

Jin, Z. (2018, July 16). Open up a new era of military-civilian integration and in-depth development of a new situation. *Qiushi*. http://www.qstheory.cn/dukan/qs/2018-07/16/c_1123114703.htm

Kamensky, J., & Slawson, E. (2019, November 7). Five takeaways from China's fourth plenum. *China Business Review*. https://www.chinabusinessreview.com/five-takeaways-from-chinas-fourth-plenum-2/

Keohane, R. O., & Nye, J. S. (1989). *Power and interdependence : World politics in transition* (2nd ed.). Harper Collins.

Kleinwächter, W. (2007). The history of Internet governance. In C. Möller & A. Amouroux (Eds.), *Governing the Internet: Freedom and regulation in the OSCE Region*. Organization for Security and Co-Operation in Europe. www.osce.org/fom

Krekel, B. (2009). *Capability of the People's Republic of China to conduct cyber warfare and computer network exploitation: Prepared for the US-China economic and security review commission*. https://nsarchive2.gwu.edu//NSAEBB/NSAEBB424/docs/Cyber-030.pdf

Krekel, B., Adams, P., & Bakos, G. (2012). *Occupying the information high ground: Chinese capabilities for computer network espionage and cyber espionage*.

Kuehl, D. T. (2009). From cyberspace to cyberpower: Defining the problem. In F. D. Kramer, S. H. Starr, & L. K. Wentz (Eds.), *Cyberpower and national security*, pp. 24–42. National Defense University Press.

Kurlantzick, J. (2019, November). *How China is interfering in Taiwan's election*. Council on Foreign Relations. https://www.cfr.org/in-brief/how-china-interfering-taiwans-election

Lai, E. (2015). *Renminbi internationalization: The prospects of China's yuan as the next global currency*. https://iems.ust.hk/assets/publications/thought

-leadership-briefs/2015/tlb09/1503093_ust_iems_thought_leadership_brief_issue9_v08-web.pdf

Lau, J. (2010, July 9). A history of Google in China. *Financial Times.* http://ig-legacy.ft.com/content/faf86fbc-0009-11df-8626-00144feabdc0#axzz6br0M5thl

Lee, K.-F. (2018). *AI Superpowers: China, Silicon Valley and the new world order.* Houghton Mifflin Harcourt. https://www.aisuperpowers.com/

Lee, Z. (2021, July 5). China's cybersecurity regulator targets more U.S.-listed tech companies after Didi investigation. *Forbes.* https://www.forbes.com/sites/zinnialee/2021/07/05/chinas-cybersecurity-regulator-targets-more-us-listed-tech-companies-after-didi-investigation/?sh=5ea525521a89

Leonard, B. (2022, May 3). *Update on cyber activity in Eastern Europe.* Threat Analysis Group. https://blog.google/threat-analysis-group/update-on-cyber-activity-in-eastern-europe/

Li, G. (2015). The wolves of Zhurihe: China's OPFOR comes of age. *China Brief, 15*(4). https://jamestown.org/program/the-wolves-of-zhurihe-chinas-opfor-comes-of-age/

Li, K. (2015). *Report on the work of the government.* http://english.www.gov.cn/archive/publications/2015/03/05/content_281475066179954.htm

Li, K. (2021). *Report on the work of the government.* http://english.www.gov.cn/premier/news/202103/13/content_WS604b9030c6d0719374afac02.html

Li, K. (2022). *Report on the work of the government.* http://english.www.gov.cn/premier/news/202203/12/content_WS622c96d7c6d09c94e48a68ff.html

Li, M. (2018, November 12). *Reflections on the strategy of civil-military integration of network information system.* Cyberspace Administration of China. http://www.cac.gov.cn/2018-11/12/c_1123701001.htm

Li, R. (2018). Towards a new Internet for the year 2030 and beyond. *Third Annual ITU IMT-2020/5G Workshop and Demo Day.* https://www.itu.int/en/ITU-T/Workshops-and-Seminars/201807/Documents/3_Richard Li.pdf

Li, S. (2017, March 20). *The role of maintaining network sovereignty on ideological security.* Cyberspace Administration of China. http://www.cac.gov.cn/2017-03/20/c_1120657215.htm

Li, Y. (2019). Global cyberspace governance: State actors and the China-US cyber relationship. *Contemporary International Relations, 29,* 105–124.

Li, Y. (2020, January 28). Cognitive confrontation: A new frontier of future war. *China Military Network.* http://www.81.cn/theory/2020-01/28/content_9726644.htm

Li, Z. (2012). A Chinese perspective on cyber war. *International Review of the Red Cross, 94*(886), 801–806. https://doi.org/10.1017/S1816383112000823

Libicki, M. C. (2009). *Cyberdeterrence and Cyberwar.* RAND Corporation. www.rand.org

Lin, J., Singer, P. W., & Costello, J. (2016, March 3). China's quantum satellite could change cryptography forever. *Popular Science.* https://www.popsci.com/chinas-quantum-satellite-could-change-cryptography-forever/

Lindsay, J. R. (2013). Stuxnet and the limits of cyber warfare. *Security Studies, 22*(3), 365–404. https://doi.org/10.1080/09636412.2013.816122

Linjuan, J., Wang, W., & Zhang, Y. (2019, September 10). Military intelligence is deeply affecting future operations. *Ministry of National Defense.* http://www.mod.gov.cn/jmsd/2019-09/10/content_4850148.htm

Liu, B. (2004, December 27). China launches new generation Internet. *China Daily.* http://www.chinadaily.com.cn/english/doc/2004-12/27/content_403512.htm

Liu, L. (1995, November 7). Information warfare' sets new topic for study in tactics. *PLA Daily [FBIS-CHI95-234].*

Liu, Q. (2018, April 25). Historical opportunity to be a cyber power. *China Daily.* http://www.chinadaily.com.cn/a/201804/25/WS5adfbbe4a3105cdcf651a470 .html

Liu, X. (2019, May 1). ITU secretary-general: BRI helps narrow world digital divide. *CGTN.* https://news.cgtn.com/news/3d3d674e31597a4d34457a6333566d54/ index.html

Liu, X. (2021, June 14). PLA deploys AI in mock warplane battles, "trains both pilots and AIs". *Global Times.* https://www.globaltimes.cn/page/202106 /1226131.shtml

Liu, Y. (2011, August 1). *Efforts to create a new situation for the prosperity and development of basic research.* Central Government Portal. http://www.gov.cn/ ldhd/2011-08/01/content_1917336.htm

Liu, Y. (2018, January 10). National standards committee: Is formulating "China standard 2035". *Xinhua.* http://www.xinhuanet.com/fortune/2018-01/10/c _129787658.htm

Liu, Y., Wu, J., Wu, Q., & Xu, K. (2013). Recent progress in the study of the next generation Internet in China. *Philosophical Transactions of the Royal Society A, 371*(1987). https://doi.org/10.1098/rsta.2012.0387

Lo, S., & Lee, K. (2018). *China is poised to win the 5G race.* https://www.ey.com/ en_cn/tmt/china-is-poised-to-win-the-5g-race-are-you-up-to-speed

Logan, D. C. (2017). The evolution of the PLA's red-blue exercises. *China Brief, 17*(4). https://jamestown.org/program/evolution-plas-red-blue-exercises/

Lookout. (2020). *Mobile APT Surveillance Campaigns Targeting Uyghurs: A collection of long-running android tooling connected to a Chinese mAPT actor.* https://unit42.paloaltonetworks.com/unit42-pluginphantom-new-android -trojan-abuses-droidplugin-framework/

Lu, C. (2020, November 12). "Clean network" plan harms network security. *People's Daily.* http://media.people.com.cn/n1/2020/1112/c40606-31927790.html

Lu, W. (2016, April 27). *Lu Wei: Taking the responsibility of a major country and building a community with a shared future in cyberspace.* Shanghai Internet Illegal and Bad Information Reporting Center. http://www.shjbzx.cn/jbpt/n57/ n63/u1ai1394.html

Lu, X. (2002). *Promoting city informatization for social and economic development.*

Lu, Y. (2010). Science & technology in China: A roadmap to 2050. In *Science & technology in China: A roadmap to 2050.* Springer Berlin Heidelberg. https://doi .org/10.1007/978-3-642-04823-4_1

Lu, Z. (2018, January 3). China, a cyber power. *Cyberspace Administration of China.* http://www.cac.gov.cn/2018-01/03/c_1122201579.htm

Lupovici, A. (2011). Cyber warfare and deterrence : Trends and challenges in research. *Military and Strategic Affairs, 3*(3), 49–62.

Lyu, J. (2019, March 22). *What are China's cyber capabilities and intentions?* IPI Global Observatory. https://theglobalobservatory.org/2019/03/what-are-chinas -cyber-capabilities-intentions/

Mackinder, H. J. (1904). The geographical pivot of history. *Geographical Journal*, *23*(4), 437. https://doi.org/10.2307/1775498

MacroPolo. (2020, June 20). *The global AI talent tracker – MacroPolo*. https://macropolo.org/digital-projects/the-global-ai-talent-tracker/

Mandiant. (2013). *APT 1: Exposing one of China's cyber espionage units*. www.mandiant.com

Mandiant. (2014, September 3). *Darwin's favorite APT group*. https://www.mandiant.com/resources/blog/darwins-favorite-apt-group-2

Manjikian, M. M. (2010). From global village to virtual battlespace: The colonizing of the Internet and the extension of realpolitik. *International Studies Quarterly*, *54*(2), 381–401.

Marczak, B., Hulcoop, A., Maynier, E., Razzak, B. A., Crete-Nishihata, M., Scott-Railton, J., & Deibert, R. (2019, September 24). *Missing link: Tibetan groups targeted with 1-Click mobile exploits*. The Citizen Lab. https://citizenlab.ca/2019/09/poison-carp-tibetan-groups-targeted-with-1-click-mobile-exploits/

Masiowski, M., Mohr, N., Soller, H., & Zesko, M. (2022). *Quantum computing funding remains strong, but talent gap raises concern*. McKinsey. https://www.mckinsey.com/capabilities/mckinsey-digital/our-insights/quantum-computing-funding-remains-strong-but-talent-gap-raises-concern

Maslej, N., Fattorini, L., Brynjolfsson, E., Etchemendy, J., Ligett, K., Lyons, T., Manyika, J., Ngo, H., Niebles, J. C., Parli, V., Shoham, Y., Wald, R., Clark, J., & Perrault, R. (2023). *The AI index 2023 annual report*. https://aiindex.stanford.edu/wp-content/uploads/2023/04/HAI_AI-Index-Report_2023.pdf

McKenzie, N., Tobin, G., & Sakkal, P. (2019, November 23). The moment a Chinese spy decided to defect to Australia. *The Age*. https://www.theage.com.au/national/the-moment-a-chinese-spy-decided-to-defect-to-australia-20191122-p53d0x.html

McReynolds, J., & Luce, L. (2021). China's human capital ecosystem for network warfare. In R. D. Kamphausen (Ed.), *The people of the PLA 2.0*, pp. 327–371. Strategic Studies Institute.

Meissner, P. (2021, September 2). *These countries rank highest for digital competitiveness*. World Economic Forum. https://www.weforum.org/agenda/2021/09/countries-rank-highest-digital-competitiveness/

Miao, W. (2016, May 6). *In-depth study of the spirit of general secretary Xi Jinping's important speech to promote the construction of a cyber power with new development concepts*. Cyberspace Administration of China. http://www.cac.gov.cn/2016-05/06/c_1118813304.htm

Miao, W., & Lei, W. (2016). Policy review: The cyberspace administration of China. *Global Media and Communication*, *12*(3), 337–340. https://doi.org/10.1177/1742766516680879

Military Talent Net. (2022, March 12). *Announcement on the direct selection and recruitment of fresh graduates from ordinary institutions of higher learning by the strategic support force in 2022*. http://81rc.81.cn/news/2022-03/12/content_10140223.htm

Miller, R. A., & Kuehl, D. T. (2009). Cyberspace and the "first battle" in 21st-century war. *Defense Horizons*, *68*. https://ndupress.ndu.edu/Portals/68/Documents/defensehorizon/DH-68.pdf?ver=2014-03-06-114910-860

Min, J. (2013, February 6). China's "Internet sovereignty" in the wake of WCIT-12. *China US Focus.* https://www.chinausfocus.com/peace-security/chinas-internet -sovereignty-in-the-wake-of-wcit-12

Ministry of Education. (2021, July 30). *Welcome to apply for postgraduate study of the academy of military science.* China Postgraduate Admissions Information Network. https://yz.chsi.com.cn/kyzx/other/202108/20210830/2103279127.html

Ministry of Foreign Affairs. (2017). *International strategy of cooperation on cyberspace.* https://www.fmprc.gov.cn/mfa_eng/wjb_663304/zzjg_663340/jks _665232/kjlc_665236/qtwt_665250/t1442390.shtml

Ministry of Foreign Affairs. (2019, April 27). *List of deliverables of the second Belt and Road forum for international cooperation.* https://www.fmprc.gov.cn/mfa _eng/zxxx_662805/t1658767.shtml

Ministry of National Defense. (2016, January 1). *China establishes rocket force and strategic support force.* http://eng.mod.gov.cn/ArmedForces/ssf.htm

Ministry of Science and Technology. (2006). *Notice on issuing the "eleventh five-year development outline" of the national key basic research and development plan (973 plan) (No. 433).* Ministry of Science and Technology. http://www .most.gov.cn/kjgh/kjfzgh/200708/t20070824_52689.htm

Ministry of Science and Technology. (2012). *Notice of the ministry of science and technology on printing and distributing the special plans for the "twelfth five-year plan" of 6 national major scientific research plans including Nano research (No. 627).* Ministry of Science and Technology. http://www.most.gov.cn/tztg /201206/t20120621_95215.htm

MITRE. (n.d.). *Naikon.* Retrieved August 20, 2022, from https://attack.mitre.org/ groups/G0019/

MND. (2006). *National defense report.* https://www.ustaiwandefense.com/tdnswp /wp-content/uploads/2020/02/Taiwan-National-Defense-Report-2006.pdf

MND. (2008). *National defense report.* https://www.ustaiwandefense.com/tdnswp/ wp-content/uploads/2020/02/Taiwan-National-Defense-Report-2008.pdf

MND. (2009). *Quadrennial defense review.* https://www.ustaiwandefense.com /tdnswp/wp-content/uploads/2020/02/2009-Taiwan-Quadrennial-Defense -Review-QDR.pdf

MND. (2013). *National defense report.* https://www.ustaiwandefense.com/tdnswp/ wp-content/uploads/2020/02/Taiwan-National-Defense-Report-2013.pdf

MND. (2015). *National defense report.* https://www.ustaiwandefense.com/tdnswp/ wp-content/uploads/2020/02/Taiwan-National-Defense-Report-2015.pdf

MND. (2017a). *National defense report.* https://www.ustaiwandefense.com/tdnswp /wp-content/uploads/2020/02/Taiwan-National-Defense-Report-2017.pdf

MND. (2017b). *Quadrennial defense review.* https://www.ustaiwandefense.com /tdnswp/wp-content/uploads/2000/01/2017-Taiwan-Quadrennial-Defense -Review-QDR.pdf

MND. (2019). *National defense report.* https://www.ustaiwandefense.com/tdnswp/ wp-content/uploads/2020/02/Taiwan-National-Defense-Report-2019.pdf

MND. (2021a). *National defense report.* https://www.ustaiwandefense.com/tdnswp /wp-content/uploads/2021/11/Taiwan-National-Defense-Report-2021.pdf

MND. (2021b). *Quadrennial defense review.* https://www.ustaiwandefense.com /tdnswp/wp-content/uploads/2021/03/2021-Taiwan-Quadrennial-Defense -Review-QDR.pdf

Moorhead, P. (2020, February 27). Why 5G patent 'value' is more important than the 'number' of patents. *Forbes*. https://www.forbes.com/sites/moorinsights/2020/02/27/5g-patent-value-is-more-important-than-number-of-patents/?sh=220e456a7941

Morgan, F. E., Boudreaux, B., Lohn, A. J., Ashby, M., Curriden, C., Klima, K., & Grossman, D. (2020). *Military applications of artificial intelligence*. RAND Corporation.

Morgan, P. M. (2010). Applicability of traditional deterrence concepts and theory to the cyber realm. In *Proceedings of the a workshop on deterring cyberattacks*. National Academies Press. https://doi.org/10.17226/12997

Mueller, M. (2011). China and global Internet governance. In R. Deibert, J. Palfrey, R. Rohozinski, & J. Zittrain (Eds.), *Access contested: Security, identity, and resistance in Asian cyberspace*, pp. 177–194. The MIT Press.

Mulvenon, J. (2009). PLA computer network operations: Scenarios, doctrine, organizations, and capability. In R. Kamphausen, D. Lai, & A. Scobell (Eds.), *Beyond the strait: PLA missions other than Taiwan*, pp. 253–285. Strategic Studies Institute.

Mulvenon, J. C., & Yang, R. H. (1999). The People's liberation army in the information age. *The People's Liberation Army in the Information Age*. https://www.rand.org/pubs/conf_proceedings/CF145.html

Nairne, D. (2002, September 18). State hackers spying on us, say dissidents. *South China Morning Post*. https://www.scmp.com/article/391734/state-hackers-spying-us-say-dissidents

National Defense University. (2020). *The science of military strategy*. National Defense University Press. https://www.airuniversity.af.edu/Portals/10/CASI/documents/Translations/2022-01-26 2020 Science of Military Strategy.pdf

National People's Congress. (2021a, June 10). *Data security law of the People's Republic of China (No. 84)*. National People's Congress of the People's Republic of China. http://www.npc.gov.cn/englishnpc/c23934/202112/1abd8829788946ecab270e469b13c39c.shtml

National People's Congress. (2021b, August 20). *Personal information protection law of the People's Republic of China*. National People's Congress of the People's Republic of China; National People's Congress of the People's Republic of China. http://www.npc.gov.cn/npc/c30834/202108/a8c4e3672c74491a80b53a172bb753fe.shtml

National Security Law of the People's Republic of China, Pub. L. No. 29 (2017). http://eng.mod.gov.cn/publications/2017-03/03/content_4774229.htm

NDRC. (2015). *Vision and actions on jointly building Silk Road Economic Belt and 21st-century maritime silk road*. https://en.ndrc.gov.cn/newsrelease_8232/201503/t20150330_1193900.html

NDRC. (2019). *The Belt and Road Initiative: Progress, contributions and prospects*. http://www.xinhuanet.com/english/2019-04/22/c_137998357.htm

NDRC. (2021). *14th five-year plan for economic and social development (2021–2025)*. https://en.ndrc.gov.cn/policies/

NDRC. (2022, March 3). Promoting the healthy development of the digital economy in China. *Qiushi*. http://en.qstheory.cn/2022-03/03/c_720696.htm

Nedopil, C. (2020). *Investments in the Belt and Road Initiative*. Green Belt and Road Initiative Center. https://green-bri.org/investments-in-the-belt-and-road-initiative-bri

NetEase. (2021, January 4). A surveying and mapping emergency support unit of the strategic support force marches into the exercise field. *NetEase.* https://www.163 .com/dy/article/FVG530JP0514R9M0.html

NetEase. (2022, March 16). What is the use of the "Leaping-Zhu Rihe" series of exercises? *NetEase.* https://www.163.com/dy/article/H2J82HO305529LNH.html

Ni, A., & Gill, B. (2019). The People's liberation army strategic support force: Update 2019. *China Brief, 19*(10). https://jamestown.org/program/the-peoples -liberation-army-strategic-support-force-update-2019/

NIST. (2016). *Report on post-quantum cryptography [8105].* https://doi.org/10 .6028/NIST.IR.8105

Nitta, Y. (2019, May 17). ZTE signs deal to help launch 5G in Myanmar. *Nikkei Asia.* https://asia.nikkei.com/Spotlight/5G-networks/ZTE-signs-deal-to-help-launch -5G-in-Myanmar

Niu, L., Tan, H., & Liu, J. (1995, March 28). Information warfare is coming at us. *PLA Daily [FBIS-CHI-95-124].*

Notice of the State Council on Issuing the Development Plan for the New Generation of Artificial Intelligence, Pub. L. No. 35. (2017). http://www.gov.cn/zhengce/ content/2017-07/20/content_5211996.htm

NPES Standards Bluebook. (2005). *Standards: What are they and why are they important?*

NUDT. (n.d.-a). *About the school of electronic science.* National University of Defense Technology. Retrieved August 22, 2022, from https://www.nudt.edu.cn /xysz/dzkxxy/index.htm

NUDT. (n.d.-b). *Introduction to school of computer science.* National University of Defense Technology. Retrieved August 22, 2022, from https://www.nudt.edu.cn /xysz/jsjxy/index.htm

NUDT. (n.d.-c). *Introduction to the school of intelligent science.* National University of Defense Technology. Retrieved August 22, 2022, from https://www.nudt.edu .cn/xysz/znkxxy/index.htm

NUDT. (n.d.-d). *National university of defense technology colleges.* Retrieved December 17, 2020, from https://english.nudt.edu.cn/Colleges/index.htm

NUDT. (2012, April 7). *Recruitment notice for the director of the state key laboratory of high performance computing.* National University of Defense Technology. https://www.nudt.edu.cn/rczp/bdc45cd3a205439eb638dd7 9be769a87.htm

NUDT. (2019a). *2019 PhD admissions prospectus.* National University of Defense Technology. http://yjszs.nudt.edu.cn/pubweb/homePageList/detailed .view?keyId=321

NUDT. (2019b). *2020 PhD admissions prospectus.* National University of Defense Technology. http://yjszs.nudt.edu.cn/pubweb/homePageList/detailed .view?keyId=506

NUDT. (2020). *2021 PhD admissions prospectus.* National University of Defense Technology. http://yjszs.nudt.edu.cn/pubweb/homePageList/detailed.view ?keyId=887

NUDT. (2021a). *2022 PhD admissions prospectus.* National University of Defense Technology. http://yjszs.nudt.edu.cn/pubweb/homePageList/detailed .view?keyId=12145

NUDT. (2021b). *2022 Postgraduate admissions prospectus.* National University of Defense Technology. http://yjszs.nudt.edu.cn/pubweb/homePageList/detailed .view?keyId=12144

NUDT. (2022a). *2023 PhD admissions catalogue.* National University of Defense Technology. http://yjszs.nudt.edu.cn/pubweb/homePageList/detailed.view?keyId =12361

NUDT. (2022b). *2023 Postgraduate admissions exam catalogue.* National University of Defense Technology. http://yjszs.nudt.edu.cn/pubweb/homePageList /detailed.view?keyId=12445

Nye, J. S. (2010). *Cyber power.* http://belfercenter.org

Nye, J. S. (2011). *The future of power.* Perseus Books Group.

O'Connor, S., Hanson, F., Currey, E., & Beattie, T. (2020). *Cyber-enabled foreign interference in elections and referendums.* www.aspi.org.au

O'Meara, S. (2019, August 21). Will China lead the world in AI by 2030? *Nature.* https://www.nature.com/articles/d41586-019-02360-7

O'Neill, P. H. (2020, February 29). Web War I: The cyberattack that changed the world. *Daily Dot.* https://www.dailydot.com/debug/web-war-cyberattack-russia -estonia/

Office of the Historian. (n.d.). *Milestones: 1866–1898: Mahan's the influence of sea power upon history.* Retrieved December 10, 2020, from https://history.state.gov /milestones/1866-1898/mahan

Origin Quantum. (n.d.). *Company overview.* Retrieved December 13, 2020, from http://www.originqc.com.cn/en/website/companyProfile.html

Pang, R., Qian, G., & Zhang, D. (2020, December 14). A record of cross-domain actual combat training organized by a certain department of the strategic support force. *China Military Network.* http://www.81.cn/zz/2020-12/14/content _9952345.htm

Parliament of UK. (2010). *Commission communication: Internet governance: The next steps.* https://publications.parliament.uk/pa/cm201011/cmselect/cmeuleg /428-xiv/42809.htm

Peng, C. Z., Yang, T., Bao, X. H., Zhang, J., Jin, X. M., Feng, F. Y., Yang, B., Yang, J., Yin, J., Zhang, Q., Li, N., Tian, B. L., & Pan, J. W. (2005). Experimental free-space distribution of entangled photon pairs over 13 km: Towards satellite-based global quantum communication. *Physical Review Letters, 94*(15). https://doi.org /10.1103/PhysRevLett.94.150501

Peng, F. (1996, January 9). Drastic changes to take place in form of battlefield. *Military Forum [FBIS-CHI-96-061].*

Peng, G., & Yao, Y. (2005). *The science of military strategy.* Military Science Publishing House, Academy of Military Science of the Chinese People's Liberation Army.

People's Daily. (2001, May 9). *Electronic information turned into China's No. 1 pillar industry.* http://www.china.org.cn/english/DO-e/18698.htm

People's Daily. (2014, June 23). Internet sovereignty: An inescapable issue. *People's Daily.* http://world.people.com.cn/n/2014/0623/c1002-25183696.html

People's Daily. (2016, July 7). Excerpts from the representative's speech at the symposium on the army's actual combat military training. *People's Daily.* http:// military.people.com.cn/n1/2016/0807/c1011-28616977-3.html

People's Daily. (2017a, July 13). The strategic support force cooperates with 9 local units to cultivate high-end talents for new combat force. *People's Daily.* http://military.people.com.cn/n1/2017/0713/c1011-29402123.html

People's Daily. (2017b, December 28). China unveils its first civil-military cybersecurity innovation center. *People's Daily.* http://en.people.cn/n3/2017/1228/c90000-9309428.html

People's Daily. (2021, February 22). Chinese military to build new-type training system amid external threats. *People's Daily.* http://en.people.cn/n3/2021/0222/c90000-9820804.html

People's Daily. (2022, March 21). Resolute China sharpens focus on innovation. *People's Daily.* http://en.people.cn/n3/2022/0321/c90000-9973767.html

People's Daily Online. (2013, November 15). *Xi Jinping talks about accelerating the improvement of the Internet management leadership system-current affairs.* http://politics.people.com.cn/n/2013/1115/c1001-23559689.html

Perrault, R., Shoham, Y., Brynjolfsson, E., Clark, J., Etchemendy, J., Grosz Harvard, B., Lyons, T., Manyika, J., Mishra, S., & Carlos Niebles, J. (2019). *The AI index 2019 annual report.* https://hai.stanford.edu/sites/default/files/ai_index_2019_report.pdf

Pitt, D. C., & Xu, Y. (2002). *Chinese telecommunications policy.* ARTECH House. https://uk.artechhouse.com/Chinese-Telecommunications-Policy-P536.aspx

PLA Daily. (1996, April 23). 10 major effects of information warfare in military arena. *PLA Daily [FBIS-CHI-96-087].*

PLA Daily. (2015, November 2). Dean of the academy of military sciences: Reform must solve the systemic obstacles fettering the strong army. *Chinanews.* http://www.chinanews.com/mil/2015/11-02/7600724.shtml

PLA Daily. (2016a, February 10). Joint combat readiness for the spring festival of the rocket forces, strategic support forces and other services. *PLA Daily.* http://www.81.cn/jmywyl/2016-02/10/content_6903114.htm

PLA Daily. (2016b, March 11). How does the strategic support force forge new quality weapons: Create more original and surprising victory. *China News.* http://www.chinanews.com/mil/2016/03-11/7792939.shtml

Pohlmann, T., & Buggenhagen, M. (2022). *Who is leading the 5G patent race?* https://www.iplytics.com/wp-content/uploads/2022/06/5G-patent-race-June-2022_website.pdf

Pohlmann, T., & Philipp, K. B. (2020). *Fact finding study on patents declared to the 5G standard.* https://www.iplytics.com/wp-content/uploads/2020/02/5G-patent-study_TU-Berlin_IPlytics-2020.pdf

PwC. (2016). *China's new silk route: The long and winding road.* www.pwc.com/gmc

Qasky. (n.d.). *Anhui Qasky Quantum Technology Co. Ltd.* Retrieved December 13, 2020, from http://www.qasky.com/en/

Qi, J. (2019, July 31). Seize the commanding heights of artificial intelligence technology development. *China Military Network.* http://www.81.cn/2019zt/2019-07/31/content_9574802.htm

Qiang, C. Z.-W. (2007). China's information revolution: Managing the economic and social transformation. In *China's information revolution.* The World Bank. https://doi.org/10.1596/978-0-8213-6720-9

Qiao, L., & Wang, X. (1999). *Unrestricted warfare.* PLA Literature and Arts Publishing House. https://www.c4i.org/unrestricted.pdf

Qiu, Z. (2019, February 12). Quantum technology, subverting future warfare. *China Military Network.* http://www.81.cn/gfbmap/content/2019-02/12/content_227082.htm

Qiushi. (2018, October 16). Xi Jinping talks about military-civilian integration: It's about national security and the overall situation of development. *Qiushi.* http://www.qstheory.cn/zhuanqu/rdjj/2018-10/16/c_1123565364.htm

Qu, J. (2018, October 15). Commentary: The ulterior motives behind Washington's cyber fear-mongering against China. *Global Times.* http://www.xinhuanet.com/english/2018-10/15/c_137533091.htm

Qualcomm. (2020, September 29). *The essential role of technology standards.* https://www.qualcomm.com/news/onq/2020/09/29/essential-role-technology-standards

QuantumCTek. (n.d.). *Company profile.* Retrieved December 13, 2020, from http://www.quantum-info.com/English/about/

QUDOOR. (n.d.). *About Qike Quantum.* Retrieved December 13, 2020, from http://www.qudoor.cn/en-us/about

Raiu, C. (2012, June 29). *New MacOS X backdoor variant used in APT attacks.* Securelist Kaspersky. https://securelist.com/new-macos-x-backdoor-variant-used-in-apt-attacks/33214/

Raman, B. (2011, January 16). *Chinese military exercises during 2010- An update.* Chennai Centre for China Studies. https://www.c3sindia.org/defence-security/chinese-military-exercises-during-2010-an-update/

Rattray, G. J. (2009). An environmental approach to understanding cyberpower. In F. D. Kramer, S. H. Starr, & L. K. Wentz (Eds.), *Cyberpower and national security*, pp. 253–274. National Defense University Press.

Reuters. (2017, May 16). China state firms set up 150 billion yuan fund to invest in new technologies: Xinhua. *Reuters.* https://www.reuters.com/article/us-china-soe-investment/china-state-firms-set-up-150-billion-yuan-fund-to-invest-in-new-technologies-xinhua-idUSKCN18C1DU?il=0

Reuters. (2021, July 2). China investigates Didi over cybersecurity days after its huge IPO. *Reuters.* https://www.reuters.com/technology/china-cyberspace-administration-launches-security-investigation-into-didi-2021-07-02/

Roberts, H., Cowls, J., Morley, J., Taddeo, M., Wang, V., & Floridi, L. (2020). The Chinese approach to artificial intelligence: An analysis of policy, ethics, and regulation. *AI and Society, 1.* https://doi.org/10.1007/s00146-020-00992-2

Ruili Municipal People's Government. (2019, August 26). *From "military-civilian combination" to "military-civilian integration."* http://www.rl.gov.cn/szb/Web/_F0_0_28D070X5OS3VWH5Q3TPTNH1KZZ.htm

Samson, Y. (2015). Becoming a cyber power. *China Perspectives, 2*, 53–58. https://journals.openedition.org/chinaperspectives/6731

Scimago Journal & Country Rank. (2022). *SJR – International science ranking.* https://www.scimagojr.com/countryrank.php?category=1702&area=1700

SCMP. (2002, August 13). Yahoo! silent on censorship claims in China. *South China Morning Post.* https://www.scmp.com/article/388121/yahoo-silent-censorship-claims-china

SCMP. (2017, July 11). Beijing reportedly orders ban on all personal VPN accounts by February. *South China Morning Post.* https://www.scmp.com/news/china

/policies-politics/article/2102085/beijing-said-banning-individual-vpn-access
-february

SCO. (n.d.). *The Shanghai cooperation organisation*. Retrieved December 12, 2020, from http://eng.sectsco.org/about_sco/

SCO. (2009). *Agreement on cooperation in ensuring international information security between the member states of the Shanghai cooperation organisation.* Shanghai Cooperation Organisation.

Segal, A. (2013, December 10). *Cyberspace cannot live without sovereignty, says Lu Wei.* Council on Foreign Relations. https://www.cfr.org/blog/cyberspace-cannot
-live-without-sovereignty-says-lu-wei

Segal, A. (2020, March 13). *China's alternative cyber governance regime.* U. S. China Economic Security Review Commission.

Sharma, M. (2016). China's emergence as a cyber power. *Journal of Defence Studies, 10*(1), 43–68. http://www.idsa.in/journalofdefencestudiesURLhttp://idsa.in/jds/jds_10_1_2015_chinas-emergence-as-a-cyber-power

Sharma, M. (2018). Decrypting China's Quantum Leap. *The China Journal, 80,* 24–45. https://doi.org/https://doi.org/10.1086/697232

Sharp, H. (2020). *Discussion paper: An analysis of the "new IP" proposal to the ITU-T.* https://www.internetsociety.org/resources/doc/2020/discussion-paper
-an-analysis-of-the-new-ip-proposal-to-the-itu-t/

Sheldon, J. B. (2011). Deciphering cyberpower: Strategic purpose in peace and war. *Strategic Studies Quarterly, 5,* 95–112.

Shen, W. (1995, November 7). Focus of contemporary world military revolution—Introduction to research in information warfare. *PLA Daily [FBIS-CHI95-239].*

Shen, X. (1999). *The Chinese road to high technology.* Palgrave Macmillan. https://doi.org/10.1057/9781403905505_4

Shirai, S. (2019, November 20). China's digital currency could threaten dollar's dominance. *The Japan Times.* https://www.japantimes.co.jp/opinion/2019/11
/20/commentary/world-commentary/chinas-digital-currency-threaten-dollars
-dominance/#.XrFeCRQzbZ5

Shu, C. (2014, November 21). China tried to get world Internet conference attendees to ratify this ridiculous draft declaration. *TechCrunch.* https://techcrunch.com
/2014/11/20/worldinternetconference-declaration/

SICAS. (n.d.). *Institute for pattern recognition and artificial intelligence – Huazhong University of Science and Technology.* Study in China Admission System. Retrieved August 23, 2022, from https://www.sicas.cn/School/183/Contents
/110721162721891.shtml

Sigurdson, J. (1980). Technology and science in the People's Republic of China. In *Technology and science in the People's Republic of China.* Pergamon Press. https://doi.org/10.1016/c2013-0-05889-6

Silk Road Briefing. (2020, February 19). China's Digital Silk Road (DSR): The new frontier in the digital arms race? *Silk Road Briefing.* https://www.silkroadbriefing
.com/news/2020/02/19/chinas-digital-silk-road-dsr-new-frontier-digital-arms-race/

Sina. (2009, December 3). Introduction and faculty of the school of computer science, Wuhan University. *Sina.* http://edu.sina.com.cn/kaoyan/2009-12-03
/1908228655.shtml

Sina. (2016, November 27). The PLA army's 2016 military exercises inventory exclusive screens to see the army's skills. *Sina.* http://mil.news.sina.com.cn/china
/2016-11-27/doc-ifxyasmv1993383.shtml

Sina. (2021, July 30). Both red and blue focus on the transformation and leap of "The Wolf of Zhurihe". *Sina Military.* https://mil.sina.cn/zgjq/2021-07-30/detail -ikqciyzk8573225.d.html

Sina. (2022, May 17). With the establishment of a 3 billion industrial fund, Wuhan accelerates the construction of a national cybersecurity talent and innovation base. *Sina.* https://finance.sina.com.cn/chanjing/cyxw/2022-05-17/doc -imcwipik0386090.shtml

Sina Military. (2016, July 21). The first battle of Zhu Rihe exercise: The first line of troops against Taiwan invaded the core position of the Blue Army. *Sina Military.* http://mil.news.sina.com.cn/china/2016-07-21/doc-ifxuhukv7041022.shtml

Singer, P. W., & Freidman, A. (2014). *Cybersecurity and cyberwar.* Oxford University Press. https://news.asis.io/sites/default/files/Cybersecurity_and_Cyberwar.pdf

Snyder, J., Komaitis, K., & Robachevsky, A. (2016, May 9). *The history of IANA.* Internet Society. https://www.internetsociety.org/ianatimeline/

Song, L. (2017, October 18). China to build world-class armed forces by mid-21st century: Xi – Xinhua | English.news.cn. *Xinhua.* http://www.xinhuanet.com/ english/2017-10/18/c_136688520.htm

Spade, J. M. (2012). *China's cyber power and America's national security.* U.S. Army War College.

Starr, S. H. (2009). Toward a preliminary theory of cyberpower. In F. D. Kramer, S. H. Starr, & L. K. Wentz (Eds.), *Cyberpower and national security*, pp. 43–88. National Defense University Press.

State Council. (1994). *Regulations of the People's Republic of China for safety protection of computer information systems.* http://en.pkulaw.cn/display.aspx ?cgid=4a65c0a755db9cc4bdfb&lib=law

State Council. (1997). *Measures for security protection administration of the international networking of computer information networks.*

State Council. (1998). *China's national defense.*

State Council. (2002). *China's national defense in 2002.*

State Council. (2004). *China's national defense in 2004.*

State Council. (2006). *The national medium-and long-term program for science and technology development (2006–2020).*

State Council. (2009). *China's national defense in 2008.*

State Council. (2010). *White paper on the Internet in China.* https://www.chinadaily .com.cn/china/2010-06/08/content_9950198.htm

State Council. (2011). *China's national defense in 2010.*

State Council. (2013). *The diversified employment of China's armed forces.*

State Council. (2014, August 20). *Ministry of industry and information technology.* http://english.www.gov.cn/state_council/2014/08/23/content _281474983035940.htm

State Council. (2015a). *Made in China, 2025.*

State Council. (2015b). *China's military strategy.* http://english.www.gov.cn/archive /white_paper/2015/05/27/content_281475115610833.htm

State Council. (2015c, July 4). *China unveils "Internet Plus" action plan to fuel growth.* http://english.www.gov.cn/policies/latest_releases/2015/07/04/content _281475140165588.htm

State Council. (2015d). *Guiding opinions of the state council on actively promoting the "Internet + action" (state development (2015) No. 40).* State Council. http:// www.gov.cn/zhengce/content/2015-07/04/content_10002.htm

State Council. (2016). *The 13th five-year plan for economic and social development of People's Republic of China (2016–2020).*

State Council. (2017a, November 26). *The general office of the central committee of the communist party of China issued the "action plan for promoting large-scale deployment of Internet protocol version 6 (IPv6)."* http://www.gov.cn/zhengce/2017-11/26/content_5242389.htm

State Council. (2017b, December 6). The general office of the state council issued "opinions on promoting the deep development of military-civilian integration of national defense technology industry." *The State Council Information Office of the People's Republic of China.* http://www.scio.gov.cn/xwfbh/gbwxwfbh/xwfbh/hfkgw/Document/1612885/1612885.htm

State Council. (2019). *China's national defense in the New Era.*

State Council. (2020, April 9). *Opinions of the central committee of the communist party of China and the state council on building a more complete system and mechanism for market-based allocation of factors.* http://www.gov.cn/zhengce/2020-04/09/content_5500622.htm

State Council. (2022, March 8). *Minister: China ranks 12th in global innovation index 2021.* https://english.www.gov.cn/statecouncil/ministries/202203/08/content_WS6227114bc6d09c94e48a6484.html

State Council. (2023). *China's digital economy grew to 50.2 trillion Yuan in 2022.* https://english.www.gov.cn/archive/statistics/202304/27/content_WS644a6152c6d03ffcca6ecb0e.html

State secrecy protection regulations for computer information systems on the Internet. (2000). http://www.asianlii.org/cn/legis/cen/laws/ssprfcisoti915/

Stokes, M. A., Lin, J., & Hsiao, L. C. R. (2011). *The Chinese people's liberation army signals intelligence and cyber reconnaissance infrastructure.* www.project2049.net

Stone, A., & Wood, P. (2020). *China's military-civil fusion strategy.* https://www.linkedin.com/company/11049011

Su, E. (1996, June 11). Logical concept of information warfare. *Military Forum [FBIS-CHI-96-135].*

Superposition. (2017, October 31). *China's $10B national laboratory for quantum information sciences set to open by 2020.* https://superposition.com/2017/10/31/china-goes-big-92-acre-10-billion-quantum-research-center/

Swayne, M. (2020, March 28). Baidu joins quantum fray with machine learning toolkit. *The Quantum Daily.* https://thequantumdaily.com/2020/05/28/paddling-back-baidu-makes-good-on-its-quantum-promise-with-machine-learning-toolkit/

SWIFT. (n.d.). *SWIFT history.* SWIFT. Retrieved December 12, 2020, from https://www.swift.com/about-us/history

Szczepański, M. (2019). *Economic impacts of artificial intelligence (AI).* https://www.europarl.europa.eu/RegData/etudes/BRIE/2019/637967/EPRS_BRI(2019)637967_EN.pdf

Tai, K., & Zhu, Y. Y. (2022). A historical explanation of Chinese cybersovereignty. *International Relations of the Asia-Pacific.* https://doi.org/10.1093/IRAP/LCAB009

Tay, K. L. (2020, May 7). *China's military looks to civilians to boost innovation.* International Institute for Strategic Studies. https://www.iiss.org/blogs/analysis/2020/05/china-civil-military-innovation

Tencent AI Lab. (n.d.). *Research areas.* https://ai.qq.com/hr/ailab.shtml

The Conversation. (2012, December 14). *Future-of-the-Internet talks crash: Let's update the system.* https://theconversation.com/future-of-the-internet-talks-crash-lets-update-the-system-11296

The Economist. (n.d.). Quantum technology is beginning to come into its own. *The Economist.* Retrieved December 13, 2020, from https://www.economist.com/news/essays/21717782-quantum-technology-beginning-come-its-own

The Paper. (2017, September 9). All eight research institutes under the newly formed academy of military sciences are unveiled. *The Paper.* https://www.thepaper.cn/newsDetail_forward_1789598

The People's Bank of China. (2020, April 28). *PBC expands pilot program of FinTech innovation regulation to Shanghai and five other cities (areas).* http://www.pbc.gov.cn/en/3688110/3688172/4015485/index.html

Thomas, T. L. (2004). *Dragon bytes: Chinese information-war theory and practice 1995–2003* (Foreign Mi).

Thomas, T. L. (2005). Chinese and American network warfare. *Joint Force Quarterly, 38*, pp. 76–83.

Thomas, T. L. (2007). *Decoding the virtual dragon.* Foreign Military Studies Office.

Tikk-Ringas, E. (2017). International cyber norms dialogue as an exercise of normative power. In *Georgetown Journal of International Affairs, 17.*

Tomoyuki, Y. (2021, July 19). *Cases of cyberattacks including those by a group known as APT40 which the Chinese government is behind.* Ministry of Foreign Affairs of Japan. https://www.mofa.go.jp/press/danwa/press6e_000312.html

TOP500. (n.d.-a). *Tianhe-1A.* Retrieved August 22, 2022, from https://www.top500.org/system/176929/

TOP500. (n.d.-b). *Tianhe-2A.* Retrieved August 22, 2022, from https://www.top500.org/system/177999/

Travagnin, M. (2019). *Patent analysis of selected quantum technologies.* https://doi.org/10.2760/938284

Tsinghua University. (n.d.). *The latest developments in Jittor.* Retrieved December 13, 2020, from https://cg.cs.tsinghua.edu.cn/jittor/

Tsinghua University. (2018). *China: AI development report 2018.* http://www.sppm.tsinghua.edu.cn/eWebEditor/UploadFile/China_AI_development_report_2018.pdf

Twomey, C. P. (2005). Chinese doctrines as strategic culture: Assessing their effects. *Strategic Insights, 4*(10).

UN Peace and Development Trust Fund. (2022). *Progress report on the Belt and Road Initiative in support of the United Nations 2030 agenda for sustainable development.* https://www.un.org/sites/un2.un.org/files/progress_report_bri-sdgs_english-final.pdf

UNCTAD. (2021). *Digital economy report 2021.* https://unctad.org/system/files/official-document/der2021_en.pdf

UNCTAD. (2022). *China's structural transformation what can developing countries learn?* https://unctad.org/system/files/official-document/gds2022d1_en.pdf

UNDP. (n.d.). *Goal 9: Industrial innovation and infrastructure.* Retrieved December 12, 2020, from https://www.undp.org/content/undp/en/home/sustainable-development-goals/goal-9-industry-innovation-and-infrastructure.html

UNGA. (2011a). Resolution 65/141. Information and communications technologies for development. In *Thirty-first session* (Vol. 1). www.broadbandcommission.org.

UNGA. (2011b). *Letter dated 2011/09/12 from the permanent representatives of China, the Russian Federation, Tajikistan and Uzbekistan to the United Nations addressed to the secretary-general (A/66/359))*. UN. http://digitallibrary.un.org /record/710973

UNGA. (2013). *A/68/98 – Group of governmental experts on developments in the field of information and telecommunications in the context of international security*. https://undocs.org/A/68/98

UNGA. (2015a). *A/69/723 – Letter dated 9 January 2015 from the permanent representatives of China, Kazakhstan, Kyrgyzstan, the Russian Federation, Tajikistan and Uzbekistan to the United Nations addressed to the secretary-general*. https://undocs.org/en/A/69/723

UNGA. (2015b). *Resolution 70/125 outcome document of the high-level meeting of the general assembly on the overall review of the implementation of the outcomes of the world summit on the information society.*

US Chamber of Commerce. (2017). *Made in China 2025: Global ambitions built on local protections*. https://www.uschamber.com/sites/default/files/final_made _in_china_2025_report_full.pdf

US Department of State. (2020). *The clean network*. https://www.state.gov/the -clean-network/

US DoD. (2002). *Annual Report to Congress: Military Power of the People's Republic of China.*

US DoD. (2003). *Annual Report to Congress: Military Power of the People's Republic of China.*

US DoD. (2004). *Annual Report to Congress: Military Power of the People's Republic of China.*

US DoD. (2006). *Annual Report to Congress: Military Power of the People's Republic of China.*

US DoD. (2010). *Annual Report to Congress: Military and Security Developments Involving the People's Republic of China.*

US DoD. (2011). *Annual Report to Congress: Military and Security Developments Involving the People's Republic of China.*

US DoD. (2013). *Annual Report to Congress: Military and Security Developments Involving the People's Republic of China.*

US DoD. (2015). *Annual Report to Congress: Military and Security Developments Involving the People's Republic of China ANNUAL REPORT TO CONGRESS Military and Security Developments Involving the People's Republic of China 2015.*

US DoD. (2018). *Annual Report to Congress: Military and Security Developments Involving the People's Republic of China*. http://www.andrewerickson.com/wp -content/uploads/2019/05/DoD-China-Report_2018.pdf

US DoD. (2019). *Annual Report to Congress: Military and Security Developments Involving the People's Republic of China.*

US DoD. (2020). *Military and security developments involving the People's Republic of China*. https://media.defense.gov/2020/Sep/01/2002488689/-1/-1/1 /2020-DOD-CHINA-MILITARY-POWER-REPORT-FINAL.PDF

US DoD. (2021). *Military and security developments involving the People's Republic of China*. https://media.defense.gov/2021/Nov/03/2002885874/-1/-1/0 /2021-CMPR-FINAL.PDF

US DoD. (2022). *Military and security developments involving the People's Republic of China.* https://media.defense.gov/2022/nov/29/2003122279/-1/-1/1/2022-military-and-security-developments-involving-the-peoples-republic-of-china.pdf

USTC. (n.d.). *Key laboratory of quantum information.* University of Science and Technology. Retrieved December 13, 2020, from https://en.physics.ustc.edu.cn/7852/listm.htm

V-Dem institute. (2019). *Democracy facing global challenges: V-Dem annual report 2019.* https://www.v-dem.net/media/filer_public/99/de/99dedd73-f8bc-484c-8b91-44ba601b6e6b/v-dem_democracy_report_2019.pdf

Vavra, S. (2020, September 8). Chinese cyber power is neck-and-neck with US, Harvard research finds. *CyberScoop.* https://www.cyberscoop.com/chinese-cyber-power-united-states-harvard-belfer-research/

Voo, J., Hemani, I., Jones, S., Desombre, W., Cassidy, D., & Schwarzenbach, A. (2020). *National cyber power index 2020 methodology and analytical considerations.* https://www.belfercenter.org/sites/default/files/2020-09/NCPI_2020.pdf

Waltz, K. N. (1979). *Theory of international politics.* Addison-Wesley Publishing Company.

Wang. (2014, January 8). *Quantum technology: Changing the face of information warfare.* China Military. http://www.81.cn/jkhc/2014-01/08/content_5726287.htm

Wang, B., & Li, F. (1995, June 20). Information warfare. *PLA Daily.* https://fas.org/irp/world/china/docs/iw_wang.htm

Wang, C. N. (2023). *China Belt and Road Initiative (BRI) investment report 2022.* https://greenfdc.org/china-belt-and-road-initiative-bri-investment-report-2022/

Wang, L. (2019, October 24). *Speech by Wang Lei, coordinator for cyber affairs, at the 6th world Internet conference.* Ministry of Foreign Affairs of the People's Republic of China. https://www.fmprc.gov.cn/mfa_eng/wjb_663304/zzjg_663340/jks_665232/kjfywj_665252/t1710346.shtml

Wang, P. (1995). The challenge of information warfare. *China Military Science.* https://fas.org/irp/world/china/docs/iw_mg_wang.htm

Wang, S. (2021, September 13). In Zhu Rihe, the most important thing for the Army is to conquer itself. *NetEase Military.* https://www.163.com/war/article/GJP3T16L000181KT.html

Wang, Y. (2017). *What we do to embrace the intelligence new norm: China's AI development policies and our work.* https://www.itu.int/en/ITU-T/studygroups/2017-2020/03/Documents/What we do to embrace the Intelligence new norm – WANG Yuntao.pdf

Wang, Y. (2021, February 9). Cyber power: The only way to modernization. *China Military Network.* https://www.81.cn/ll/2021-02/09/content_9984026.htm

WCITLeaks. (2012). *Proposals for the work of the conference (World Conference on International Telecommunications 2012).*

Wee, R. (2023, July 19). China's digital yuan transactions seeing strong momentum. *Reuters.* https://www.reuters.com/markets/asia/chinas-digital-yuan-transactions-seeing-strong-momentum-says-cbank-gov-yi-2023-07-19/

Wei, J. (1996, June 25). Information War: A new form of people's war. *PLA Daily.* https://fas.org/irp/world/china/docs/iw_wei.htm

Wei, S. (2021, March 23). A clear understanding of the asymmetry of cyber warfare. *China Military Network*. http://www.81.cn/xue-xi/2021-03/23/content_10009053.htm

Wen, J. (2011, July 16). *Wen Jiabao's "Qiushi" article: Several issues concerning scientific and technological work*. Central Government Portal. http://www.gov.cn/ldhd/2011-07/16/content_1907593.htm

Working Group on Internet Governance (WGIG). (2005a). *China's comments to WGIG on draft working papers*. www.wgig.org/docs/Comment-China.doc

Working Group on Internet Governance (WGIG). (2005b). *Report of the working group on Internet governance*.

Whalley, J., Zhou, W., & An, X. (2009). *Chinese experience with global 3G standard-setting Chinese experience with global 3G standard-setting (No. 2537)*. www.RePEc.org

WHU. (2021, July 7). *Practical training at school of cyber science and engineering*. School of Cyber Science and Engineering, Wuhan University. https://cse.whu.edu.cn/info/1100/1792.htm

Wiggers, K. (2020, May 27). Baidu open-sources paddle Quantum toolkit for AI quantum computing research. *VentureBeat*. https://venturebeat.com/2020/05/27/baidu-open-sources-paddle-quantum-toolkit-for-ai-quantum-computing-research/

Willett, M. (2019). Assessing cyber power. *Survival*, 61(1), 85–90. https://doi.org/10.1080/00396338.2019.1569895

Williams, B. K. (2021). *Evaluating China's road to cyber super power*. https://www.osti.gov/servlets/purl/1830481

WIPO. (n.d.). *Standards and patents*. World Intellectual Property Organization. Retrieved December 13, 2020, from https://www.wipo.int/patent-law/en/developments/standards.html

WIPO. (2019). *WIPO technology trends 2019: Artificial intelligence*. https://www.wipo.int/edocs/pubdocs/en/wipo_pub_1055.pdf

WIPO. (2021). *Global innovation index 2021: China*. https://www.wipo.int/edocs/pubdocs/en/wipo_pub_gii_2021/cn.pdf

WIPO. (2022). *Global innovation index 2022*. https://www.wipo.int/edocs/pubdocs/en/wipo_pub_2000_2022/cn.pdf

World Internet Conference. (n.d.). *Overview of WIC*. Retrieved December 12, 2020, from http://www.wuzhenwic.org/2020-10/15/c_547699.htm

World Internet Conference. (2015, November 10). *2nd world Internet conference*. http://www.wuzhenwic.org/2015-11/10/c_47252.htm

Wortzel, L. M. (2014). *The Chinese people's liberation army and information warfare*. Strategic Studies Institute and U.S. Army War College Press.

Wu, J. (1995, November 20). Joint operations: The basic form of combat on high tech terms. *China Military Science [FBIS-CHI-96-066]*, 4.

Wu, J., Ren, G., & Li, X. (2007). Source address validation: Architecture and protocol design. In *Proceedings of the international conference on network protocols, ICNP* (pp. 276–283). https://doi.org/10.1109/ICNP.2007.4375858

Wu, T.-H., & Hung, C.-L. (2021). Cyber warfare capabilities of the PLA strategic support force. In T.-Y. Su & J.-M. Hung (Eds.), *Report on the defense technology trend assessment*. Institute for National Defense and Security Research.

https://indsr.org.tw/uploads/enindsr/files/202206/64b998f3-d906-46a4-b78e
-08c06eb28c3e.pdf

Wuhan Municipal Cyberspace Administration. (2021, December 9). *The first graduates of the national cyber security talent and innovation base set off for a long voyage.* http://www.whwx.gov.cn/gzdt/202112/t20211209_1869388.shtml

Wuhan Municipal People's Government. (2022, May 2). *Notice of the municipal People's government on several policies for further supporting the development of national cybersecurity talents and innovation bases.* http://www.wuhan.gov
.cn/zwgk/xxgk/zfwj/gfxwj/202205/t20220513_1971126.shtml

Wuthnow, J. (2019). China's "new" academy of military science: A revolution in theoretical affairs? *China Brief, 19*(2). https://jamestown.org/program/chinas
-new-academy-of-military-science-a-revolution-in-theoretical-affairs/

Xi, J. (2015, December 16). *Remarks by H.E. Xi Jinping President of the People's Republic of China at the opening ceremony of the second world Internet conference.* Ministry of Foreign Affairs of the People's Republic of China. https://www.fmprc
.gov.cn/eng/wjdt_665385/zyjh_665391/201512/t20151224_678467.html

Xi, J. (2017a). *Secure a decisive victory in building a moderately prosperous society in all respects and strive for the great success of socialism with Chinese characteristics for a New Era.* http://www.xinhuanet.com/english/download/Xi
_Jinping's_report_at_19th_CPC_National_Congress.pdf

Xi, J. (2017b, November 4). *Full text of Xi Jinping's report at 19th CPC National Congress.* https://www.chinadaily.com.cn/china/19thcpcnationalcongress/2017
-11/04/content_34115212.htm

Xi, J. (2022, January 15). Continue to strengthen and optimize my country's digital economy. *Qiushi.* http://www.qstheory.cn/dukan/qs/2022-01/15/c
_1128261632.htm

Xie, X. (2018, March 23). *Towards a New Era of network power construction.* Cyberspace Administration of China. http://www.cac.gov.cn/2018-03/23/c
_1122578659.htm

Xinhua. (2008, June 30). *Ministry of industry and information technology inaugurated.* http://www.china.org.cn/government/news/2008-06/30/content
_15906787.htm

Xinhua. (2014a, April 20). *20 years of the Internet in China.* http://www.china.org
.cn/business/2014-04/20/content_32150035.htm

Xinhua. (2014b, July 22). China vows heavier penalties for Internet rumourmongers. *Xinhua News Agency.*

Xinhua. (2015a, February 27). *China deletes over 60,000 Internet accounts.* http://
english.www.gov.cn/news/top_news/2015/02/27/content_281475062456492.htm

Xinhua. (2015b, March 28). Chronology of China's Belt and Road Initiative. *Xinhua.*    http://english.www.gov.cn/news/top_news/2015/04/20/content
_281475092566326.htm

Xinhua. (2016a, January 1). Opinions of the central military commission on deepening the reform of national defense and the army. *Xinhua.* http://www
.xinhuanet.com/mil/2016-01/01/c_1117646695.htm

Xinhua. (2016b, July 14). The army's "leap-over-2016 Zhurihe" series of exercises will begin. *Xinhua.* http://www.xinhuanet.com/mil/2016-07/14/c
_1119219033.htm

Xinhua. (2016c, July 21). The central military commission of the communist party of china and the state council issued the "opinions on the integrated development of economic construction and national defense construction." *Xinhua*. http://www.xinhuanet.com//politics/2016-07/21/c_1119259282.htm

Xinhua. (2016d, August 29). Strive to build a strong, modern strategic support force: Xi. *Xinhua*. http://eng.chinamil.com.cn/view/2016-08/29/content_7231309.htm

Xinhua. (2016e, November 17). Digital stars in spotlight at World Internet Conference. *Xinhua*. http://www.china.org.cn/business/2016-11/17/content_39722606.htm

Xinhua. (2017a, January 22). Xi to head central commission for integrated military, civilian development. *Xinhua*. http://www.xinhuanet.com/english/2017-01/22/c_136004750.htm

Xinhua. (2017b, January 23). The military-civilian integration development committee sets up the military industry sector and welcomes heavy benefits. *Xinhua*. http://www.xinhuanet.com//finance/2017-01/23/c_129458492.htm

Xinhua. (2017c, February 4). *China shuts down 18 illegal live streaming apps.* http://www.xinhuanet.com//english/2017-04/02/c_136178399.htm

Xinhua. (2017d, May 3). Chinese scientists make quantum leap in computing. *Xinhua*. http://www.xinhuanet.com/english/2017-05/03/c_136253686.htm

Xinhua. (2017e, June 21). Xi urges efforts to boost integrated military and civilian development. *Xinhua*. http://www.xinhuanet.com/english/2017-06/21/c_136381507.htm

Xinhua. (2017f, July 19). Xi Jinping delivered the military flag to the academy of military science, the national defense university, and the national university of defense technology. *Xinhua*. http://www.xinhuanet.com/politics/2017-07/19/c_1121347127.htm

Xinhua. (2017g, July 20). China maps out AI development plan. *Xinhua*. http://www.xinhuanet.com/english/2017-07/20/c_136459382.htm

Xinhua. (2017h, September 7). "Leap-2017 Zhurihe": From the red army brigade actions to see the new changes in the army's exercise and training after the remodel. *Xinhua*. http://www.xinhuanet.com//politics/2017-09/07/c_1121625327.htm

Xinhua. (2017i, October 18). Socialism with Chinese characteristics enters new era: Xi. *Xinhua*. http://www.xinhuanet.com/english/2017-10/18/c_136688475.htm

Xinhua. (2018a). Strong guidance for the construction of a cyber power in the New Era. *Xinhua*. http://www.cac.gov.cn/2018-04/22/c_1122720502.htm

Xinhua. (2018b, January 15). Opinion | Military-civilian integration is the only way for information construction. *Xinhua*. http://m.xinhuanet.com/mil/2018-01/05/c_129783567.htm

Xinhua. (2018c, January 27). PLA publishes new military training outline, highlights combat. *Xinhua*. http://www.xinhuanet.com/english/2018-01/27/c_136929690.htm

Xinhua. (2018d, January 28). Details of China's long-range, quantum-secured "unhackable" messaging revealed. *Xinhua*. http://www.xinhuanet.com/english/2018-01/20/c_136909246.htm

Xinhua. (2018e, April 21). Jinping: Independent innovation promotes the construction of a network power. *Xinhua*. http://www.xinhuanet.com/politics/2018-04/21/c_1122719810.htm, *Xi*

Xinhua. (2019a, January 15). Where is the winning mechanism of intelligent warfare? *Xinhua*. http://www.xinhuanet.com/mil/2019-01/15/c_1210038327.htm

Xinhua. (2019b, March 21). *Steady progress on the journey to a cyber power*. Cyberspace Administration of China. http://www.cac.gov.cn/2019-03/21/c_1124261187.htm

Xinhua. (2019c, July 20). The national cyber security talent and innovation base exhibition center was put into use. *Xinhua*. http://www.xinhuanet.com/politics/2019-07/20/c_1210205370.htm

Xinhua. (2019d, October 1). China exhibits advanced drones, unmanned underwater vehicles in military parade. *Xinhua*. http://www.xinhuanet.com/english/2019-10/01/c_138439078_3.htm

Xinhua. (2019e, December 12). SCO anti-cyber-terrorism drill held in China. *Xinhua*. http://www.xinhuanet.com/english/2019-12/12/c_138626263.htm

Xinhua. (2020a, September 8). China proposes "global initiative on data security". *Xinhua*. http://www.xinhuanet.com/english/2020-09/08/c_139353373.htm

Xinhua. (2020b, November 25). Xi stresses military training to raise capability of winning wars. *Xinhua*. http://www.xinhuanet.com/english/2020-11/25/c_139542743.htm

Xinhua. (2023a, May 31). China's 176-Qubit quantum computing platform goes online. *Xinhua*. https://english.news.cn/20230531/0946675301284c1786b4ee27251c89a3/c.html

Xinhua. (2023b, July 6). China home to 2.84 mln 5G base stations. *Xinhua*. http://english.news.cn/20230706/7945b114d7f247c88c5009b68b9501ac/c.html

Xu, C., Yang, W., & Hu, J. (2020, January 21). Intelligent warfare, where is the change. *PLA Daily*. http://www.81.cn/jfjbmap/content/2020-01/21/content_252681.htm

Xu, C.-X. (2004). *National informatization index system of China*.

Xu, H. (2006, March 3). Domain name "change face": China fights against cyber sovereignty. *Sohu*. https://it.sohu.com/20060303/n242107118.shtml

Xu, L. (2015, November 7). *Speech by Comrade Xu Lin at the symposium on "learning, propagating and implementing the spirit of the fifth plenary session and promoting the construction of a strong cyber power"*. Cyberspace Administration of China. http://www.cac.gov.cn/2015-11/07/c_1117072074.htm

Xu, Y. (2018, August 5). 18 Qubits: USTC scientists set new quantum entanglement record. *USTC News Center*. http://quantum.ustc.edu.cn/web/en/node/575

Xudong, G. (2014). A latecomer's strategy to promote a technology standard: The case of Datang and TD-SCDMA. *Research Policy*, 43(3), 597–607. https://doi.org/10.1016/j.respol.2013.09.003

Yan, J., & Yao, H. (2019, December 3). *HKUST story*. National University of Defense Technology. https://www.nudt.edu.cn/zjkd/kdgs/f7994cba37ee4cbebb441509971c6e7f.htm

Yang, F., & Li, J. (2020, March 19). Cognitive warfare: Dominating the contest in the intelligent era. *China Military*. http://www.81.cn/theory/2020-03/19/content_9772502.htm

Yang, J., Diao, S., & Zheng, Z. (2003). *The evaluation and comparison of China's informatization from 1999 to 2001*.

Yang, Y., & Tian, L. (2018, February 22). From "able to play" to "able to fight". *China Youth Online.* http://zqb.cyol.com/html/2018-02/22/nw.D110000zgqnb_20180222_2-04.htm

Yang, Z., Yang, D., & Ma, S. (2011, October 11). PLA UST promotes integrated development of interdisciplinary research. *PLA Daily.* https://thechinatimes.com/online/2011/10/1597.html

Ye, Z., & Zhao, B. (2014, July 22). Thoughts on cyber sovereignty, cyber frontier, cyber defense. *People's Daily.* http://theory.people.com.cn/n/2014/0722/c386965-25316567.html

Yin, J., Ren, J.-G., Lu, H., Cao, Y., Yong, H.-L., Wu, Y.-P., Liu, C., Liao, S.-K., Zhou, F., Jiang, Y., Cai, X.-D., Xu, P., Pan, G.-S., Jia, J.-J., Huang, Y.-M., Yin, H., Wang, J.-Y., Chen, Y.-A., Peng, C.-Z., & Pan, J.-W. (2012). Quantum teleportation and entanglement distribution over 100-kilometre free-space channels. *Nature,* *488*(7410), 185–188. https://www.nature.com/articles/nature11332

Zhai, Z. (1995, June 27). Computer viruses and computer security. *PLA Daily* *[FBIS-CHI-95-193].*

Zhang, A. (2019, August 14). New technology provides method to surpass SWIFT. *Global Times.* https://www.globaltimes.cn/content/1161456.shtml

Zhang, B., Gu, D., & Ma, W. (2015). A study of the correlation between China's informatization level and its national "well-being". Proceedings of PTC 2015. Honolulu, Hawaii, Pacific Telecommunications Council.

Zhang, D., Maslej, N., Brynjolfsson, E., Etchemendy, J., Lyons, T., Manyika, J., Ngo, H., Niebles, J. C., Sellitto, M., Sakhaee, E., Shoham, Y., Clark, J., & Perrault, R. (2022). *The AI index 2022 annual report.* https://aiindex.stanford.edu/wp-content/uploads/2022/03/2022-AI-Index-Report_Master.pdf

Zhang, G. (2017, October 2). In-depth study and implementation, strengthening reform and innovation, and accelerating the formation of a new pattern of in-depth development of military-civil fusion. *People's Daily.* http://politics.people.com.cn/GB/n1/2017/1002/c1024-29571345.html

Zhang, L., & Chen, S. (2019). *China's digital economy: Opportunities and risks.* https://www.imf.org/en/Publications/WP/Issues/2019/01/17/Chinas-Digital-Economy-Opportunities-and-Risks-46459

Zhang, Q., Xu, F., Li, L., Liu, N. Le, & Pan, J. W. (2019). Quantum information research in China. In *Quantum science and technology* (Vol. 4, Issue 4, p. 040503). Institute of Physics Publishing. https://doi.org/10.1088/2058-9565/ab4bea

Zhang, Z. (2017, September 30). Beijing-Shanghai quantum link a "new era." *China Daily.* http://www.chinadaily.com.cn/china/2017-09/30/content_32669593.htm

Zhang, Z. (2018a, February 1). Cyber security urgently needs the development of military-civilian integration. *China Military Network.* http://www.81.cn/theory/2018-02/01/content_7929256.htm

Zhang, Z. (2018b, August 8). Civil-military integration: An urgent need to lay the foundations of cybersecurity. *NetEase.* https://www.163.com/dy/article/DONJULOK0511DV4H.html

Zhao, L. (2016a, August 19). Nation's next generation of missiles to be highly flexible. *China Daily.* http://www.chinadaily.com.cn/china/2016-08/19/content_26530461.htm

Zhao, L. (2016b, November 24). Line for quantum communication to be ready next year. *China Daily*. http://www.chinadaily.com.cn/china/2016-11/24/content _27476521.htm

Zhen, L. (2016, January 1). Chinese military launches two new wings for space and cyber age. *South China Morning Post*. https://www.scmp.com/news/china /diplomacy-defence/article/1897356/chinese-military-launches-two-new-wings -space-and-cyber

Zheng, B. (2021, April 21). Cyber power is a grand strategy in the new era and new development stage. *Cyberspace Administration of China*. http://www.cac.gov.cn /2021-04/21/c_1620581585957180.htm

Zheng, Y. (2013, July 27). 19 industries to shed capacity. *China Daily*. https://www .chinadaily.com.cn/business/2013-07/27/content_16839914.htm

Zheng, Y. (2019, October 10). How to integrate the mechanization, informatization, and intelligence of weapons and equipment. *China Military*. http://www.81.cn/ jfjbmap/content/2019-10/10/content_244912.htm

Zhou, D. (1996, March 19). Increase awareness of information confrontation. *PLA Daily [FBIS-CHI-96-109]*.

Zhou, H., & Zhang, C. (2018a, March 15). Actively promote the in-depth development of cybersecurity military-civil fusion. *PLA Daily*. http://www.81.cn /gfbmap/content/2018-03/15/content_201624.htm

Zhou, H., & Zhang, C. (2018b, May 22). Build the Great Wall of network of military-civil fusion. *PLA Daily*. http://www.81.cn/jfjbmap/content/2018-05/22 /content_206727.htm

Zhou, Q., Zhou, Y., & Liu, J. (2019, February 19). Video I The naval offshore joint training formation in the southern theater command is in actual combat training. *China Military Network*. http://www.81.cn/hj/2019-02/19/content_9467951 .htm

Zhou, X. (2017, June 7). Chinese censor shuts down dozens of online entertainment news accounts. *South China Morning Post*. https://www.scmp.com/news/ china/economy/article/2097367/chinese-censor-shuts-down-dozens-online -entertainment-news

Zhou, X., & Choi, C. (2018, October 31). Develop and control: Xi Jinping urges China to use artificial intelligence in race for tech future. *South China Morning Post*. https://www.scmp.com/economy/china-economy/article/2171102/develop -and-control-xi-jinping-urges-china-use-artificial

Zhu, R. (2001, March 5). *Report on the outline of the tenth five-year plan for national economic and social development (2001)*. http://www.npc.gov.cn/ zgrdw/englishnpc/Special_11_5/2010-03/03/content_1690620.htm

Zhuang, R. (2021, February 1). *Ideological weapons and action guides for the construction of a strong cyber country*. Cyberspace Administration of China. http://www.cac.gov.cn/2021-02/01/c_1613753152020388.htm

# INDEX

For Product Safety Concerns and Information please contact our EU
representative GPSR@taylorandfrancis.com Taylor & Francis Verlag GmbH,
Kaufingerstraße 24, 80331 München, Germany

Printed and bound by CPI Group (UK) Ltd, Croydon, CR0 4YY
08/06/2025
01897008-0010